THE
DISP
SOVEREIGNTY OVER
SIPADAN AND
LIGITAN ISLANDS

The **ISEAS – Yusof Ishak Institute** (formerly Institute of Southeast Asian Studies) is an autonomous organization established in 1968. It is a regional centre dedicated to the study of socio-political, security, and economic trends and developments in Southeast Asia and its wider geostrategic and economic environment. The Institute's research programmes are grouped under Regional Economic Studies (RES), Regional Strategic and Political Studies (RSPS), and Regional Social and Cultural Studies (RSCS). The Institute is also home to the ASEAN Studies Centre (ASC), the Temasek History Research Centre (THRC) and the Singapore APEC Study Centre.

ISEAS Publishing, an established academic press, has issued more than 2,000 books and journals. It is the largest scholarly publisher of research about Southeast Asia from within the region. ISEAS Publishing works with many other academic and trade publishers and distributors to disseminate important research and analyses from and about Southeast Asia to the rest of the world.

THE INDONESIA-MALAYSIA DISPUTE CONCERNING SOVEREIGNTY OVER SIPADAN AND LIGITAN ISLANDS

Historical Antecedents and
the International Court of
Justice Judgment

D.S. RANJIT SINGH

ISEAS YUSOF ISHAK
INSTITUTE

First published in Singapore in 2020 by
ISEAS Publishing
30 Heng Mui Keng Terrace
Singapore 119614
E-mail: publish@iseas.edu.sg
Website: <http://bookshop.iseas.edu.sg>

The responsibility for facts and opinions in this publication rests exclusively with the author and his interpretations do not necessarily reflect the views or the policy of the publishers or their supporters.

ISEAS Library Cataloguing-in-Publication Data

Names: Ranjit Singh.
Title: The Indonesia-Malaysia Dispute Concerning Sovereignty over Sipadan and
    Ligitan Islands : Historical Antecedents and the International Court of Justice
    Judgment / by D.S. Ranjit Singh.
Description: Singapore : ISEAS – Yusof Ishak Institute, 2020. | Includes
    bibliographical references and index.
Identifiers: ISBN 9789814843645 (paperback) | ISBN 9789814843652 (PDF)
Subjects: LCSH: Malay Archipelago--Boundaries--History. | Sabah (Malaysia)
    --Claims--History. | Sipadan Island (Sabah, Malaysia)--International status. |
    Ligitan Island (Sabah, Malaysia)--International status. | Indonesia--Boundaries
    --Malaysia. | Malaysia--Boundaries--Indonesia. | Arbitration (International law).
Classification: LCC KZ3684.5 M3R19

Cover photograph: Sipadan Island taken from a boat, reproduced with permission from the author.

Typeset by Superskill Graphics Pte Ltd

To my wife, Gurmit Kaur

Contents

Appendixes

List of Figures

List of Abbreviations

ASEAN	Association of Southeast Asian Nations
BNBC	British North Borneo Company
BNBPA	British North Borneo Provisional Association
C.O.	Colonial Office
DEIC	Dutch East India Company
EEIC	English East India Company
EEZ	Exclusive Economic Zone
FEER	*Far Eastern Economic Review*
F.O.	Foreign Office
H.M.G.	His Majesty's Government
H.O.C.	Hydrographic Office Chart
ICJ	International Court of Justice
IGC	Inter-Governmental Committee
MCA	Malayan Chinese Association
MCP	Malayan Communist Party
MIC	Malayan Indian Congress
MPAJA	Malayan Peoples Anti-Japanese Army
MSCC	Malaysia Solidarity Consultative Committee
ODA	Overbeck-Dent Association
PCA	Permanent Court of Arbitration
PRB	Party Rakyat Brunei
R.O.E.C.	Resident of the East Coast
SSA	Sabah State Archives
TAC	Treaty of Amity and Cooperation
UK	United Kingdom
UMNO	United Malays National Organization
UNCLOS I	First United Nations Conference on the Law of the Sea, 1958
UNCLOS II	Second United Nations Conference on the Law of the Sea, 1960
UNCLOS III	Third United Nations Conference on the Law of the Sea, 1973–1982
US	United States

Acknowledgements

In the process of writing this volume, documents were obtained from a number of archives and organizations. In this context, I would like to thank the following: National Archives of the United Kingdom (London); Algemeen Rijksarchief of the Netherlands (Leiden); National Archives of the United States (Washington, D.C.); Sabah State Archives (Kota Kinabalu); and International Court of Justice (The Hague). On a personal note, I would like to record my sincere thanks to Associate Professor Dr Jatswan Singh Sidhu for having gone through my manuscript and for having rendered me assistance in many other ways.

Preface

The conclusion of the First United Nations Conference on the Law of the Sea in 1958 (UNCLOS I) and the Third United Nations Conference on the Law of the Sea in 1982 (UNCLOS III) caused a flurry of activities among coastal states in Southeast Asia and many other areas to extend their jurisdiction over seas and oceans based on the new limits permitted for the extension of the territorial sea and the exclusive economic zone (EEZ). The result was that the territorial seas and EEZs of many nation-states overlapped, producing in their wake a trail of rival territorial claims and disputes. The dispute between Indonesia and Malaysia concerning sovereignty over the two islands of Sipadan and Ligitan, situated on the northeast coast of Borneo, was one such case that arose in 1969 while the two countries were in the midst of delimiting their continental shelf boundaries. Both countries advanced rival sovereignty claims over the two islands, but as the issue could not be resolved even after prolonged negotiations, the two countries decided in 1996 to place the case before the International Court of Justice (ICJ) for settlement. The case was filed with the ICJ in 1998 and the verdict delivered in 2002. Malaysia's case, and that of Indonesia as well, was fought by renowned international lawyers. However, long before the lawyers came into the picture, a great deal of meticulous, precise and laborious preparation for collecting, arranging and developing evidence for the case had already taken place. Although a number of agencies, representing different types of expertise, specializations and disciplines were involved in this massive task, there was one field and discipline which played an important role without which no country can have a case to present and without which no international lawyers would have a case to prepare; and this is the discipline of History. I can vouch for this statement as I was appointed as team leader by the Malaysian Government to prepare the historical evidence for its case concerning sovereignty over the Sipadan and Ligitan Islands.

While analysing the verdict of the ICJ in the Sipadan and Ligitan case and about that of Pulau Batu Puteh/Pedra Branca, it became evidently clear to me that the ICJ gives priority consideration to the possession of a legal title based on historical developments. Thus, for a country to successfully defend its claim over a disputed territory, it must produce concrete historical evidence in support of its title. And here I cannot downplay the role of historians, their area of specialization, and the importance of rigorous and meticulous research. It is about this realization concerning the importance of the historical setting, not only for the sake of building up an unassailable case but also for a comprehensive understanding of the issue at hand, that persuaded me to develop a number of chapters in this work before even approaching the analysis pertaining to the bases of the claims advanced by the respective claimants and the ICJ's verdict. As will be seen from Chapters 2 to 4 of this book, the story of disputed areas of control goes back to precolonial times. Although the Sipadan and Ligitan case was settled in 2002, this work has taken a long time to complete, partly due to the sheer volume of documents which had to be acquired and analysed before the narrative could be written. The delay, however, has benefitted the writer and enriched the volume in the sense that the Pulau Batu Puteh case was concluded in 2008 and this enabled the author to make more meaningful comparisons and generalizations between these two cases. A number of areas in Southeast Asia and East Asia, including the Straits of Malacca, the South China Sea, the Natuna Sea, the Celebes Sea, the Sulu Sea, and the East China Sea abound with contested maritime claims. It is the writer's ardent hope that this volume will serve, in some ways, as a guide for interested parties to understand the essential requirements for upholding a valid claim.

1

Introduction

1.1 A Brief Description of the Sipadan and Ligitan Islands

Before broaching the subject of this work, that is, the dispute over the ownership of the Sipadan and Ligitan Islands between Indonesia and Malaysia, a brief description of the two islands is in order. The islands of Sipadan and Ligitan are both located in the southeastern portion of Sabah in the Celebes Sea (Figures 1.1 and 1.2). Sipadan Island is an oceanic island and the only one of its kind in Malaysia. It is not part of the continental shelf of Borneo but emerges separately from the ocean rising some 600 to 700 metres from the seabed. It is a small island with an area of about 0.13 square kilometres. It is situated at 4°06′ latitude north and 118°37′ longitude east. The island sits on top of an extinct volcano and, was formed by living corals growing on the submarine mountain head. In 1903, a US naval report described Sipadan Island as follows:[1]

> This island is densely wooded with tall timber and is the resort of many turtles. There is no water and it is in consequence, uninhabited.

The coral reefs that grow around the island are home to many sea creatures such as the fusilier, snapper, barracuda, manta ray and hammerhead shark (Figure 1.3). The island is also home to many turtles of the hawksbill and green-backed species. There is a turtle tomb underneath the column of the island, formed by an underwater limestone cave where many turtles get drowned as they are unable to find the surface. Sipadan is rated as one of the top destinations for diving in the world.[2] Sipadan lies about

FIGURE 1.1
Sabah, the Philippines and Indonesian Borneo

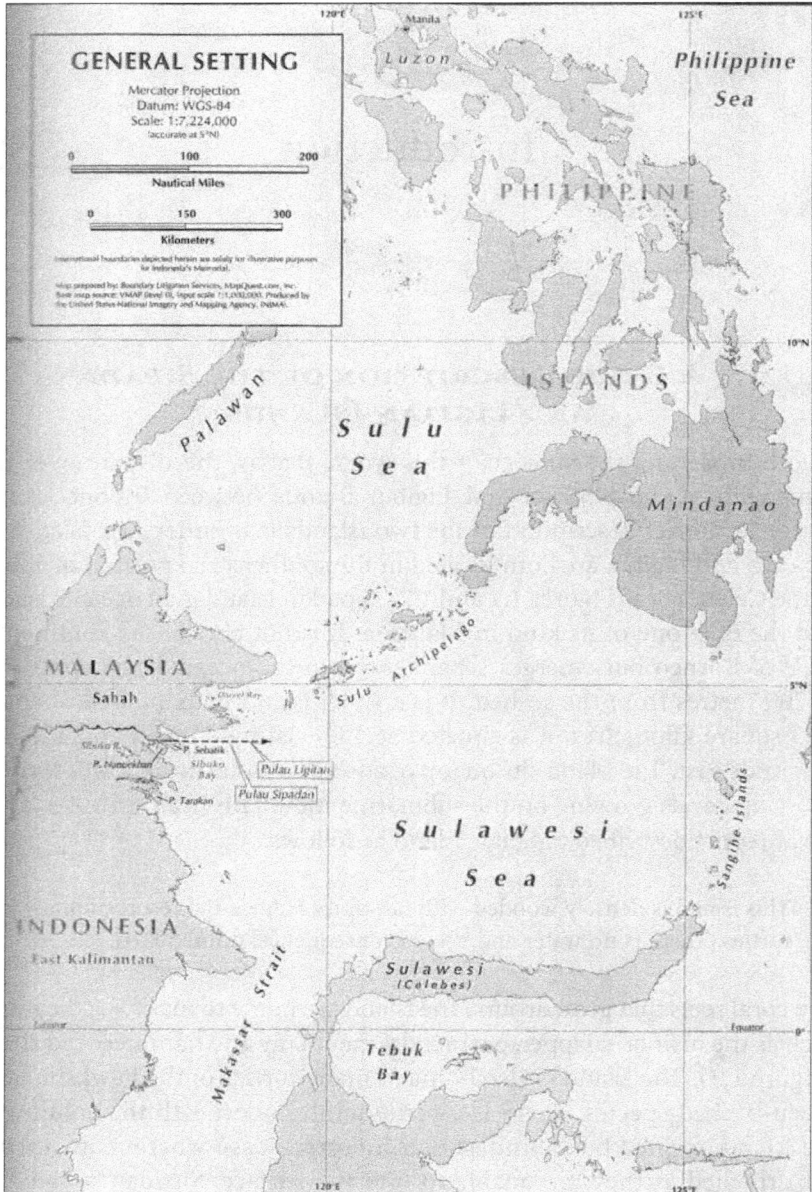

Source: International Court of Justice (ICJ), *Memorial of Indonesia*, vol. 1, 2 November 1999, Map 2.1.

FIGURE 1.2
Location of Islands Relevant to the Dispute

Source: ICJ, *Memorial of Malaysia*, vol. 1, 2 November 1999, p. 5.

21 nautical miles from Semporna of the Borneo mainland (Sabah). In the past, and even today, Sipadan has remained an important place for the collection of a valuable delicacy, that is, turtle eggs. On most nights, a number of turtles crawl ashore to lay their eggs in the sandy areas close to the bushes. Each turtle usually lays from 150 to 300 eggs in a safe, deep hole dug by itself. In the past, the Sultan of Sulu owned this island, and he

FIGURE 1.3
Sipadan Island

Source: ICJ, *Memorial of Indonesia*, vol. 1, 2 November 1999, p. 8.

obtained a handsome revenue from the collection and sale of turtle eggs coming from this place. This valuable commodity was collected by agents appointed by the Sultan.[3] In 1882, the British North Borneo Company (BNBC) became the owner of a large stretch of territory on the northern part of the Borneo Island. These territories were originally acquired from the Sultans of Brunei and Sulu by the Overbeck-Dent Association (ODA) in 1877 and 1878 respectively. When the BNBC took over the ownership of this area, it established a government to administer the region and slowly, over time, from 1882 to 1946, fashioned the new state of North Borneo, now known as Sabah. The territorial limit of the Brunei and Sulu Grants in North Borneo pertaining to coastal waters was 9 nautical miles from the coast (three marine leagues). The BNBC however began to administer about twenty-six islands on the east coast of North Borneo, including Sipadan and Ligitan, which were beyond the 9 nautical miles limit under the mistaken impression that they were included in the 1878 Sulu Grants.[4] When the Company assumed the administration of Sipadan in 1882 as well, it continued with the practice of appointing agents to collect turtle eggs from the island. In 1913, the BNBC started issuing licences to appointed persons for the collection of turtle eggs on Sipadan Island. The original licence given in 1913 to two persons named Panglima Abu Sari and Maharaja Anggai was renewed over the years, even as late as 1975.[5] In 1933, the North Borneo Government proclaimed Sipadan Island as a bird sanctuary and a notification to that effect was erected on the island.[6] After the Japanese Occupation from 1942 to 1945, the BNBC became bankrupt. The British Government was also at the same time keen to take over North Borneo from the BNBC to streamline its administration in Southeast Asia after the Second World War. The transfer took place in 1946 and, North Borneo became a British Crown Colony on 15 July 1946.[7]

In 1962, the Colonial Government constructed a lighthouse on Sipadan Island. In 1963, Sabah became part of Malaysia, and the island continued to be administered by the new government. Before 1979, Sipadan was not permanently inhabited although Panglima Abu Sari had planted some coconut trees and maize. A well was also dug to provide fresh water for the collectors of turtle eggs. A semi-permanent wooden hut was also built to shelter the turtle egg collectors especially if they stayed overnight. In 1979, in order to attract scuba divers, tourist facilities such as chalets were built by Malaysia.[8] The author visited Sipadan Island in 1991 with a team of researchers and stayed two nights there. At that time there were a number of chalets, as well as a house where the man in charge of collecting turtle eggs lived. The resorts were later closed down due to security reasons and to protect the island from over-exploitation. Visitors may now stay at several excellent nearby resorts on Mabul and Kapalai Islands. Mabul is the nearest inhabited island with about 1,000 residents and lies about 8 nautical miles to the north of Sipadan. In 1994, a hotel complex called the Sipadan Water Village was built there.

Ligitan is a small island lying in the southern part of a large reef extending from the nearby islands of Danawan and Si Amil. Most of the reef is submerged. Ligitan is situated about 21 nautical miles from Semporna, and about 57.6 nautical miles from Sebatik Island on the Sabah-Indonesian border in eastern Borneo. Its coordinates are 4°09′ latitude north and 118°53′ longitude east. The island is about 7.9 hectares in size and is mostly made up of sand. Ligitan is covered with rocks, wild grass, and trees called *bilang-bilang* but is not inhabited. The island is often used to dry fish caught by the Bajau Laut, a sea-faring people of the region. In July 1963, the Colonial Government of North Borneo constructed a lighthouse on Ligitan Island as well (Figure 1.4). Both the lighthouses on Sipadan and Ligitan Islands are still in operation today.[9]

FIGURE 1.4
Ligitan Island and the Light Tower

Source: ICJ, *Memorial of Malaysia*, vol. 1, 2 November 1999, p. 25.

1.2 BACKGROUND OF THE DISPUTE

The region of Southeast Asia is saddled with numerous conflicting maritime claims which have arisen as a result of historical factors, as well as the implementation of the United Nations Convention on the Law of the Sea of 1982 (the Convention) by member states of the region.[10] These overlapping claims relate to maritime features such as islands and rocks, as well as national territorial waters (12 nautical miles), and the exclusive economic zone (EEZ) which extends to 200 nautical miles from the national baselines of a particular country. At the moment (2019), the major areas of disputes in Southeast Asia are in the Straits of Malacca, the South China Sea, the Natuna Sea, the Celebes Sea and the Sulu Sea. Such disputes also abound in other regions, especially in Northeast Asia. Sometimes these counter-claims take on very strong nationalist sentiments and often lead to heightened inter-state tensions due to the strategic and economic importance of these maritime features. For example, in 2012–13 the dispute between Japan and China over the ownership of the Senkaku/Diaoyu Islands in the East China Sea almost escalated to an armed confrontation between

FIGURE 1.5
The Semporna Region

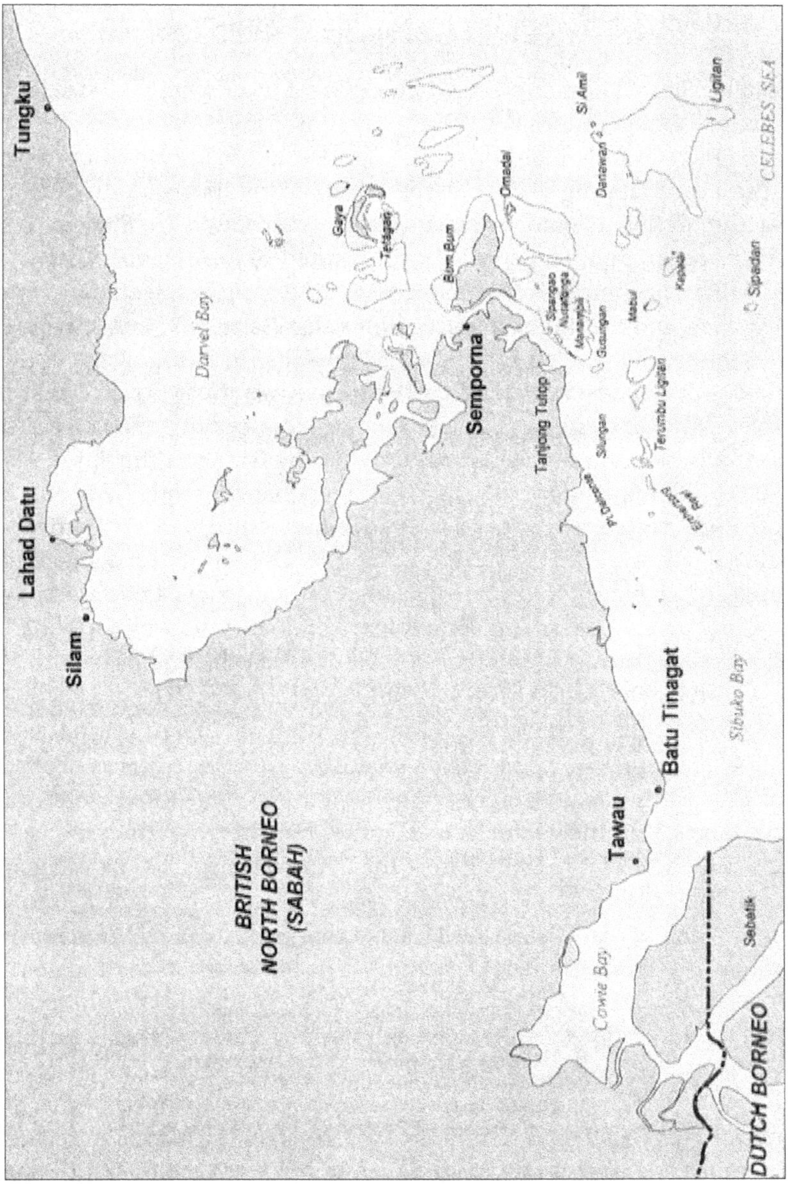

Source: ICJ, *Memorial of Malaysia*, vol. 1, 2 November 1999, p. 62.

the two powers. A similar situation developed between the Japanese and the South Koreans concerning jurisdiction over the Takashima Island.[11] In the South China Sea, the Spratly Islands, which comprise over more than 750 rocks, atolls, cays, islets, and reefs covering a vast area of over 425,000 square kilometres, are claimed partially or wholly by six claimants. These are China, Taiwan, Vietnam, the Philippines, Malaysia and Brunei. The Spratly Islands region itself is a potential hot spot, not only because of these overlapping claims of the six claimants but also due to the fact that the area is a major passageway for international shipping. For this reason, other powers, especially the United States, Japan, Australia and India, have become involved in the region, seeking to safeguard freedom of navigation and overflight against China's aggressive assertion of sovereignty over almost the whole of the South China Sea. In 2015, events in the area almost developed into a clash between the two great powers, that is, the United States and China. The catalyst that produced this explosive situation was the initiation of reclamation activities by China in the Spratly Islands in 2015. China undertook extensive reclamation work in a number of reefs and created artificial islands together with their 12 nautical miles national water zones.[12] In May 2015, the United States demanded that China immediately stop these reclamation and construction activities as the Spratly region was a disputed area, and such actions interfered with the rights of free navigation and overflight.[13] At the end of October 2015, the United States sent a destroyer ship close to one of the artificial islands created by China to challenge China's assertion of sovereignty in the region. China denounced the American action, describing it as a provocation and a threat to its sovereignty.[14] In April 2016, the United States and the Philippines held their annual war games, but this time the exercises were seen as a show of strength against the Chinese presence in the region.[15]

China's assertive policy in the region has also brought it into direct conflict with two of the Southeast Asian claimants, namely Vietnam and the Philippines. From the 1970s, there have been naval clashes and stand-offs between the navies of China, and those of Vietnam and the Philippines. In 2013, the Philippines filed a case with the Permanent Court of Arbitration (PCA) at The Hague challenging China's massive territorial claims in the Spratlys and sought to reaffirm its own rights to some of the islands, especially in the West Philippines Sea. This action further threatened to challenge China's assertions in the area. Both China and the Philippines are members of the PCA. China, however, refused to acknowledge the court's right to hear the case, but in November 2015, the PCA ruled that it had jurisdiction in the case. The PCA subsequently set up a tribunal to hear the case brought up by the Philippines. In a five-day hearing in November 2015, the Philippines presented its case to the tribunal, but China refused to accept or participate in the proceedings.

The Philippines case was based on the following issues:

(a) China did not have "historic rights" over waters in the South China Sea beyond limits provided for by the UNCLOS.
(b) China's "nine-dash line" did not have any basis under international law.
(c) Maritime features controlled by China in the South China Sea are not islands and are therefore not capable of generating national territorial waters and EEZs.
(d) China violated the UNCLOS by preventing the Philippines from exercising its fishing and exploration rights; and
(e) China had damaged the environment beyond repair by its various activities.

On 12 July 2016, the tribunal delivered its judgment. The tribunal's ruling was as follows:

(a) There was no legal basis for China to claim "historic rights" to resources within its so-called "nine-dash line" in the South China Sea.
(b) China had interfered with the traditional Philippines's fishing rights and sovereign rights in the area within the South China Sea.
(c) None of the reefs and maritime features held by China in the Spratly Islands were entitled to a 200-nautical mile EEZ.

China reacted by rejecting the Court's findings and threatened to safeguard its interests by all means. The situation in the South China Sea remains explosive.[16]

The dispute between Malaysia and Indonesia over the ownership of the two islands of Sipadan and Ligitan arose as a result of the process of implementing the 1958 United Nations Continental Shelf Convention by the two states. After the Second World War, it became apparent that many maritime states wished to exploit the seabed and subsoil adjacent to their coastlines for mineral resources.

Industrialization, development and technological innovations were the main driving forces behind the desire to acquire the rich resources of the seabed. As a result of these forces, many maritime states issued unilateral declarations of sovereignty over contiguous submarine territory and adjacent seas beyond the traditionally accepted 3 nautical miles limit. In 1945, another development occurred in this field. President Harry S. Truman of the United States introduced the modern concept of the "continental shelf" through his Proclamation of 1945 which allowed the United States to have jurisdiction and control over the "natural resources of the subsoil and sea bed of the continental shelf" contiguous to its coastlines. It was a unilateral declaration, but many maritime states began to lay claims to their continental shelves. However, as the breadth of the continental shelf that a country could claim was still not defined, there arose the possibility of conflicting claims between countries. To bring some order to this potential problem, the International Law Commission in 1953 recommended the limit of a country's continental shelf to a line at the 200 metres depth. Not all countries adhered to this rule, and to prevent political chaos in the oceans, the United Nations (UN) took up the matter in 1958 to formulate a new set of laws to govern the jurisdiction of states over seas adjacent to their coastlines. Towards this end, the UN held three major conferences—the first in 1958, the second in 1960 and the third from 1973 to 1982. The First United Nations Conference on the Law of the Sea (UNCLOS I) was held in Geneva. Its main achievements were that it gave formal recognition to jurisdiction of states over their internal waters, the territorial sea, the contiguous zone and the continental shelf. The most important outcome of the Conference was the adoption of the Continental Shelf Convention, 1958 which gave coastal states rights over their continental shelves up to the depth of the 200 metres isobath. As a result of this Convention, many states in Southeast Asia began to lay claims to their continental shelves.

The Second United Nations Conference on the Law of the Sea (UNCLOS II) was held in 1960, but it failed to produce any substantive agreement. The final and most productive conference on the matter was called the Third United Nations Conference on the Law of the Sea (UNCLOS III). It commenced its work in 1973 and completed its massive task in 1982. This conference resulted in the United Nations Convention on the Law of the Sea (the Convention) signed at Montego Bay, Jamaica in December 1982 by 119 countries. The Convention came into force in 1994. The 1982 Convention, sometimes called "the Constitution of the Sea", allows coastal states to establish a territorial sea up to 12 nautical miles, and an EEZ of up to 200 nautical miles from their respective baselines.

As mentioned earlier, the adoption of the Continental Shelf Convention of 1958 led many states in Southeast Asia to lay claim to their respective continental shelves. One such state was the Federation of Malaya which ratified the said Convention in 1960. In 1966, the new nation of Malaysia (formed in 1963) promulgated the Continental Shelf Act, adopting the 200 metres depth criteria. The said Act also provided for the delimitation of the continental shelf between Malaysia and Indonesia. This exercise was conducted in 1969. Before this delimitation process began, however, the Government of Malaysia passed a legislation called the Emergency (Essential Powers) Ordinance No. 7 of August 1969 by which it extended its territorial waters from the traditional 3 nautical miles to the 12 nautical miles zone. In accordance with this Ordinance, Malaysia also announced the publication of a large-scale map showing its territorial waters and continental shelf boundaries. This map, published on 21 December 1979, came to be known as *Peta Baru*.[17]

It was during the process of delimiting the continental shelf boundaries between Malaysia and Indonesia in 1969 that problems arose as to the ownership of the two islands of Sipadan and Ligitan. Both countries advanced rival sovereignty claims over the two islands. Although the issue could not be resolved immediately, the two countries nevertheless went ahead with the signing of a treaty in the same year (1969), establishing their continental shelf boundaries in the Straits of Malacca and the South China Sea. This treaty is entitled "Agreement between the Government of the Republic of Indonesia and the Government of Malaysia relating to the Delimitation of the Continental Shelves between the Two Countries, 27 October 1969." It entered into force on 7 November 1969.[18] The two countries also agreed to settle the issue of ownership over the two islands through discussions at a later date.

More trouble was in store for Malaysia when it published the *Peta Baru* on 21 December 1979 entitled "Territorial Waters and Continental Shelf Boundaries of Malaysia". One of the disputes that developed in 1980 as a consequence of this map was conflicting claims of sovereignty between Singapore and Malaysia over Pedra Branca/Pulau Batu Puteh. In 1979, Malaysia also became embroiled in the Spratly Islands dispute as a result of this map. It thus became the fifth claimant to some of the features in the area. In 1980, it proclaimed its 200 nautical miles EEZ and subsequently occupied six islets in the Spratly Islands area.

As mentioned earlier, the Convention of 1982 came into force in 1994. Malaysia and most of the members of the Association of Southeast Asian

Nations (ASEAN) became signatories to the Convention. The Law of the Sea regime immediately caused a flurry of activities in Southeast Asia and the South China Sea with every nation-state parcelling out seas and oceans into their respective EEZs.[19] As discussed above, the Spratlys has remained a hot spot for tensions. Despite attempts to come to some compromise, the dispute continues to simmer without much hope of an amicable settlement in the near future. Within ASEAN itself, there is a strong desire to establish mechanisms and processes for dispute settlement in the region. In 2003, ASEAN leaders meeting at the Ninth ASEAN Summit in Bali identified the High Council of the Treaty of Amity and Cooperation (TAC) in Southeast Asia (1976) as the main organ for the job. An ASEAN Maritime Forum was also established at the same summit to tackle the rising number of maritime territorial disputes in Southeast Asia.[20] Despite the ongoing efforts for greater integration in ASEAN, its members do not seem to have full trust in each other or in the abilities of ASEAN and prefer to submit disputes to the ICJ.

The dispute over the ownership of Sipadan and Ligitan Islands resurfaced in 1982 when Indonesian naval units appeared off Sipadan supposedly to investigate the presence of "foreign troops" on the island.[21] In 1991, Indonesia protested in the press that Malaysia had built tourist facilities on Sipadan Island. Indonesia accused Malaysia of going back on its promise in 1969 not to undertake any development activity on the said island. Indonesia pointed out that during the September 1969 delimitation talks in Kuala Lumpur between the two countries, a "status quo" or standstill agreement was reached with respect to Sipadan and Ligitan Islands. This status quo agreement, according to Indonesia was respected by both countries for about ten years. Indonesia further claimed that beginning from 1979, Malaysia had started erecting tourist installations on Sipadan Island in contravention of the status quo agreement.[22] Malaysia denied that there was ever such a verbal agreement and maintained that the two islands had always belonged to itself.[23] In October 1991 however, the then Malaysian Foreign Minister, Datuk Abdullah Ahmad Badawi assured his counterpart, Ali Alatas, that no further development projects would be undertaken on the two islands until the question of sovereignty was resolved.[24] The two sides also agreed to establish a Joint Working Group to resolve the issue. However, meetings held by this group from 1992 to 1994 failed to produce any result. In January 1994, talks between the two countries ended in failure. In September 1994, Malaysia proposed for the dispute to be referred to the ICJ. Indonesia, however, wanted the case to be brought to the ASEAN

High Council. Malaysia disagreed as it doubted the impartiality of the said Council.[25] The matter was then referred to the special envoys of both sides. In June 1996, the special envoys recommended to their respective governments for the dispute to be placed before the ICJ for arbitration. Seeing that further efforts at a diplomatic solution would be fruitless, the leaders of both countries at the time, Datuk Seri Dr Mahathir Mohamad and President Suharto, agreed on 7 October 1996 to refer the dispute to the ICJ for arbitration. On 31 May 1997, both countries signed a Special Agreement to refer the dispute to the ICJ, and on 2 November 1998, this agreement was filed with the said Court. Both countries then submitted their respective written memorials in 1999, followed by counter-memorials and replies. The oral pleadings were held from 3 to 12 June 2002, and the verdict delivered on 17 December 2002.[26]

Why was there a dispute concerning sovereignty over these two tiny islands? To get a clearer picture, we have to study the past. As with many other unresolved issues in Asia, the case of Sipadan and Ligitan Islands was a residue of colonialism, a legacy from colonial activities. In the second half of the nineteenth century, both the Dutch and the British began to expand and consolidate their colonial empires in Borneo. In 1898, the United States also joined the bandwagon by taking over the Philippines from the jurisdiction of Spain. As the territorial concessions obtained by the three colonial powers from the native rulers were in some ways vaguely defined and thus overlapped, these colonial powers began to adopt a new idea that had been developed in Europe in the eighteenth century, that is, the concept of the territorial state.[27] Applied to Asia and Africa, it took the form of the territorial empire or colony. Such a concept necessitated the creation of precise boundaries between colonial possessions. In their fervour to create these legally defined boundaries in their colonial empires, as well as to avoid intensive colonial conflict arising out of overlapping territorial claims, the Netherlands and Britain on the one hand, and the United States and Britain on the other, entered into negotiations for the delimitation of their respective boundaries in the northeastern Borneo region. The outcome of these separate exercises was the delimitation of the boundary between British Borneo and Dutch Borneo (1891–1915); and the sea boundary between the State of North Borneo and the Philippines (1903–30). The two small islands of Sipadan and Ligitan became victims of this boundary delimitation activity because their precise status remained somewhat undefined. The unfortunate consequence of this state of affairs was that both Malaysia and Indonesia assumed that they each had unquestioned sovereignty over the two islands. Since the process of boundary creation by the colonial powers concerned had such an overriding bearing on the dispute, the historical circumstances that went into the making of these boundaries now deserve our attention.

Notes

1. "Report on the Islands under the Sovereignty of the United States lying off the coasts of British North Borneo, recently visited by the USS *Quiros* by Lieutenant Francis Boughter", July 1903 inclosure in R.F. Nicholson, Chief of the Bureau of Navigation, to the Assistant Secretary of Navy, 6 August 1903, Hydrographic Office Survey Correspondence (U.S.A), 1854–1907, R.G. 37, File 161.34, Box 9.
2. Hashim Abdul Wahab, *Adventure Journeys in Sabah* (Kuala Lumpur: Alafhakam Sdn Bhd, 2001), pp. 140–41.
3. Memorandum from Assistant District Officer Semporna to the Resident, East Coast 21.1.1916, Resident of the East Coast (R.O.E.C), 39/16 Sabah State Archives (SSA).
4. See Chapter 2 for further details.
5. Acting Resident, East Coast to the Government Secretary [North Borneo], 26.1.1916, R.O.E.C., 39/16. SSA; and Report of the Committee of Investigation, (State of Sabah) Re: Sipadan and Ligitan, 1975, vol. 2, pp. 94–96.
6. Notification No. 69, *British North Borneo Official Gazette*, 1 February 1933, p. 28.
7. K.G. Tregonning, *Under Chartered Company Rule (North Borneo 1881–1946)* (Singapore: University of Malaya Press, 1959), p. 222.
8. International Court of Justice (ICJ), *Case Concerning Sovereignty over Pulau Ligitan and Pulau Sipadan (Indonesia/Malaysia), Memorial of Malaysia*, vol. 1, 2 November 1999, pp. 15–19 (hereafter cited as *Memorial of Malaysia*, vol. 1).
9. Ibid., pp. 13–15.
10. United Nations, *The Law of the Sea* (New York: United Nations, 1983), p. xix.
11. See, for example, *International Herald Tribune*, 20 August 2012; Takashi Nakamichi, "Tokyo Re-examines Cooperation With Seoul", *Wall Street Journal*, 20 August 2012; *New Straits Times*, 15 September 2012; *New Straits Times*, 25 September 2012; *The Star*, 26 September 2012; *Sunday Star*, 3 February 2013; and *The Star*, 6 February 2013.
12. See *The Star*, 22 January 2015, 29 May 2015, and 7 August 2015; and *New Straits Times*, 11 May 2015.
13. Frank Ching, "War Drums over South China Sea", *New Straits Times*, 4 June 2015, https://www.nst.com.my/news/2015/09/war-drums-over-south-china-sea.
14. *Sunday Star*, 1 November 2015.
15. *New Sunday Times*, 3 April 2016; and *The Star*, 5 April 2016.

16. See *Sunday Star*, 1 November 2015; *The Star*, 13 July 2016; and *New Straits Times*, 2 December 2015, 3 December 2015, 23 June 2016, and 13 July 2016.

17. Kriangsak Kittichaisaree, *The Law of the Sea and Maritime Boundary Delimitation in South-East Asia* (Singapore: Oxford University Press, 1987), pp. 57–64; J. de V. Allen, A.J. Stockwell and L.R. Wright, eds., *A Collection of Treaties and Other Documents Affecting the States of Malaysia, 1791–1963*, vol. 2 (London: Oceana Publications, 1981), p. 563; and R. Haller-Trost, *The Contested Maritime and Territorial Boundaries of Malaysia, An International Law Perspective* (London: Kluwer Law International, 1988), pp. 1–15.

18. The text of the treaty can be found in the US Department of State's series called *Limits in the Sea*, no. 1. Also see R. Haller-Trost, *The Territorial Dispute between Indonesia and Malaysia over Pulau Sipadan and Ligitan in the Celebes Sea: A Study in International Law* (Durham: International Boundaries Research Unit, University of Durham, 1995), pp. 4–5.

19. United Nations, *The Law of the Sea*, p. xix. See also Mark J. Valencia, *Malaysia and the Law of the Sea: The Foreign Policy Issues, the Options and Their Implications* (Kuala Lumpur: Institute of Strategic and International Studies, Malaysia, 1991), p. 1.

20. See *Press Statement by the Chairperson of the 9th ASEAN Summit and the 7th ASEAN+3 Summit Bali, Indonesia*, 7 October 2003, pp. 1–5; and *Declaration of ASEAN Concord II (Bali Concord II)*, pp. 1–6.

21. *Straits Times*, 7 July 1982; and *Asia Week*, 23 July 1982.

22. *The Star*, 7 June 1991, and International Court of Justice, *Verbatim Record*, 3 June 2002, 10 a.m; pp. 16–17.

23. *The Star*, 11 October 1991; and *Far Eastern Economic Review (FEER)*, 17 March 1994.

24. *New Straits Times*, 12 and 18 October 1991.

25. *New Sunday Times*, 2 June 2002.

26. *Memorial of Malaysia*, vol. 1, paras. 4.1–4.6, pp. 27–28.

27. K.J. Holsti, *International Politics: A Framework for Analysis*, 7th ed. (New Jersey: Prentice-Hall, 1995), p. 47. Holsti has this to say concerning the development of the idea of the territorial state in Europe: "For the era from 1648 to 1814, the notion of territoriality as the basis of political organization was only beginning to emerge. Dynastic holdings were often noncontiguous ... and the notion of lineal frontiers was only rudimentary. But by the end of the eighteenth century, it was commonly accepted—as it is today—that a state occupies a definite piece of territory, and that its jurisdiction extends only to the extremities of that territory. So, sovereignty referred not only to a domination over subjects, but also over real estate. To think otherwise might seem strange to us, but at the time of the Westphalia treaties, the notion of territory rather than people as the basis of political jurisdiction was not well understood or defined".

2

Historical Background:
The Partitioning of the Malay Archipelago

2.1 INTRODUCTION

This chapter explores the coming of European powers to Southeast Asia and how, from 1529 to 1824, they parcelled out the region into the Spanish, Portuguese, Dutch and English spheres of control. By 1824, the Dutch and the English had basically partitioned the Malay world between themselves; the Spanish had entrenched themselves in the Philippines, while the Portuguese still retained some outposts in the region.

The chapter then goes on to give special attention to the partitioning of Borneo as this has a direct bearing on the theme and topic of this work. The cutting-up of the huge island was in fact started by the indigenous powers, especially Brunei and Sulu. Later, Spain, the Netherlands and Britain continued the process and established their own spheres of control. In expanding their territorial possessions in Borneo, the European powers also inherited the problem of undefined boundaries and overlapping territorial jurisdiction from local powers. Such a situation was bound to create conflict, a reality that the powers concerned had to face in the 1880s.

A large section of the chapter is devoted to the entrenchment of British influence in North Borneo as well as the establishment of the British North Borneo Company (BNBC). This emphasis is given as elements of British Paramountcy and BNBC administration in North Borneo became vital evidence for determining the question of sovereignty over the two islands of Sipadan and Ligitan by the International Court of Justice (ICJ) later on.

2.2 THE CREATION OF EUROPEAN SPHERES OF INFLUENCE IN SOUTHEAST ASIA, 1529–1824

Some of the territorial and boundary disputes between the independent nations of Southeast Asia that emerged in the postcolonial era, such as the Philippines' claim to Sabah (1962) and later the issue of sovereignty over the Sipadan and Ligitan Islands between Malaysia and Indonesia (1969), had their roots in both the precolonial and colonial periods. Western colonialism, especially, led to the eventual partitioning of Southeast Asia into spheres of influence and territorial empires basically between Spain, Holland, Britain, France and the United States. European colonial expansion began in the late fifteenth century and was pioneered by two countries, Spain and Portugal. As they were both Catholic states, the Pope wished to avoid conflict between them and so he divided the world into two parts along a line west of the Azores by the Papal Bull of 1493. The Portuguese were given the right to expand east of this line, and the Spanish west of it (the Pope assumed that the earth was flat). The two powers agreed to abide by this ruling by signing the Treaty of Tordesillas in 1494.[1] Driven by a crusading spirit as well as economic motives, the Portuguese began to expand their power into the Indian Ocean with the objective of wresting the lucrative spice trade monopoly from the Arabs and other Muslim traders. Within the first two decades of the sixteenth century, the Portuguese had not only crushed the Moors in the Indian Ocean but had established an extensive maritime empire in the East based on the acquisition and occupation of strategic locations. This network of ports and commercial centres extended from Lisbon to such areas as the Cape of Good Hope, Ormuz, Calicut, Goa, Sri Lanka, Malacca, Moluccas (Ternate) and Macao.[2]

On the other hand, Spain, after the discovery of America by Christopher Columbus in 1492, concentrated its empire building mainly in South America. In 1521, Ferdinand Magellan of Spain embarked on the world's first attempt to circumnavigate the globe by sailing west. He set sail from Deville, Spain with a fleet of five ships. On 6 March 1521, he reached the Philippines (Landrone Island). By this time, he had only three ships left with him, the *Victoria*, the *Trinidade* and the *Concepcion*; while the other two ships had misadventures along the way. Magellan himself was killed fighting on Mactarn Island, an islet of Cebu on 27 April 1521. Many of his men were also killed by the ruler of Cebu. After leaving Cebu, the surviving members of the expedition burnt the third ship, the *Concepcion* on the reef off Bohol Island as there were not enough men left to handle all the three ships. Sailing to Mindanao and then to Palawan, the two ships, the *Victoria* and the *Trinidade*, reached the Brunei Bay in June 1521. The Spaniards were welcomed by the Brunei Sultan with whom in fact they had an audience later on.[3] From Brunei, Magellan's men embarked on their journey home, but on the way the *Victoria* intruded into the Portuguese sphere of influence in the Spice Islands. As a consequence of this, Portugal protested against Spain for infringing the Treaty of Tordesillas of 1494. After a series of claims and counterclaims pertaining to territorial rights in the region, the two states reached a compromise in 1529 by the Treaty of Saragossa. By this treaty, a line was drawn 17° east of the Moluccas as the boundary between the Spanish and the Portuguese spheres of influence.[4] Territories east of this line were allocated to the Spanish, and west of the line to the Portuguese. The islands "discovered" by Magellan in 1521, in fact, fell on the Portuguese side of the line drawn in 1529. Spain was however bent on consolidating its position in the islands around Cebu and subsequently sent a strong naval expedition in 1542 to the region under the command of Ruy Lopez de Villalobos from Mexico. Lopez claimed the islands for Spain and named them Philippines in honour of Emperor Charles VI's son Philip, who later became king of Spain as Philip II. In 1565, the Spaniards established their first settlement in the Philippines on Cebu Island. From here, Spain extended its control to other islands, such as Leyte, Panay, Mindoro and Luzon. In 1571, the Spaniards captured the small town of Manila and made it the capital of their new territories.[5] From this stronghold, Spain then tried to subjugate the main centres of indigenous political power in the region, including Mindanao, Sulu and Brunei which invariably were all Muslim kingdoms. Mindanao was ultimately conquered, but Spain failed to rein in either Brunei or Sulu. Sulu finally capitulated in 1878, after three centuries of resistance. Spain ruled the Philippines till 1898 when the United States took over the islands and became the new colonial masters of the Filipinos.

Now, we go back to European rivalry in the region. The hostility between Spain and Portugal in the Spice Islands and the Philippines ended with the union of the two crowns in 1580. Both Spain and Portugal, however, began to face threats from a new European power which descended on the scene, the Dutch. In fact two new strong European powers, the Dutch and the English entered the race for possession of the Spice Islands at the beginning of the seventeenth century, almost immediately upon the formation of the English East India Company (EEIC) in 1600 and the Dutch East India Company (DEIC) in 1602. From this period till 1624 both these companies began to establish factories in Java and the Spice Islands in a bid to control the spice trade. The Dutch for example made their headquarters at Jacatra (renamed Batavia) and opened up trading centres at most of the islands of the archipelago. The EEIC similarly had their headquarters at Bantam and opened up factories in many places such as Batavia, Amboina, Macassar, Acheh, and Patani. The Dutch, however, wished to control the whole of the Malay Archipelago, that is, the East Indies, and its spice trade solely for themselves, and resolutely followed a policy designed to evict all other European powers from the area. D.G.E. Hall describes the Dutch attitude as follows:[6]

> Their East India Company conducted a concentrated national offensive against Portugal and Spain, and they bitterly resented the intrusion of the English into the spice trade ...

In the end, however, the Dutch failed to expel any of the three European powers from the region, but paradoxically, their hold on the Dutch East Indies became stronger.

With the exception of the Philippines and the Moluccas, the partitioning of the rest of the Malay Archipelago, including Borneo, was basically a long-drawn-out contest between Holland and Britain. The Dutch went all out to oust the English from the East Indies. Measures undertaken by the Dutch to achieve this aim included establishing a monopoly on the trade of the Indies, imposing restrictions on English trade and even using force. The DEIC was financially and militarily (especially naval capabilities) stronger that the EEIC and was fully supported by its home government, unlike the EEIC. The climax of the Dutch campaign came in 1623 when, in an incident known as the Massacre of Amboina, the local Dutch authorities executed (beheaded) twenty-one factors of the EEIC's factory at Amboina on charges of conspiring to seize the Dutch fortress in the said town.[7] The EEIC had already started moving to India since 1612 and completely withdrew from the archipelago in 1624 after the Amboina debacle.

From 1624 onwards, the Dutch encountered little challenge from other European powers to their policy of exclusive political and commercial control in the Malay Archipelago until 1786 when the EEIC suddenly reappeared on the scene with the establishment of a new settlement at Penang. Since shifting its activities to India, the EEIC was not only fast emerging as a territorial power in the subcontinent, but had, by the second half of the eighteenth century developed a much more lucrative trade than the spice trade. This trade was the fast-growing commercial relationship with China in three major commodities that is tea, silk, and ceramics, which were in high demand in Europe. The trade with China, however, had many obstacles. One of the great difficulties was that the Chinese would not exchange their much sought-after goods, particularly tea, silk and ceramics, for European manufactures. Europeans wishing to acquire these valued Chinese items had to pay in silver bullion. The Chinese, however, were willing to accept another set of foreign items especially from Southeast Asia, including tin, pepper, tropical produce and maritime products. These products were obtained from Southeast Asia by European country traders who then sold the items to the EEIC.

The EEIC realized the negative consequences of a continuous drain of the bullion on the economy of Britain and India and started using Southeast Asian produce as an alternative exchange commodity for obtaining Chinese goods. In this quest, the company wished to improve the operations of the country traders by providing them with a station in Southeast Asia where such produce could be safely obtained in abundance. The company also needed such a port for the security of their China trade, and for refitting purposes. Numerous naval expeditions were thus sent by the company to Southeast Asia in the hope of obtaining a suitable site for its needs. Most of these attempts, including the Balambangan venture (1773–75) failed to materialize, except the establishment of Penang which took place in 1786.[8] By this time, however, a more valuable substitute had been found in place of tin, pepper and Southeast Asian tropical produce for the China trade—and this was opium. Tregonning writes of the entry of opium into the commerce with China as follows:[9]

> Opium, easy to grow and ship from India, and yielding greater profits in China, was replacing the illusive South-East Asian commodities in Canton by the nineteenth century. By the 1830s, China instead of receiving, was paying out large quantities of silver for the privilege of smoking opium. The balance of trade became ever more favourable to the Company as opium came to the market in steadily increasing quantities.

Although Penang subsequently declined in importance relative to the China trade, it was retained by the EEIC. The re-entry of the EEIC into the Malay Archipelago with the establishment and retention of Penang, and the outbreak of the French Revolution (1789), followed by the French Revolutionary Wars (1792–95) and the Napoleonic Wars (1799–1815) in

Europe, completely changed the European power balance in the Malay world. In 1795, Holland was invaded and occupied by France (1795–1814). The ruler, William V of Orange fled to England, while the French established a protectorate under its control called the Batavian Republic. In England, William V struck a deal with the British Government by which he agreed to place Dutch colonies under British control during the duration of the war as a measure to prevent their occupation by the French. The British Government promised to return the colonies to the Netherlands when the war was over. To facilitate the transfer of the colonies to British hands, William V issued instructions to Dutch East Indies officials known as the "Kew Letters" ordering them to hand over the jurisdiction of the Dutch colonies to the British without resistance. However, the Dutch were divided over the issue of either siding with the British or the French who claimed of having liberated Holland from the "yoke of Orange". In 1799, the Batavian Republic abolished the DEIC and placed all its colonial possessions in the East Indies under state control. This ended the once mighty DEIC. Britain asked the EEIC to occupy the Dutch colonies in the Malay Archipelago, but there was some resistance from local Dutch officials. In 1795, an EEIC force captured Malacca without much resistance. In 1811 Java was taken with the help of an expeditionary force from India which had used Malacca as a staging point. Thomas Stamford Raffles, who had joined the Penang administrative service as Assistant Secretary in 1805, and who had helped plan the invasion of Java, was appointed Lieutenant-Governor of Java. He served in that position from 1811 to 1816. Meanwhile, in 1813, Napoleon was defeated at Leipzig. Consequently, Britain and Holland signed the Convention of London on 13 August 1814, by which the Dutch were restored almost all of the former colonies of the DEIC, except the Cape Colony. As the Napoleonic Wars ended only with Napoleon's final defeat at Waterloo in 1815, the handing of Java to the Dutch was delayed to 19 August 1816.[10]

The returning Dutch lost no time in imposing their political control and monopolistic trade policies in the East Indies once again. The British traders at Penang strongly resented the Dutch initiative as these merchants had a free hand in the Malay Archipelago from 1795 to 1816. The EEIC was also apprehensive of the repercussions of the Dutch monopoly system on the fate of their vital China trade. Sir Stamford Raffles, who had been appointed Lieutenant-Governor of Bencoolen in 1818, was a strong proponent of the expansion of the British Empire in the Malay Archipelago at the expense of the Dutch and joined in the anti-Dutch drive. He openly challenged their position by establishing the EEIC's foothold in Singapore in 1819. Though the Dutch protested strenuously against Raffles' actions, they wanted to come to a permanent settlement with the British over the control of the archipelago to put an end to their perennial rivalry in the region. Negotiations were held, which finally led to the conclusion of the Anglo-Dutch Treaty of 1824. By the terms of this agreement, an imaginary line was drawn arbitrarily by the two colonial powers without any consultation whatsoever with the local rulers. This line divided the Malay world into two spheres of influence, one belonging to the Dutch and the other to the British. The Malay Peninsula, Singapore, and Malacca came under the British sphere of influence, while Sumatra and Java came under the Dutch sphere of influence. The British also agreed not to establish any further settlements (in reference to the EEIC's establishment at Singapore in 1819) "on any other islands south of the Straits of Singapore".[11] What a dramatic change compared to the situation before the French Revolutionary Wars!

Two more important observations must be made before we move on to the next phase of the narrative. One point concerns the implications of the 1824 treaty on Borneo. This issue was raised by the Dutch later on when attempts were made by certain parties to extend British influence on the island. D.G.E. Hall is of the opinion that the matter was settled during the discussions leading to the 1824 treaty. He writes as follows:[12]

> It was finally agreed that Borneo should not be mentioned, and that the demarcation line [delimiting the two spheres of influence] should not extend beyond the Singapore Straits.

The second point to note is that from 1816 onwards, all Dutch colonial activity in the East Indies was conducted directly by the state. In the case of the British, the situation remained as before, that is, British colonial expansion was partially imperial and partially private. It must be noted that the EEIC was abolished after the Indian Mutiny in 1858, and India came directly under the control of the British Government.[13]

2.3 THE CUTTING OF THE BORNEAN MELON

The cutting of the Bornean melon started even before the advent of the Western powers, although the process became more accelerated and permanent as a result of the European expansion.

2.3.1 The Expansion of the Brunei Empire in Borneo

One of the earliest and most powerful kingdoms to emerge on the island of Borneo was Brunei. Having gained independence from Majapahit around 1370, Brunei began to extend its jurisdiction over large parts of Borneo during the fifteenth and sixteenth centuries.[14] A historian by the name of Johannes Willi wrote that the Kingdom of Brunei at that time extended its control "over the whole island of Borneo, the Sulu Archipelago and parts of the Philippines".[15]

In the sixteenth century, the Portuguese and the Spaniards began to enter into relations with Brunei.[16] After capturing Malacca in 1511, the Portuguese concentrated their efforts in establishing their control and trade monopoly over the Moluccas. As far as Brunei was concerned, the Portuguese were more interested in establishing diplomatic and commercial relations. In this endeavour, numerous diplomatic missions were sent from Malacca to Brunei from 1526 till 1641, and a number of commercial and diplomatic treaties were agreed upon by both sides.[17]

Relations with the Spaniards began in 1521 when the remainder of Ferdinand Magellan's fleet consisting of the *Victoria* and the *Trinidade* visited Brunei. As mentioned earlier, the Spaniards were well received by the Bruneians and even had a meeting with the Sultan. Antonio Pigafetta, the historian of Magellan's fleet, wrote the first extensive eyewitness account of the Brunei town and the surrounding region. Pigafetta gave a glowing account of Brunei, and its court, and described in detail the town's layout.[18] As discussed earlier, the Spaniards established themselves at Manila in 1571 and were desirous of expanding their influence over Sulu and Brunei. Relations between the Spaniards and Brunei were not so friendly and finally ended up in two Spanish attacks on the Brunei capital in 1578 and 1580 respectively. The Spanish Governor of the Philippines at the time, Francisco de Sande led the first expedition against Brunei in 1578. Sande demanded Brunei's subjugation to Spain, but the Bruneians refused, whereupon Sande attacked and captured the town. Although the Spaniards had intentions of colonizing Brunei, they found the place pretty unhealthy and were obliged to withdraw and sail back to Manila.[19] Following this, the second attack came in 1580, but this time the Spanish were driven back by the Bruneians. The Spanish attacks weakened Brunei somewhat, and the outer fringes of the empire began to disintegrate in the seventeenth century. In the south of the island, the kingdoms of Sambas, Pontianak, and Bandjermasin became independent Muslim Sultanates by the beginning of the seventeenth century.[20]

2.3.2 The Rise of Sulu and the Division of Sabah into the Brunei and Sulu Spheres

In the north, the political situation also began to change as a result of a long-drawn-out civil war in Brunei from 1662 to 1674. One of the contenders to the throne in this civil war, Muhyiddin, invited assistance from the ruler of Sulu which at that time was a vassal of Brunei. The Sulu ruler was offered the area northeast of Brunei (the Sabah region) if Muhyiddin was successful in defeating his rival, Abdul Mubin of Pulau Cermin, with the help of Sulu forces.[21]

Muhyiddin finally won the civil war with Sulu assistance but did not honour his pledge of giving the territories in north Borneo to Sulu. Sulu thus broke away from Brunei overlordship and effectively established its independence. Of greater importance to Brunei's future was that Sulu began to challenge Brunei's political and commercial supremacy in the Sabah region.

The dynamics of external trade in the 1750s also led to the rise of Sulu as a powerful kingdom. European country traders, mainly English, began to make Jolo, the Sulu capital, as an important emporium for procuring Southeast Asian produce to use as exchange commodities for the China trade. The country traders supplied Sulu with guns, gunpowder and opium in exchange for the much sought-after Southeast Asian tropical produce. As the demand for tropical produce increased tremendously, Sulu used the arms and gunpowder obtained from the country traders to expand its territorial control over the rich hinterland of north Borneo. Thus, the struggle for supremacy in the Sabah region between Sulu and Brunei began in earnest in the 1750s. By the 1820s, Sulu was able to eliminate Brunei's influence in the Tempasuk and Marudu regions of the west coast, as well as all the coastal areas of the east coast of north Borneo until Balik Papan.[22] In its endeavour to exploit the riches of the Borneo hinterland, the Sulu Sultanate established a web of settlements along the coastal areas. To consolidate its political and administrative control in the region, it carved out a number of large dependencies. In 1761, when Alexander Dalrymple of the EEIC visited Jolo, the Sulu capital, and concluded a treaty of friendship and commerce with Sultan Muhammad Mohiodin,[23] the names of Sulu dependencies in north Borneo given to him were Papar, Marudu, Mangindora, and Tirum. Another account of the dependencies of the Sultan of Sulu was given by James Hunt in his article published in 1837 entitled "Some Particulars Relating to Sulo, in the Archipelago of Felicia". According to Hunt, two of the provinces of Sulu on the northeast coast of Borneo were Mangindora and Tirum. The island of Separan (Sipadan) was also mentioned. It was part of the province of Mangindora. Tirum was the last and southern most dependency of Sulu bordering the Kingdom of Bulungan.[24] In 1878, the Sulu Sultanate claimed jurisdiction over the dependencies of Pandasan, Marudu, Paitan, Sugut, Bonggaya, Labuk, Sandakan, Kinabatangan and Mumiang[25] (Mangindora thus became divided into Paitan, Sugut, Bonggaya, Labuk, Sandakan, and Kinabatangan, while Tirum was replaced by Mumiang by 1878). As a result of these developments, the Sabah region became a bone of contention between the two rival powers of Brunei and Sulu for more than two centuries, a problem inherited by the colonial powers, and then by the independent nations which succeeded them.

Thus, the process of cutting the Bornean melon, which was initiated by native powers, preceded, accompanied, and later, even superseded the colonial era. Another point to note is that, although the region of north Borneo was generally termed as "Saba" or "Sabah" by Brunei documents, it did not constitute a state or a *negeri*. Rather, by the eighteenth and the nineteenth centuries, this huge area was divided into three spheres of influence and jurisdiction. The coastal area of the west coast, consisting of twenty-three dependencies, was under the jurisdiction of Brunei. The coastal area from Pandasan in the north to Balik Papan on the east, as mentioned above, belonged to the Kingdom of Sulu, and was divided into a number of large dependencies. The interior remained independent and was held by tribal chiefs of various communities.[26] This region was later moulded into the apparatus of a new state called North Borneo by the British North Borneo Company (BNBC) from 1882 to 1946. In 1963, on the eve of the formation of Malaysia, the state's name was changed to Sabah.[27] The term "North Borneo" or "Sabah" will be used hereafter to refer to this region.

2.3.3 The Spanish Sphere of Influence in Borneo

We have seen how the Spanish established themselves in Manila in 1571 and subsequently tried to bring Brunei and Sulu under their control but failed to subjugate them. Spain lost interest in Brunei which continued to survive as a much-weakened state. The Spanish campaign to subdue Sulu continued, but "the Sulu Sultanate, more archipelagic and also more aggressive in character, developed both in the wake of Brunei's retreat and in opposition to the Spanish advance".[28] Sulu defied Spanish conquest for over three hundred years. In fact, as discussed earlier, the Sulu Sultanate emerged as a major regional power in the eighteenth century, funnelled by the dynamics of external trade.

The fortunes of Sulu, however, began to wane during the second half of the nineteenth century as a result of naval action by the British, the Spaniards and the Dutch which paralysed the slave raiding activities of the Sultanate. At the same time, however, new European nations, especially Germany, began to have trading contacts with Jolo. Britain, too, maintained her commercial relations with Sulu despite the destruction of some of Sulu's slave raiding centres such as Tempasuk and Marudu by the British navy in 1845. Fearing the danger of British, German and even Dutch intervention in the Sulu region, Spain began an earnest campaign in 1871 to subjugate the stubborn kingdom by instituting a naval blockade and by systematically destroying the Sulu trading craft.[29] Realizing that he would soon lose his kingdom to the Spanish, the Sultan of Sulu, Muhammad Jamaluladzam (1862–81), ceded all his possessions in North Borneo to the Overbeck-Dent Association (ODA) on 22 January 1878 with the hope of obtaining help from the British.[30] However, the expected help from Britain did not materialize, and Sulu was conquered by the Spanish six months later. On 22 July 1878, Sultan Muhammad Jamaluladzam signed the Treaty of Capitulation with Spain, by which he surrendered his kingdom and all its dependencies to the latter.[31] As we will see later in Chapter 3, Spain refused to recognize the Overbeck-Dent concessions obtained from the Sultan of Sulu on 22 January 1878 and accused the ODA of intruding into its sphere of jurisdiction in Borneo.

2.3.4 Dutch Expansion in Borneo

The DEIC and the EEIC initially concentrated in establishing their centres of trade in Java and the Spice Islands, so much so that Borneo was rather neglected. Even then, the Dutch established factories at Sambas and Sukanda almost on their arrival in the East but had to withdraw by 1622 as a result of an attack by a Javanese force. In the south, the Dutch signed monopoly contracts with Bandjermasin in 1635 and 1664 to secure the lucrative pepper trade of the kingdom. However, even here, conflict with the ruler finally led to war and withdrawal in 1669. Thus, the Dutch attempts to control the southwest and southeast areas of Borneo in the seventeenth century ended up in failure. Their position in Borneo was no better in the eighteenth century. As stated earlier, most of the Dutch possessions in the Malay Archipelago came under temporary English control from 1795 to 1816. Upon their return to the East in 1816 however, the Dutch, with great speed and energy, quickly established Netherlands sovereignty over Bandjermasin (1817), Sambas (1818) and Pontianak

(1818) and resumed their former policies of monopolistic commercial control.[32] As discussed earlier as well, strong protests from the merchants of Penang as well as Raffles ultimately led to the conclusion of the 1824 Anglo-Dutch Treaty dividing the Malay Archipelago into Dutch and English spheres of influence. Both parties excluded Borneo from the confines of this treaty, but the Dutch continued to entertain the notion that they had paramountcy over Borneo as well. Thus, when Britain and its private agents of colonial expansion began to make inroads into Borneo in the 1840s, the Dutch protested vehemently, but to no avail. Part of the opportunity afforded to other colonial powers, in this case the English, to establish themselves in the northern parts of Borneo rested with the Dutch. From 1825 to the 1840s, as they were too preoccupied with affairs in Java due to the Java War, 1825–30, they not only almost neglected their existing establishments in Borneo but also their ambition of expanding further northwards. This policy of disinterest in the vast northern part of the island, according to Graham Irwin, laid the said area "open to colonization by other European powers".[33] In 1841, James Brooke was to make his debut in Old Sarawak which was then part of the Brunei Empire. This event and subsequent British entrenchment in Brunei (1847) served as a wake-up call to the Dutch. Although the Dutch had generally neglected their possessions in Borneo in the 1820s to 1840s, some sort of consolidation was going on in east Borneo. In 1826, the Netherlands signed a Contract with the Sultan of Bandjermasin, by which the latter ceded the kingdom of Berou and its dependencies to the Dutch East Indies Government. The Kingdom of Berou was subsequently divided by the Dutch into smaller sultanates of Sambaliung, Gumungtabur, and Bulungan.[34] On 12 November 1850, the Government of the Netherlands East Indies concluded a Contract of Vassalage with the Sultan of Bulungan named Mohammad Khahar-Oedien [Kaharudin]. Article II of this Contract described the northern limits of the territories of the Sultanate of Bulungan extending as far as the Tawau River and Batu Tinagat. The said Article is worded as follows:[35]

ARTICLE II

The Territory of Boeloengan lies within the following limits:- Towards Goenoeng-Teboer; from the sea-shore inland, the River Karanliegan from its mouth to its source beyond the Batoe-Bevekkier and the Palpakh Mauntain; Towards the Zulu [Sulu] possessions on the sea-shore, the cape called Batoe Tinagat and beyond the River Tanwan [Tawau]

> The following islands shall belong to Boeloengan, namely Terakkan, Nenvoekkan and Sebittikh [Sebatik], together with the small islands belonging to them.

This area encroached upon a vast region claimed by the Sultan of Sulu, the southern limit of which was the Balik Papan River. Thus, once again we see that the territories claimed by local rulers overlapped, and European colonial powers who were entrenching themselves in the region inherited this problem of undefined boundaries.

2.3.5 The Extension of British Influence in Borneo

As discussed earlier, the English became interested again in the Malay Archipelago including Borneo in the second half of the eighteenth century because of their growing trade with China. A number of expeditions were sent from India by the EEIC to Southeast Asia to find a suitable site for fulfilling the commercial and strategic needs of the China trade. One such expedition was sent to the Borneo-Sulu-Philippine region in 1759 under the command of Alexander Dalrymple. In the following year, the EEIC Council at Madras instructed him to negotiate a treaty with the Sultan of Sulu for the purpose of acquiring a base for a factory. Dalrymple set sail in the EEIC's *Cuddalore*, reaching the Sulu capital, Jolo, in January 1861, where he concluded a treaty of friendship and commerce with Sultan Muhammad Mohiodin on 28 January 1761. The following year, he signed another agreement dated 26 July 1762 with two chiefs from the Sabah region, one named Modin Orang Tuan of Tempassuk, and another named Abdul Bendahara of Abai. By this agreement, these two chiefs granted to the EEIC all the land of Borneo "northward of Abai River" as well as the island of Usukan. Based on the strength of these two agreements, Dalrymple took possession of the island of Balambangan in the name of the EEIC on 23 January 1763. The treaty with Sulu was further consolidated with more agreements with its rulers in 1763, 1764 and 1769.[36]

Although Dalrymple had taken possession of Balambangan Island in 1763, a factory was only established there on 12 December 1773, under John Herbert. Herbert tried to expand the trade of the new settlement and sent messengers to various kingdoms in the region to increase supplies. In June 1774, a letter was sent to the Sultan of Brunei expressing the desire of the management to enter into an alliance with him. The Brunei Sultan sent an ambassador to Balambangan inviting the English to settle in his territories. As a follow-up, John Jesse, the Secretary at Balambangan, was appointed

Deputy Agent for Brunei in 1774 where he succeeded in concluding a treaty with the Sultan. By this treaty, the EEIC obtained exclusive trading rights in pepper and permission to establish a factory in the Sultan's territories in return for military assistance to Brunei in the case of an attack from its enemies, chiefly by Sulu. A factory was established near the capital at Brunei in 1774, and John Jesse was appointed as Resident. Meanwhile, the EEIC's settlement at Balambangan was destroyed by Sulu raiders in February 1775 and had to be abandoned. John Herbert and most of the company's establishment were able to escape to Brunei. Herbert appealed to the Sultan to permit the EEIC to establish a settlement in the ruler's domains. Jesse, who had established very cordial relations with the ruler, was instrumental in persuading the Sultan to agree to this request. On 28 March 1775, the Sultan of Brunei signed a treaty by which he granted the island of Labuan to the EEIC for all time.[37] Immediately after that, Labuan was taken possession of, and a settlement was started. Johannes Willi documents the proceedings as follows:[38]

> on 28 March 1775 he [the Sultan] signed a treaty by which he granted the Island of Labuan to the English East India Company for all time. On 16th April following, the *Endeavour* set sail for the acquired island, and Herbert hoisted the Company's flag on the spot where a new settlement with a fort was to be founded.

Herbert at once set about erecting fortifications at Labuan but instructions arrived from Madras in November 1775 for a total withdrawal from the region. The settlement at Labuan was therefore abandoned. The factory and agency at Brunei were also withdrawn simultaneously in November 1775.[39]

In December 1803, the EEIC once again occupied Balambangan. However, as the settlement failed to prosper, the island was evacuated in 1805 after the garrison had nearly starved. From 1803 to 1805, the Balambangan administrators also tried to re-establish the company in Brunei, and the 1775 cession of Labuan was reactivated. However, with the decision to abandon Balambangan in 1805, the EEIC's second venture in Labuan also did not materialize.[40]

2.3.6 The Establishment of James Brooke in Sarawak, 1841
British interest in the affairs of Brunei was once more activated in the 1840s as a result of a number of factors which included events in Brunei itself;

developments in Southeast Asia, especially the establishment of Singapore in 1819; the activities of an English adventurer named James Brooke in Sarawak; and Britain's takeover of Hong Kong in 1842.[41]

In Brunei, a rebellion broke out in one of its far-flung dependencies called Sarawak (hereafter referred to as Old Sarawak). The Brunei governor of the province, Pengiran Mahkota, was unable to suppress the uprising. The ruler of Brunei, Sultan Omar Ali Saifuddin II (r.1824–52) then sent his uncle, Raja Muda Hashim, the Pengiran Bendahara (Chief Minister) at the time, to quell the rebellion in the province. There is a reason to believe that Raja Muda Hashim was in fact exiled to this distant province.[42] In 1839, an English adventurer, James Brooke, visited Kuching, the capital of Old Sarawak in his schooner, the *Royalist*, looking for trading opportunities. He was well received by Raja Muda Hashim but finding that a rebellion was going on in the province, James decided to sail to the Celebes Islands. In 1840, he returned to Kuching to find that the fighting was still going on. At this juncture, Raja Muda Hashim asked for James Brooke's assistance to suppress the rebellion, hoping ultimately to enlist the Englishman's support for his return to, and reinstatement at the Brunei capital. As a reward, Raja Muda Hashim promised to appoint James as governor of Sarawak. James agreed to the terms, suppressed the uprising, and was appointed temporary governor by Raja Muda Hashim in 1841.[43] In 1842, James sailed to the Brunei capital where he secured his position from Sultan Omar Ali Saifuddin II. The Sultan gave him the title of Tuan Besar (Great Lord, not Raja) and appointed him as his representative in charge of affairs in Old Sarawak.[44]

James Brooke was anxious to expand British influence in Borneo. For this purpose, James Brooke's agent in London, Henry Wise, tried to secure official British recognition for Sarawak from 1841 to 1842. The British Government, however, showed no interest at the time. The First Opium War with China and the signing of the Treaty of Nanking in 1842, however, changed the British position. Borneo at once became strategically important for Britain for commercial and strategic reasons. In 1842, Wise also advanced a practical reason for the expansion of British commerce and influence in the region. The reason cited was the availability of coal in northwest Borneo. With the expansion of trade with China and the advent of the steamship, a supply of coal in northwest Borneo would be of great advantage to Britain. The presence of coal in Borneo was reported since 1837. Wise, therefore, urged the British Government to quickly establish a colony in northwest Borneo and impressed upon Sir Robert Peel, the British Prime Minister at the time, of the great advantage that would accrue to Britain by such a move. James Brooke also offered Sarawak as the first choice for such a colony. James felt that the establishment of a British colony in Borneo should serve as a stepping stone on a long-term basis for the expansion of British influence in the region. Irwin writes concerning James' feelings as follows:[45]

> In his opinion [James'] the establishment of a Crown Colony in Borneo ought not to be regarded as an end in itself, but merely as the first step in a much larger programme of British expansion through the Indian Archipelago.

The British Government, however, did not make a definite decision pertaining to James' offer of converting Sarawak into a crown colony.

2.3.7 Britain's Acquisition of Labuan, 1846
In the absence of such a decision, James advocated the expediency of establishing permanent British influence over the Brunei Sultanate. In March 1843, he suggested that such an objective could be attained quickly by obtaining the cession of Labuan from the Sultan of Brunei which could be easily arranged. The British Government was keen on acquiring Labuan and appointed James Brooke as British Confidential Agent for Borneo in 1845.[46] In November 1846, Captain G. Rodney Mundy, who was in charge of the British Naval vessels on the northwest coast of Borneo, received instructions to proceed to Brunei and obtain the cession of Labuan from the Sultan. Mundy arrived at Brunei together with James Brooke and secured a treaty from Sultan Omar Ali Saifuddin II signed on 18 December 1846 by which the Sultan ceded the island of Labuan to Britain. On 24 December 1846, Mundy sailed to Labuan and took formal possession of the island, which thus became a British Crown Colony.[47]

2.3.8 The Anglo-Brunei Treaty of 1847
The British consolidated their position in the region by signing a Treaty of Friendship and Commerce with the Sultan of Brunei in 1847 by which Britain practically gained paramountcy in the territories of the still vast empire of Brunei. The Dutch protested at the establishment of James Brooke at Sarawak as well as at the 1847 Anglo-Dutch treaty, but their protests were rejected outright by the British Government.[48] Thus began a new phase in the partition of Borneo with a definitive intervention by Britain and its colonial agents.

Britain, however, used the 1847 treaty with Brunei as a keep-off sign against other European powers rather than for extending political control over the Sultan's domains. On the other hand, Britain actively permitted the expansion of its colonial empire by private agents; in this case James Brooke, who had established himself as an independent ruler of Old Sarawak in 1846. Unprotected by Britain and crumbling rapidly, the Brunei Empire became an easy prey for the expansionist designs of Rajah James Brooke. From 1846 to 1890, Old Sarawak, under Rajah James Brooke (r.1841–68) and his successor, Rajah Charles Brooke (r.1868–1917) swallowed up almost the whole of the Brunei Empire, except its capital and the region in north Borneo.[49]

2.3.9 The Emergence of Western Speculators in North Borneo
Since neither the British Government not its colonial agents took effective control of the north Borneo region, it soon became the hunting ground for American and European speculators or territorial concession hunters.

2.3.10 The American Venture
The man who initiated this process was C.L. Moses, the US First Consul to Brunei. The United States had concluded a commercial treaty with Brunei in 1850, but it was activated only in 1865. When Moses took up his post in 1865, he wished to utilize his position for personal gain. In the same year, on 11 August 1865, he was able to obtain from Sultan Abdul Mumin (r.1852–85) of Brunei, for a period of ten years, the lease of a large territorial concession in North Borneo stretching from the Sulaman River on the west coast to the Paitan River on the east. The Sultan was to receive a sum of $4,500 (Spanish dollars) a year and the Temenggong a sum of $4,000. Moses was interested only in making a quick profit, and as such, soon sold off his concessions to a Hong Kong merchant named Joseph W. Torrey and his associates on 9 September 1865. This group then formed the American Trading Company of Borneo which tried to develop plantation agriculture at Kimanis in 1865, but the venture failed. Torrey returned to Hong Kong and tried to dispose of his possessions in Sabah to other interested parties. In 1870, Gustavus Baron von Overbeck, the Consul-General for Austria-Hungary in Hong Kong, became interested in the Sabah leases, and subsequently acquired them from Torrey and the American Trading Company of Borneo in 1875 for a sum of $15,000 provided a renewal could be secured within nine months.[50] The Sultan

refused to renew the grants, and Overbeck, having failed to arouse any interest in the venture in Vienna, turned to the firm of Dent Brothers of London for financial support.

2.2.11 The Overbeck-Dent Association (ODA), The Brunei Grants (1877), and The Sulu Grants (1878)

Alfred Dent, the younger partner of the British firm, saw great potential in the Sabah venture and agreed to go into partnership with Overbeck. On 27 March 1877, the ODA was formed by the two men for the purpose of obtaining the Sabah leases and selling them off for a profit.[51] On 16 December 1877, Overbeck arrived at Labuan in a chartered steamer, the "America", and had an interview with W.H. Treacher, the British Acting Consul-General for Borneo. The Baron told Treacher that the object of his organization was to acquire territorial concessions in Sabah from the Sultan of Brunei, "and form a British Company, the main desire being to develop the agricultural resources of the northern portion of Borneo".[52] Overbeck then proceeded to Brunei where he managed to persuade Sultan Abdul Mumin and Pengiran Temenggung Hashim to conclude five documents on 29 December 1877. Through these agreements, the Sultan and the Temenggung leased to Overbeck and Dent an area extending from the Sulaman River on the west coast of Sabah to the Sibuku River on the east, including some of their *tulin* rivers (private dependencies), chiefly Papar, Benoni, and Kimanis. The ODA was to pay the Sultan $12,000 and the Temenggung $3,000 yearly. The major difference in the new arrangements was that there was no time limit on the leases. The Sultan also, by a Commission (document 5) appointed Baron von Overbeck as "Supreme Ruler" of the territories granted, with the title "Maharajah of Sabah" and "Rajah of Gaya and Sandakan".[53] Baron von Overbeck soon learnt, however, that the Sultan of Sulu had rival claims over the territories granted by the Sultan of Brunei. Fearing that the Brunei Grants might lead to an international dispute, Overbeck decided to secure the Sultan of Sulu's rights over Sabah as well. Treacher himself was of the opinion that the Sultan of Brunei's territory extended at the utmost from the Sulaman River to the Marudu Bay (on the west coast) and the remaining territories mentioned in the Brunei Grants, that is from the Marudu Bay to the Sibuku River were actually under Sulu rule. The idea that Overbeck should also secure the Sultan of Sulu's rights over Sabah might have originated from Treacher, who now began to take an active interest in the activities of Overbeck. Treacher, who wished to see that British interests were safeguarded, accompanied Overbeck to Jolo, the chief island of Sulu, with the intention of overseeing the negotiations himself, and by ensuring that relevant clauses were included in the Sulu Grants so that Britain had sufficient jurisdiction over the leases.

Overbeck and Treacher had come to Jolo at an opportune moment. Since 1871, the Spanish authorities in the Philippines had launched one of their periodic campaigns aimed at subjugating the stubborn kingdom. The island of Jolo was under siege, and the capital was in Spanish hands. Overbeck and Treacher met the Sultan at Meimbong on the southern side of the island. Fearing that he would most likely be forced to capitulate to the Spanish, Sultan Muhammad Jamaluladzam (r.1862–81) was not unwilling to negotiate with Overbeck. The presence of an agent of the British Government in the person of Treacher raised the Sultan's hopes of obtaining British military and political support against Spain. In an agreement signed on 22 January 1878, and quite similar to the Brunei Grants, but including additional clauses which gave the British Government the ultimate right over the future transfer of the concessions granted, the Sultan parted with his Borneo possessions for an annual rental of $5,000. The area ceded to the ODA extended from the Pandasan River on the west coast to the Sibuku River on the east, though the Sultan insisted he had jurisdiction from Kimanis to Balik Papan, and wished the limits to be so included. It was only upon Treacher's advice that he agreed to the southern limit being fixed at the Sibuku River. By a Commission bearing the same date, the Sultan of Sulu also appointed Overbeck as "Datu Bendahara and Rajah of Sandakan".[54] As discussed earlier, the Kingdom of Sulu was conquered by the Spanish six months later on 22 July 1878.

As far as the ODA was concerned, it had already spent a considerable sum of money in obtaining the concessions and as such was unable to finance the establishment of a centralized governmental structure immediately. To leave Sabah temporarily to its own fate without assuming some semblance of physical control over it would have aggravated the existing political situation in Sabah, which was far from stable. Besides, the latter course would have weakened the ODA's attempts to float a shareholding company and to obtain support from the British Government. Overbeck had to some extent, made preparations for such a contingency. When he came in the chartered ship, the "America" from Singapore to Labuan in 1877, he had brought along with him on board the ship three Englishmen. They were William Pretyman, William B. Pryer, and H.L. Leicester. After the agreement with the Sultan of Sulu was concluded in January 1878, Overbeck decided to start a rudimentary administration at key settlements, mainly as a "keep off" sign to other powers. As a result, Pryer was put in charge of the east coast and stationed at Kampung German, or the original Sandakan, a small village then on Timbang Island in Sandakan Bay on 11 February 1878. In April of the same year, Pretyman and Leicester were placed on the west coast at Tempasuk and Papar respectively. North Borneo was administratively divided into the East Coast and West Coast Residencies by Overbeck. Both Pryer and Pretyman were given the title of Resident, and Leicester that of Assistant Resident.[55]

2.3.12 Dent's Application for a Royal Charter, 1878

While the pioneering Residents were trying to establish a semblance of administration at their outposts in North Borneo, Alfred Dent and Overbeck were trying to dispose off their concessions in Europe to the highest bidder. However, they found themselves in a quandary as the restrictive clauses imposed by Treacher in the Sulu agreement precluded the possibility of selling them anywhere except in Britain. Dent decided that the best option open was to float a shareholding company in Britain and obtain a royal charter for it, so as to give it credibility, legitimacy, and protection as a governing body of such a vast territory. Consequently, on 2 December 1878, Alfred Dent applied for a Royal Charter from the British Government.[56] In his application, he outlined the activities of the ODA and proposed to set up a company, which would, if granted a charter, administer, and develop North Borneo along British lines of government, would initiate a process to abolish trade monopolies, and would protect the interests of the indigenous people. It was proposed that the British Government would have control over the conduct of foreign relations and the appointment of the principal administrative and judicial officers in the territory; and in return for the security and prestige it lent the chartered company, the British Government would be able to extend its political influence over a large area of strategic and economic importance without the burden of full sovereign responsibilities.[57] Dent began to canvass for support for his project and brought his ideas to bear upon influential personalities in London, such as Members of Parliament, Foreign Office personnel, and ex-administrators who had served in high-ranking positions in the East. With their help a meeting was convened on 26 March 1879 at the Westminster Palace Hotel at which Dent's project was hailed and a resolution taken to send a deputation to meet Lord Salisbury, the Secretary of State for Foreign Affairs in the Conservative government of Lord Beaconfield, with the specific aim of requesting his government for support.[58] Though favourably disposed to Dent's venture, the government was obliged to study the issue deeply as it involved serious international and external political implications.

2.3.13 The British North Borneo Provisional Association (BNBPA), 1881–82

Meanwhile, Dent had acquired Overbeck's rights in the venture as Overbeck wished to retire from the enterprise. In 1881, the chances of Dent obtaining a charter improved tremendously, as the new Gladstone's government was supportive of Dent's project. Dent, therefore took this opportunity to form a company called the British North Borneo Provisional Association (BNBPA), in March 1881 to which he sold his rights at a good profit although he still continued to play an active role in the association's affairs as managing director.[59] In May 1881, Dent successfully obtained the services of W.H. Treacher from the Colonial Office to be appointed as the first Governor of North Borneo.[60] Treacher took up his new appointment on 7 August 1881 and set about establishing the apparatus of a central government in the new territory.

2.3.14 The Charter and the Formation of the British North Borneo Company (BNBC)

While Treacher and his handful of officers were busy trying to increase the jurisdiction of the government over selected areas in Sabah, the Charter issue was being resolved in London. After carefully considering Dent's application and the tangled nature of claims to North Borneo by Spain, Holland and the United States, Gladstone's government decided that Dent's concessions in North Borneo merited support, especially as they were considered vital for safeguarding and advancing British commercial and strategic interests. On 1 November 1881, the government finally granted the long-awaited Charter incorporating the BNBC.[61] The company was actually formed on 4 April 1882;[62] it acquired the rights of the Provisional Association on 19 April and finally took over the administration of North Borneo in June of the same year.[63] The company's affairs in London were supervised by a Court of Directors headed by a chairman. Sir Ratherford Alcock served as the company's first chairman from 1882 to 1893. The granting of the Royal Charter to the BNBC in 1881 by the British Government signified a number of aspects for British imperial policy in Borneo. The British Government under Gladstone wished to continue its policy of holding paramountcy in the territories of the Brunei Empire, but without committing itself to any direct political control. It therefore, adopted the strategy of extending its influence through the concept of the "informal empire".[64] Thus, in the case of North Borneo, the idea of informal control through a chartered company was revived although the age of such companies was long past. By granting a Royal Charter to the BNBC, Britain obtained a strong hold on the territory of North Borneo by retaining control over foreign affairs and defence. The company was also bound to remain British in character and domicile. Moreover, the appointment of all the principal administrative officers of the new state, especially its Governor, required the express permission of the British Government.[65]

The BNBC ruled the new territory, styled North Borneo, from 1882 to 1946 with the exception of the Japanese Occupation period from 1942 to 1945. It is during this time that the new state of North Borneo was born. The establishment of the ODA in North Borneo and the granting of a Royal Charter to the BNBC in 1881 by the British Government brought strong protests from Spain, the Netherlands and even Rajah Charles Brooke of Sarawak. The British Government thus became involved in ironing out these differences with Spain and the Netherlands in the decades to come. This narrative will form the substance of Chapter 3.

2.3.15 Britain Established Protectorates over North Borneo, Brunei and Sarawak in 1888

One of the reasons why the British Government granted the Charter to the BNBC in 1881 was to consolidate its weak legal and political position in North Borneo. The 1870s and 1880s was a period of "New Imperialism" in Europe. During this time, the pace of imperialist expansion by Western powers intensified so greatly that "by 1900 the advanced countries partitioned most of the earth among themselves".[66] In the Borneo region, Britain was apprehensive of the designs of the new rising powers of Germany and Italy who had also joined the colonial race. The fear of Germany establishing an outpost in the North Borneo region was one factor why the British Government approved the granting of the Charter to the BNBC in 1881 as a measure to strengthen its position in the region.[67] However, even this move was not strong enough in international law to guarantee Britain's paramountcy in the area. Eventually the Madrid Protocol of 1885 settled the question of British sovereignty in North Borneo and removed the danger of German intervention there as the latter was also a signatory to the Protocol.[68] However, another section of the Brunei Empire now became a hot spot; that is, the Brunei capital itself and whatever remained of the once-sprawling kingdom. In the 1880s, especially after the establishment of the BNBC in North Borneo, a race ensued between the company and the Brookes of Sarawak to divide whatever was left of the shrinking kingdom. In 1882 for example, Sarawak annexed the Brunei province of Baram. In 1884, the BNBC obtained a lease of the Padas region from the Brunei overlords.[69] The British Government was alarmed that the volatile and fluid situation in Brunei might invite German or French intervention. Of the two, Germany was considered the more dangerous one. Lord Salisbury, the British Prime Minister at that time warned in October 1885 as follows:[70]

> [Bismark] might as likely as not seize the balance [of Brunei] while we are waiting to see it reach the proper stage of decay.

The British Government even contemplated partitioning off Brunei totally between North Borneo and Sarawak but eventually decided to preserve the tiny kingdom. To prevent the possibility of another European power establishing a foothold in the area of its influence, Britain decided to establish protectorates over all the three states within the area of British paramountcy, that is, North Borneo, Sarawak and Brunei. The three Protectorate agreements were concluded on 12 May 1888, 5 September 1888, and 17 September 1888, respectively.[71] All the three treaties were drafted in a similar format. Article III of each treaty was the most important as it gave the British Government total control over the conduct of each state's relations with foreign states, as well as among the three of them. Article III of the Protectorate Agreement with North Borneo reads as follows:[72]

> The relations between the State of North Borneo and all foreign States, including the States of Brunei and of Sarawak, shall be conducted by Her Majesty's Government, or in accordance with its directions; and if any difference should arise between the Government of North Borneo and that of any other State, the Company, as representing the State of North Borneo, agrees to abide by the decision of Her Majesty's Government, and to take all necessary measures to give effect thereto.

By this move, Britain's sovereignty over these three states became explicit and unassailable.

2.4 ADMINISTRATIVE STRUCTURE OF THE BNBC

Before moving on to the next chapter, a short description of the administrative structure established by the BNBC in North Borneo, especially on the east coast, merits some attention as it became an important reference point in the written and oral submissions of both Malaysia and Indonesia.

As mentioned earlier, W.H. Treacher, hitherto the Acting Governor of Labuan and British Consul General for Borneo, was appointed as the first Governor of North Borneo under the BNBPA in May 1881. When the BNBC took over the administration of North Borneo from the BNBPA in June 1882, the services of Treacher as Governor were retained.[73] North Borneo was divided into two broad administrative divisions called the East Coast and West Coast Residencies. Each Residency was placed under the control of an administrative officer called a Resident. In the East Coast Residency, W.B. Pryer continued in his post as Resident based at Sandakan till his retirement in 1895. The West Coast Residency, with its headquarters at Papar, was headed by Resident A.H. Everett who had joined the service on 5 September 1879 under the ODA.[74] As new stations were opened, additional officers called Assistant Residents were appointed to help the Residents. In 1909, North Borneo was divided into five Residencies. The five Residencies thus created were the West Coast Residency; the Kudat Residency; the Interior Residency, the Sandakan Residency; and the East Coast or Tawau Residency.[75] It is the Tawau Residency that concerns us most as the disputed islands of Sipadan and Ligitan are situated in that region. As will be seen in Chapter 3, the Dutch initially claimed jurisdiction till Batu Tinagat and established a station at Tawau in 1879. On the other hand, the BNBC claimed territories as far south as the Sibuku River. The dispute over overlapping territorial claims in the region was finally settled between the British and the Dutch through a long process of negotiations leading to the Anglo-Dutch Boundary Convention of 1891 and culminating in the Anglo-Dutch Boundary Treaty of 1915. Meanwhile the BNBC established government outposts at Lahad Datu (1886), Semporna (1887) and Tawau (1892).[76]

In the vicinity of the Semporna Administrative District, there were about sixteen islands which lay beyond the three marine leagues limit and were therefore not included in the 1878 Sulu Grants. The company, however, mistakenly thought they were part of its territories and began to extend its jurisdiction over them. As a consequence, these sixteen islands, including Sipadan and Ligitan were brought under the administration of the Semporna District by 1900 (see Figure 1.5). With particular reference to Sipadan and Ligitan, the company subsequently undertook a number of administrative measures pertaining to its jurisdiction over these two islands. Some of these may be elaborated below. An important issue concerned the collection of turtle eggs on Sipadan Island. Trade in turtle eggs was an important source of revenue for the Sultan of Sulu, who, before the extension of the company's rule to the said island, traditionally vested the right to collect turtle eggs on Sipadan Island to the local chief in charge of Danawan Island. The BNBC continued this practice and in 1904 settled a dispute by recognizing the customary rights of two chiefs of Danawan Island, Panglima Abu Sari and his brother Haji Mohamed to collect turtle eggs from Sipadan. The decision confirming the rights of the two chiefs mentioned above was made in 1904 by the Resident of the East Coast at that time, E.H. Barraut. This confirmation is recorded in the Company's documents as follows:[77]

> Mr. Barraut, when Resident East Coast, ruled that the right to collect turtle eggs on *Sipadan Island* belonged to Panglima Busari [Abu Sari] and this brother Haji Mohamed under a vested right, just as the right to collect Birds' nests in Madai caves. [author's emphasis.]

In 1910, Semporna's Assistant District Officer once again presided over a further dispute involving the right to collect turtle eggs on Sipadan Island. This time the dispute was between Panglima Abu Sari and Haji Mohamed, the Company's Chiefs on Danawan Island on one side and Panglima Udang, the Company's Head Chief in Semporna District on the other. According to the original arrangement, Panglima Abu Sari collected turtle eggs on Sipadan Island for fifteen nights of each month and Haji Mohamad for the next fifteen nights. Panglima Udang, however, wanted a share of three nights each month. The Assistant District Officer of Semporna wrote in 1910 as follows:[78]

> Pang. Busari [Abu Sari] however says he gave the three nights a month to Pang. Udang because he thought that it was a Government order... Neither of the two Chiefs of Denawan wish the Panglima [Udang] to collect on Sipadan, and told me so straight. I have told the Panglima [Udang] to stop collection on Sipadan...

Further evidence of the BNBC's jurisdiction over Sipadan Island appeared in 1913 when the Resident of the East Coast of North Borneo, T.N. Kough issued a licence to Panglima Abu Sari and Maharaja Anggai [Haji Mohamed's son] for the collection of turtle eggs on Sipadan Island.[79]

In 1916, the company's Government replaced the 1913 licence with a new one issued under Ordinance XXX of 1914. This new licence empowered Panglima Abu Sari and Maharaja Anggai of Danawan Island to collect turtle eggs on Sipadan Island for a period of five years that is from 1 January 1916 to 1 January 1921, with a provision for a further renewal of five years.

A *Surat Katrangan [Keterangan]* [A letter of Explanation] to Panglima Abu Sari and Maharaja Anggai in Malay was also issued by the Acting Resident East Coast on 6 May 1916.[80] On 1 June 1917, the Government of North Borneo passed an important legislation called the "Turtle Preservation Ordinance, 1917". The Ordinance gave the Governor of North Borneo the power to declare certain territories of the State of North Borneo as "Native Reserves" for the collection of turtle eggs. This legislation became significant to Sipadan. On 2 June 1919, the said island was declared a Native Reserve under the 1917 Ordinance.[81] Further evidence of the BNBC's occupation of Sipadan Island appears in 1933 when under section 28 of the Land Ordinance 1930, the North Borneo Government declared Sipadan Island a bird sanctuary.[82]

The State of North Borneo was taken over by the British Government from the BNBC in 1946 and became a Crown Colony till 1963 when it became part of Malaysia. The Colonial Government continued the practice of the BNBC in exercising jurisdiction over Sipadan and Ligitan Islands. For example, the Colonial Government of North Borneo constructed a lighthouse, on Sipadan Island in 1962 and another one on Ligitan Island in July 1963.[83] Subsequently, the Malaysian Government continued maintaining and operating these lighthouses.

The emergence of Indonesia and Malaysia as legal successors to the Dutch in the Dutch East Indies and the British in North Borneo respectively will be discussed in Chapter 5.

Notes

1. D.G.E. Hall, *A History of South-East Asia* (Basingstoke: Macmillan, 1981), p. 267.
2. D.R. SarDesai, *Southeast Asia: Past and Present* (Basingstoke: Macmillan, 1989), pp. 60–63.
3. Manual Teixeira, "Early Portuguese and Spanish Contacts with Borneo", *Da Sociedade De Geografia De Lisboa*, July–December 1964, pp. 208–313.
4. SarDesai, *Southeast Asia*, p. 62.
5. John F. Cady, *Southeast Asia: Its Historical Development* (New York: McGraw-Hill, 1964), pp. 235–38.
6. Hall, *A History of South-East Asia*, p. 321.
7. Ibid., pp. 333–34.
8. For more details, see K.G. Tregonning, *A History of Modern Malaya* (London: Eastern Universities Press, 1964), pp. 75–76. For an excellent work on the offer of Penang by the Sultan of Kedah to the EEIC, see R. Bonney, *Kedah 1771–1821:*

The Search for Security and Independence (Kuala Lumpur: Oxford University Press, 1974).

9. Tregonning, *A History of Modern Malaya*, pp. 75–76.
10. Hall, *A History of South-East Asia*, pp. 365 and 580–81; and J. Kennedy, *A History of Malaya* (Kuala Lumpur: S. Abdul Majid and Co., 1993), pp. 82–88.
11. L.A. Mills, *British Malaya 1824–67* (Kuala Lumpur: Malaysian Branch of the Royal Asiatic Society, 2003), p. 87.
12. Hall, *A History of South-East Asia*, p. 567.
13. Percival Spear, *A History of India*, vol. 2 (Harmondsworth: Penguin Books, 1975), pp. 139–49.
14. See D.S. Ranjit Singh, *Brunei 1839–1983: The Problems of Political Survival* (Singapore: Oxford University Press, 1991), pp. 12–20.
15. Johannes Willi of Gais, *The Early Relations of England with Borneo to 1805* (Langensalza: Druk von Herman Rayer & Sohne, 1922), p. 98.
16. For a good source on this, see Teixeira, "Early Portuguese and Spanish Contacts with Borneo", pp. 301–13.
17. Ranjit Singh, *Brunei 1839–1983*, pp. 21–22.
18. See Teixeira, "Early Portuguese and Spanish Contacts with Borneo", pp. 301–13.
19. E.H. Blair and J.A. Robertson, eds., *The Philippine Islands*, vol. 4 (Cleveland, 1903–9), pp. 125–35; 148–215.
20. Ranjit Singh, *Brunei 1839–1983*, pp. 30–31.
21. H. Low, "Selesilah (Book of Descent) of the Rajas of Bruni", *Journal of the Straits Branch of the Royal Asiatic Society (JSBRAS)*, no. 5 (June 1880): 16–17.
22. J.F. Warren, *The Sulu Zone, 1768–1898: The Dynamics of External Trade, Slavery and Ethnicity in the Transformation of a Southeast Asian Maritime State* (Singapore: Singapore University Press, 1981), pp. 77–79.
23. For more details on Alexander Dalrymple's expedition to Sulu, see below.
24. For a good account of Sulu's dependencies in north Borneo from the late eighteenth to the middle of the nineteenth centuries, see Alexander Dalrymple, "Essay Towards an Account of Sooloo", in *Journal of the Indian Archipelago and Eastern Asia*, Series 1, vol. 3, edited by J.R. Logan (Singapore: Society of London, 1849); J.K. Reynolds, "Towards an Account of Sulu and its Borneo Dependencies, 1700–1878" (Thesis submitted as partial fulfilment of M.A., University of Wisconsin, Madison, 1970), pp. 33–48; and J. Hunt, "Some Particulars Relating to Sulo, in the Archipelago of Felicia", in *Notices of the Indian Archipelago and Adjacent Countries*, edited by J.H. Moor (London: Cass, 1968; first published 1837).
25. See C.O. 874/54, Documents 6 and 7.
26. W.H. Treacher, Acting Consul-General for Borneo, to the Earl of Derby, 22 January 1878, Letter 118, *Papers Relating to the Affairs of Sulu and Borneo Part I (Spain No. 1, 1882): Borneo And Sulu*, F.O. 12/86.
27. D.S. Ranjit Singh, *The Making of Sabah, 1865–1941: The Dynamics of Indigenous Society*, 3rd ed. (Kota Kinabalu: Sabah State Government, 2011), pp. 3–5.

28. Nicholas Tarling, *Britain, The Brookes and Brunei* (Kuala Lumpur: Oxford University Press, 1971), p. 7.
29. Warren, *The Sulu Zone*, pp. 104–25; 191–97.
30. For more details, see below.
31. Acting Consul-General Treacher to the Marquis of Salisbury, 5 August 1878, letter 127; *Papers Relating to the Affairs of Sulu and Borneo Part 1*, F.O. 12/86, f. 290.
32. Hall, *A History of South-East Asia*, pp. 324; 562–66.
33. Graham Irwin, *Nineteenth-Century Borneo: A Study in Diplomatic Rivalry* (Singapore: Donald Moore Books, 1965), p. 68.
34. International Court of Justice (ICJ), *Judgment, Case Concerning Sovereignty Over Pulau Ligitan and Pulau Sipadan (Indonesia/Malaysia)*, The Hague, 17 December 2002, p. 16.
35. For a translated version of this Contract of Vassalage, see inclosure in M. Hartsen to Count de Bylandt, 19 March 1889, Item 44, C.O. 874/191. Also see "Memorandum respecting the Boundary between the Netherlands and Soloh [Sulu] Possessions on the North-east Coast of Borneo", in Count de Bylandt to Earl of Granville, 6 April 1883, item 12, C.O. 874|191.
36. For these various treaties and agreements, see F.O. 12/86, ff. 315–318; and J. de V. Allen, A.J. Stockwell, and L.R. Wright, *A Collection of Treaties and Other Documents Affecting the States of Malaysia, 1761–1963*, vol. 2 (London: Oceana Publications Inc., 1961), pp. 371–88.
37. Willi, *The Early Relations of England with Borneo to 1805*, pp. 98–109.
38. Ibid., p. 109.
39. Ibid., p. 114. Also see Tarling, *Britain, the Brookes and Brunei*, pp. 15–16.
40. D.E. Brown, *Brunei: The Structure and History of a Bornean Malay Sultanate*, Monograph of the *Brunei Museum Journal*, vol. 2, no. 2, 1970, p. 145.
41. For the entrenchment of British interests in China as a result of the "Opium War" of 1839–42, and the Treaty of Nanking 1842, see Warren I. Cohen, *East Asia at the Center* (New York: Colombia University Press, 2000), pp. 248–53.
42. Ranjit Singh, *Brunei 1839–1983*, pp. 47–52.
43. For more details on James Brooke's visits to Kuching in 1839 and 1840, his relations with Raja Muda Hassim and the rebellion in Sarawak, see *Letter from Borneo with Notices of the Country and its Inhabitants*, addressed to James Gardner, by J. Brooke, dated 10 December 1841, F.O. 12/1, ff. 31–38.
44. See Allen, Stockwell, and Wright, *A Collection of Treaties and Other Documents*, vol. 2, pp. 573–74.
45. Irwin, *Nineteenth-Century Borneo*, p. 88.
46. James Brooke to the Earl of Aberdeen, 31 March 1845, F.O. 12|3, f. 7.
47. Irwin, *Nineteenth-Century Borneo*, pp. 122–24.
48. Tarling, *Britain, the Brookes and Brunei*, p. 71. For the text of the Treaty, see W.G. Maxwell and W.S. Gibson, *Treaties and Engagements Affecting the Malay States and Borneo* (London: Jes. Truscott, 1924), pp. 143–47.

49. See Ranjit Singh, *Brunei 1839–1983*, pp. 59–73. Also see generally, Steven Runciman, *The White Rajahs: A History of Sarawak from 1841 to 1946* (Cambridge: Cambridge University Press, 1960).

50. C.O. 874/1, 2, 3 and 12. See also K.G. Tregonning, "American Activity in North Borneo, 1865–1881", *Pacific Historical Review* 23, no. 4 (November 1954): 358–61.

51. See Articles of Agreement between Alfred Dent and Baron von Overbeck, 27 March 1877, C.O. 874/16.

52. W.H. Treacher, Acting Consul-General for Borneo to the Earl of Derby, 2 January 1878, letter 116, *Papers Relating to the Affairs of Sulu and Borneo Part 1*, F.O. 12/86, f. 288.

53. Documents 1–5, C.O. 874/54.

54. Documents 6 and 7, C.O. 874/54; and Treacher to the Earl of Derby, 22 January 1878, letter 118, *Papers Relating to the Affairs of Sulu and Borneo, Part 1*, F.O. 12/86, f. 288.

55. Treacher to the Earl of Derby, 2 January 1878, letter 116, *Papers Relating to the Affairs of Sulu and Borneo, Part 1*, F.O. 12/86, f. 288; and Tom Harrison, ed., "The Diary of Mr. W. Pretyman, First Resident of Tempasuk, North Borneo (1878–1880)", *Sarawak Museum Journal* 7, no. 8 (New Series), No. 23 (Old Series) (December 1956): 337–38.

56. Alfred Dent to the Marquis of Salisbury, 2 December 1878, Letter 137, *Papers Relating to the Affairs of Sulu and Borneo, Part 1*, F.O. 12/86.

57. Ibid.

58. Sir Rutherford Alcock to the Marquis of Salisbury, 31 March 1879, Letter 141, *Papers Relating to the Affairs of Sulu and Borneo, Part 1*, F.O. 12/86. Sir Rutherford Alcock was elected chairman of this meeting.

59. C.O. 874/31 and C.O. 874/170.

60. Alfred Dent to W.H. Treacher, 31 May 1881, C.O. 874/117.

61. Lord Tenterden to Dent, 1 November 1881, Letter 193, *Papers Relating to the Affairs of Sulu and Borneo, Part 1*, F.O. 12/86.

62. See Deed of Settlement of the BNBC, 4 April 1882, C.O. 874/33.

63. C.O. 874/172.

64. For a fuller discussion of this concept, see W.D. McIntyre, *The Imperial Frontier in the Tropics, 1865–1875* (London: Palgrave Macmillan, 1967).

65. For a copy of the Charter of 1881, see Lord Tenterden to Dent, 1 November 1881, Letter 193 and inclosure, *Papers Relating to the Affairs of Sulu and Borneo, Part 1*, F.O. 12/86.

66. R.R. Palmer and Joel Colton, *A History of the Modern World*, 5th ed. (New York: Alfred A. Knopf, 1978), p. 603.

67. N. Tarling, "Borneo and British Intervention in Malaya", *Journal of Southeast Asian Studies* 5, no. 2 (September 1974): 162.

68. See Chapter 3 for more details.

69. See Tarling, *Britain, the Brookes and Brunei*, pp. 274; 302–4.

70. Quoted in Irwin, *Nineteenth-Century Borneo*, p. 213.
71. See Tarling, *Britain, the Brookes and Brunei*, pp. 307–18; and Ranjit Singh, *Brunei 1839–1983*, pp. 67–73. Copies of the Protectorate Agreements can be found in F.O. 12/86, ff. 426–28.
72. F.O. 12/86, f. 426.
73. Tenterden to Sir Rutherford Alcock, 15 August 1882, enclosure in Secretary BNBC to Treacher, 18 August 1882, Courts Despatch 44/1882, C.O. 874/292.
74. Diary of W. Pretyman, 5 September 1879, C.O. 874/72, f. 79.
75. *Administration and Annual Reports, North Borneo, 1909*, C.O. 648/2, f. 4, p. 6.
76. K.G. Tregonning, *Under Chartered Company Rule (North Borneo 1881–1946)* (Singapore: University of Malaya Press, 1958), pp. 86, 191, and 192; and *British North Borneo Herald*, 1 June 1887, pp. 119–21.
77. Assistant District Officer Semporna to Resident East Coast, 21 January 1916, Resident of The East Coast, (R.O.E.C.) 39/16 Sabah State Archives, (SSA): For evidence that E.H. Barraut was Resident of the East Coast in 1904, see *The British North Borneo Official Gazette*, 1 August 1905, pp. 135–37, C.O. 855.
78. Assistant District Officer, Semporna to the Resident, East Coast, 26 January 1916, R.O.E.C. 324/10, SSA.
79. Acting Resident East Coast to Government Secretary, 26 January 1916, R.O.E.C. 39/16, SSA.
80. See Copy of this *Surat* in R.O.E.C. 39/16, SSA.
81. Government Notification 129 of 1919, SSA.
82. See Notification No. 69, *British North Borneo Official Gazette*, 1 February 1933, p. 28, C.O. 855.
83. Report of the Committee of Investigation (State of Sabah), Re: Sipadan and Ligitan, Kota Kinabalu, 1975, vol. 2, pp. 24–27.

3

The Resolution of the Anglo-Spanish Claims and the Anglo-Dutch Boundary in North Borneo, 1878–1915

3.1 INTRODUCTION

By 1881, we see that three overlapping colonial spheres of influence had emerged in North Borneo. These included the Spanish sphere which involved jurisdiction over the former dependencies of the Sulu Sultanate from Pandasan to the Balik Papan River. The next was the Dutch sphere of influence which extended on the east coast up to Batu Tinagat and the Tawau River in the north. And finally, there emerged the British sphere of influence in the state of North Borneo with the establishment of the Overbeck-Dent Association (ODA) and the granting of the Royal Charter to the British North Borneo Company (BNBC) by the British Government in 1881. As noted in Chapter 2, Britain had already established a sort of paramountcy in the realm of the Brunei Empire through the Treaty of Friendship and Commerce concluded with Brunei in 1847. However, Britain did not venture into the area directly to exercise effective control. With the granting of the Charter to the BNBC in 1881, Britain somewhat sealed the weakness of its policy in North Borneo, and the question of its sovereignty became implicit. All the three spheres of colonial control criss-crossed as they were themselves a product of overlapping indigenous kingdoms. This kind of situation was bound to create conflict especially at the local level, and the home governments had to intervene to resolve the problems that arose on the ground between the BNBC, the Dutch East Indies Government and the Spanish authorities in the Philippines.

This chapter therefore examines how Spain and Britain settled the question of disputed sovereignty over parts of North Borneo by the Madrid Protocol of 1885. However, no attempt was made to demarcate the actual boundaries between the territorial possessions of these two powers. The dispute between the Netherlands and Britain pertaining to overlapping territorial claims in Borneo was settled by a long process of negotiations which began in the 1880s, leading to the Anglo-Dutch Boundary Convention of 1891, followed by an actual boundary delimitation exercise from 1912 to 1914 and culminating in the Boundary Treaty of 1915. The status of many small islands such as Pulau Sipadan and Pulau Ligitan was overlooked at the time, thus giving rise to the much later dispute in 1969 between Indonesia and Malaysia, the current focus of this work.

3.2 RESOLUTION OF THE CONFLICTING ANGLO-SPANISH CLAIMS OF SUZERAINTY IN NORTH BORNEO, 1878–85

When the ODA emerged on the scene in North Borneo, Spain immediately protested on the grounds that the Association was intruding into the territorial possessions of the Sultan of Sulu over which it had gained jurisdiction as a result of the Treaty of Capitulation signed by the Sulu ruler, Sultan Muhammad Jamaluladzam (r.1862–81) on 22 July 1878. Although the capitulation of Sulu took place six months after Sultan Muhammad Jamaluladzam had granted his territorial possessions in Borneo to Overbeck (22 January 1878), Spain refused to recognize the validity of the ODA concessions.[1] In September 1878, two Spanish warships arrived at Sandakan where Overbeck had placed William B. Pryer as Resident on 11 February 1878. The captain of one of the gunboats, the *El Dorado*, announced that Spain had jurisdiction over the Sandakan region, and warned that the settlement would be bombarded if the Spanish flag was not hoisted. Pryer, however, decided to put up a determined fight with the help of the local Sulu and Bajau chiefs.[2] The Spanish captain, using his better judgment, refrained from hostilities and "over a gentlemanly farewell sherry and bitters the Spaniard said he would return from Manila with a larger force. He sailed but never returned."[3] Thus, the matter was left to be resolved by the respective home governments. On the other hand, Britain and Germany, both of whom had established considerable trading contacts with the Sulu Kingdom, refused to recognize Spanish sovereignty over Sulu in the name of free trade. This conflict had arisen earlier in the 1870s when

Spain established a naval blockade in the Sulu Sea and detained several British and German commercial ships trading in the region. Negotiations between Spain, Britain, and Germany led to the Sulu Protocol of 1877, where free trade with Sulu was reopened.[4]

3.2.1 The Madrid Protocol of 1885

With the emergence of a British sphere of influence in North Borneo in the 1870s and 1880s, a new scenario emerged. It was now not just a question of the freedom of trade in the Sulu Archipelago, but a question of overlapping political jurisdiction between Britain and Spain. Discussions were held between Spain, Britain, and Germany in Europe to iron out these new differences, as well as to conform to the 1877 agreement on free trade in the region. These talks finally resulted in the Madrid Protocol of 7 March 1885 signed by the three powers.[5] The 1885 Protocol was basically a compromise between Spain and Britain concerning each other's sphere of jurisdiction in the Borneo-Sulu region. The treaty also guaranteed Britain, Germany, and all other powers the freedom of trade in the Sulu Archipelago.

By Article 1 of the said treaty, both Britain and Germany recognized Spain's sovereignty over Sulu. This article reads as follows:[6]

> The Governments of Great Britain and of Germany recognise the sovereignty of Spain over the places effectively occupied, as well as over those places not yet occupied, of the Archipelago of Sulu (Jolo), of which the limits are laid down in Article II.

In return, by Article III, Spain gave up all its claims in Borneo over territories which had formerly belonged to the Sultan of Sulu in favour of British sovereignty. Article III is worded as follows:[7]

> The Spanish Government renounces, as far as regards the British Government, all claims of sovereignty over the territories of the Continent of Borneo, which belong, or which have belonged in the past to the Sultan of Sulu (Jolo), and which comprise the neighbouring islands of Balambangan, Banguey, and Malawali, as well as all those comprised within a zone of three maritime leagues from the coast, and which form part of the territories administered by the Company styled the "British North Borneo Company."

It must be noted in passing, that this treaty alone is sufficient to nullify the Philippines' claim to Sabah. Subsequently, as a result of the Spanish-American War of 1898, Spain lost its colonial empire in the Philippines (including the domains of the Sultan of Sulu) to the United States.[8] The war between the two countries ended with the signing of the Treaty of Paris on 10 December 1898, where Spain ceded the Philippine Islands to the United States.[9] On 7 November 1900, an additional agreement called the "Convention between the United States and Spain" was signed in Washington. By this new treaty, Spain relinquished to the United States all titles and claims over islands and territories which may have been left out in the Treaty of Paris of 1898, especially with regards to the islands of Cagayan Sulu and Sibuku, and their dependencies.[10] Further developments between Britain and the United States concerning each other's sovereignty over various islands in the Borneo-Sulu region will be discussed in Chapter 4.

3.3 SETTLEMENT OF THE LAND BOUNDARY BETWEEN BRITISH NORTH BORNEO AND DUTCH BORNEO

Other than the Spaniards, the Dutch were also unhappy with the establishment of the ODA in North Borneo. In September 1879, the local Dutch authorities in Borneo sent a gunboat to Batu Tinagat, 40 miles within the territory of the ODA to oppose the establishment of the new enterprise. As discussed in Chapter 2, the ODA's grants from the Sultan of Sulu in 1878 included territories as far south as the Sibuku River on the east coast of Borneo, far below Batu Tinagat. The Dutch, however, claimed that territories as far north as Tawau and Batu Tinagat belonged to the Sultan of Bulungan who had become a vassal of the Netherlands by the Contract of Vassalage of 1850. The respective position of the claimed boundaries can be seen in Figure 3.1.

The Dutch planted their flag at Batu Tinagat and closed the Tawau River to all traffic. A memorandum submitted to the Dutch Parliament much later in 1891 described the action taken by the Dutch East Indies Government in 1879 as follows:[11]

> the Governor General [of the Dutch East Indies] instructed the flying of the Dutch flag at the Batoe Tinagat in a ceremonial way and the stationing of an armed vessel in the bay of St. Lucia, while at the mouth of the Tawao river a coal depot was established with a frontier guard. One of the officials [Pryer] of the British North Borneo Company protested against these actions of the Indian Government by writing on the 4th of July 1880 to the Commander of the Dutch warship which was at the moment stationed in the Sandakan bay.

FIGURE 3.1

Extract of a Map of Northeast Borneo Published by Edward Stanford in 1888 Showing the Approximate Boundaries Claimed by the Dutch (Red Line) and the BNBC (Yellow Line)

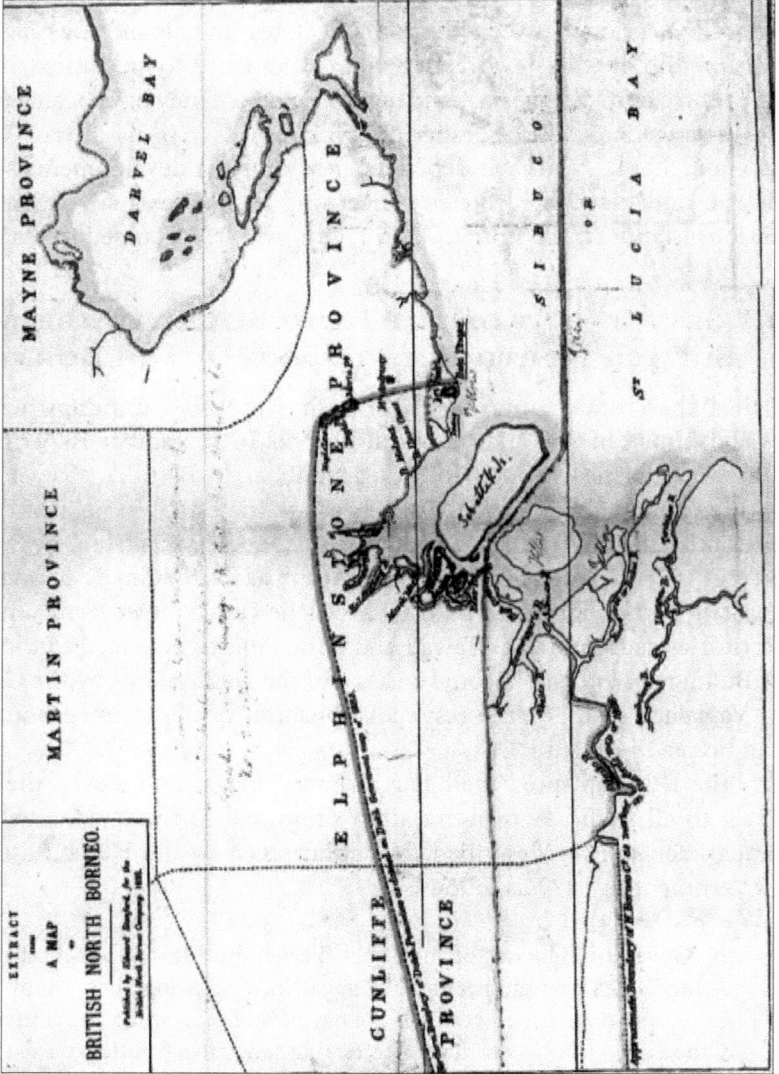

The Dutch Government at The Hague warned the British Government not to get involved in the affairs of the ODA as any such move would violate the spirit of the 1824 Anglo-Dutch Treaty. The British Government rejected the Dutch argument on the grounds that the 1824 treaty had never been applied to Borneo. Thus, when the Royal Charter was granted to the BNBC by the British Government in 1881, the Dutch accepted the fait accompli.[12]

3.3.1 Attempts to Settle the Boundary Dispute, 1882–89

Attempts to settle the boundary dispute began in 1882 when Count de Bylandt, the Netherlands Ambassador in London, addressed a letter to Earl Granville, the British Secretary of State for Foreign Affairs dated 31 May 1882, requesting discussions on the matter. In this note, the Dutch Government claimed territories as far north as Batu Tinagat, situated at the parallel of 4°20′ north.[13] The British Government responded by stating that the Dutch boundary in northeast Borneo did not extend beyond 3°20′ (the Atas River), and as such they refused to "support a claim for the recognition" of the Dutch frontier beyond that point.[14] However, the Dutch Government in a note dated 1 December 1882 opined that further progress in resolving the dispute could not be made immediately as the exact position of the Sibuku River could not be ascertained. In response, in January 1883, the British Government expressed the view that it was futile trying to settle the issue through diplomatic correspondence and suggested to the Dutch Government the merit of setting up a joint Anglo-Dutch Commission for the purpose, failing which the dispute might be submitted for arbitration purposes. Granville thus wrote:[15]

> It appears to Her Majesty's Government that a continuance of this correspondence is not likely to lead to any satisfactory arrangement, and that the best way of arriving at a settlement … would be for British and Netherlands Governments each to nominate a Commissioner authorized to examine into the question on the spot … and if this course did not result in an agreement being come to, recourse might finally be had to arbitration.

Granville's proposals were however not accepted by the Dutch.[16] Meanwhile, the situation on the ground was becoming more complicated and had the potential of erupting into hostilities. One incident which aggravated the issue was the murder of one of the Company's officers named Ference Xavier Witti in June 1882 by members of a tribe at the headwaters of the Sibuku River while he was on an exploring expedition in the region. According to Owen Rutter, Witti was a Hungarian who had served in the Austrian navy. In 1879, he was employed by Overbeck to work in North Borneo soon after the Baron had acquired the territorial concessions from the Sultans of Brunei and Sulu. Witti was attached for duty to W. Pretyman, the Resident of Tempassuk. In September 1881, he was incorporated into the administration of the British North Borneo Provisional Association (BNBPA) by the first governor of North Borneo, W.H. Treacher and appointed as officer charged with performing general service and undertaking explorations.[17] He was doing good exploratory work, but his life was cut short in the 1882 incident. On 26 February 1883, Sir Ratherford Alcock, Chairman of the BNBC wrote to Earl Granville indicating that the Directors of the Company had received a report from the North Borneo Government concerning the murder of Mr Witti somewhere near the headwaters of the Sibuku River. The Governor of Sabah, Treacher, organized an expedition which proceeded to the scene of the attack to apprehend those involved in the crime. However, because of the weather, the Company's forces were forced to return. Also at stake was the question of jurisdiction. Alcock raised the issue that it was uncertain whether the locality (the headwaters of the Sibuku River) was within the Company's territories or that of the Dutch. Under these circumstances, Alcock reported that the Company "deemed it inexpedient to take steps to assert their jurisdiction" without "some settlement of the boundary question". An indefinite delay in settling the boundary issue he claimed would lead to an inability on the part of both the Company and the Dutch to afford any security to life and property in the affected region.[18] On the same date, 26 February 1883, Alcock addressed a private letter to Granville in which he suggested the adoption of latitude 4° north as the boundary line between the territories of the BNBC and the Dutch in north east Borneo. He wrote as follows:[19]

> I trust it will be evident that on all accounts it is most desirable that a prompt settlement of the boundary should be effected, and that a parallel of latitude should be accepted by both parties, as the best mode of avoiding delay and future complications. The parallel of 4° north latitude may well be accepted by the Dutch as an equitable compromise, since it would give them 40 miles north of their original claim—from 1846 to 1877, and would prevent future misunderstandings which would doubtless arise should the north or south bank of any river be decided upon as a line of demarcation.

Granville accepted Alcock's proposal of adopting 4° north as the demarcating line and instructed Mr Stuart, the British representative at Holland to persuade the Netherlands Government to accept the same.[20] The Dutch Minister for Foreign Affairs at the time M. Rochussen, however, informed the British Government on 27 March 1883 that his government could not accept this proposal as it tantamounted to "a request for a cession of territory which belonged to the Netherlands".[21] The Dutch Government supported its position further by sending a lengthy memorandum to the British Government on 6 April 1883 by which the Netherlands basically reaffirmed its claim that the northern limit of its territory in Borneo extended to 4°20′ north.[22]

Meanwhile, the situation on the border had become more alarming by 1883. In September 1883, Governor W.H. Treacher of North Borneo conducted a tour of the border area as a show of force. On 8 September, he planted boundary symbols on the south bank of the Sibuku River, but they were soon removed by the Dutch.[23] Granville sent yet another dispatch to Count de Bylandt on 24 January 1884 requesting for speedy settlement of the matter in order to prevent the outbreak of hostilities, as the deteriorating situation could adversely affect Anglo-Dutch relations. He wrote:[24]

> The continued existence of conflicting claims as to boundary cannot fail to lead to misunderstanding, possibly even to collision; it must impede the efforts of the local officials of both countries to detect and punish crime...

Despite this urgent call, both the governments seem to have put the matter in abeyance, and further correspondence on the boundary issue seems to have been halted after this for almost five years before it was taken up again in 1889. In the meantime, from 1884 to 1888, the British Government, as discussed earlier, was busy consolidating its political control over the three states of Brunei, Sarawak and North Borneo over which separate Protectorates were established in 1888. By these moves, British sovereignty in these three states became explicit by this time.

Upon receiving news of this new development, the Dutch Government renewed correspondence for the settlement of the boundary dispute. The call was made by M. Hartsen, the new Dutch Minister for Foreign Affairs in a dispatch dated 3 January 1889 in which he also complained about the lack of interest shown by the British Government since 1884. In February 1889, the Marquis of Salisbury, who was the new British Secretary of State for Foreign Affairs, took up the matter and conducted a review of the existing correspondence pertaining to the boundary question since 1882.

Based on this survey, Salisbury concluded that the arguments put forward by the Dutch to support their claims to the limits of the boundary were as follows:[25]

(a) Territories as far north as Batu Tinagat situated at 4°20′ north belonged to the Sultan of Tidong, a vassal of the Sultan of Bulungan.
(b) The Sultan of Bulungan, named Muhammed Khahar-Oedien [Kaharudin] had signed a Contract of Vassalage with the Netherlands East Indies Government on 12 November 1850, by which the Sultan acknowledged submission to the said government in 1834. Article II of the Contract of Vassalage of 1850 described the northern limits of the territories belonging to the Sultan of Bulungan as extending to Batu Tinagat and the Tawau River on the northeast coast of Borneo.
(c) On 2 February 1877, the Netherlands Indian Government issued a Decree declaring Bulungan and Tidong as Dutch territories. This event preceded the issue of the grants by the Sultan of Sulu to the ODA [22 January 1878].
(d) The Sultan of Bulungan signed the second Contract of Vassalage with the Dutch on 2 June 1878, in which the boundaries of the Kingdom of Bulungan were described as including Batu Tinagat and the River Tawau.

The British position, Salisbury understood, was as follows:[26]

(a) That the Netherlands Government had consistently maintained that Tidong was always independent and that the territories north of the Atas River at 3°20′ including the Sibuku River, Batu Tinagat, and the Tawau River belonged to the Sultan of Sulu who was recognized by the Netherlands Government as fully independent.
(b) That according to the "Arrete" of the Governor-General of Netherlands India on 28 February 1846, the Netherlands territories on the northeast coast of Borneo did not extend any further north than Kampong Atas River situated at 3°20′ north latitude.
(c) That the "Contract of Vassalage" which actually made the Netherlands Government sovereign over the possessions of Bulungan and Tidong was signed only on 2 June 1878, that is after, and not before, the Overbeck and Dent concessions made by the Sultan of Sulu [22 January 1878].

3.3.2 Negotiations for the Settlement of the Boundary Dispute, 1889–91

The British Government in February 1889 requested its representative at The Hague to suggest to the Netherlands Government that the boundary issue should be satisfactorily settled and that both Governments nominate Commissioners with instructions to examine the question immediately and to report the result to their respective governments. The Netherlands Government agreed to this proposal upon which delegates from both governments met at the British Foreign Office in London where discussions were held over three meetings dated 16, 19 and 27 July 1889.[27] Britain was represented by Sir Philip W. Currie and Sir Edward Hertslet, and the Netherlands by Count de Bylandt and M.A.H. Gysberts. Each side also nominated two non-government officials to attend the meetings. The British non-officials were Rear-Admiral R.C. Mayne and Alexander Cook, both of whom were serving the BNBC. The Dutch non-officials were M.A.E. Elias and Captain O. Moreau. This Anglo-Dutch Joint Commission (hereafter referred to as the Joint Commission) was charged with determining the following points:[28]

1. Whether the Sultan of Boelongan [Bulungan] had a right to claim, as a dependency of his State, the State of Tidoeng, in which Batu Tinagat and the River Tawao [Tawau] are declared by the Dutch to be situated; and to place the same under Dutch protection.
2. Whether the Sultan of Sulu had a right to claim territory as far south as the Sibuco [Sibuku] River, and to cede the same to Messrs. Dent and Overbeck, who handed over their Concessions to the British North Borneo Company.
3. What was the actual position of the Sibuco River, which was alluded to in the Dent and Overbeck Concessions.

It has been further agreed that all matters connected with the rights of the local Sultans, and the limits of their respective States, at the time when the grants were made by the Sultans of Sulu and Brunei, respectively, to Messrs. Dent and Overbeck, as well as all the points of the frontier which have been under dispute, shall be open to discussion by the British and Netherland Delegates; and, further, that, in the event of a satisfactory understanding being arrived at with regard to the disputed boundary between the Netherland Indian Government and the British North Borneo Company, *on the northeast coast*, in the neighborhood of the Sibuco River, the British and Netherland Governments will proceed without delay to define, short of making

> an actual survey, and marking the boundary on the spot, the *inland boundary-lines* which separate the Netherland possessions in Borneo from the territories belonging to the States of Sarawak, Brunei, and the British North Borneo Company respectively. [author's emphasis]

It is clear even from these lines above, that the boundary that was being considered by both the British and Dutch Governments was an inland boundary, and did not include the division of offshore islands. Discussions at the three meetings were lengthy, and each side presented volumes of evidence to support their claims. Both sides also refused to budge from their original positions. This state of affairs is aptly summed up by the following quotation:[29]

> Both parties stuck to their assertions: according to the Dutch, the disputed area between the Tawao and Siboekoe Rivers belonged to the Kingdom of Boeloengan, which by virtue of the contracts with the Sultans formed a part of the territory of the Netherlands Indies, and therefore the Sultan of Solok could not cede it to the British North Borneo Company, while according to the British, that area was a part of the Kingdom of Solok and the cession to the above mentioned Company signed on 22 January 1878 was anterior to the contract between the Sultan of Boeloengan and the Netherlands-Indies Government on the 2nd of June 1878.

As the discussions threatened to stall, Sir P. Currie, on behalf of the British delegates proposed a compromise solution at the third meeting of the Joint Commission held on 27 July 1889, which was as follows:[30]

(a) That the starting point of the boundary on the northeast coast of Borneo be fixed at a point called Broershoek at the parallel 4°10′ north latitude and the boundary line should pass between the islands of Sebatik and East Nenvoeckkan.

(b) That shipping at all rivers in the disputed area located between 3°20′ and 4°20′ north latitude would be declared free.

These proposals were agreed upon by the delegates at the conference in London, but Count Bylandt expressed his view that these would have to be presented to the Dutch Government first. When this was done, the Dutch Government reserved its decision on these points until the Governor-General of the Netherlands Indies was consulted on the matter. Upon receiving advice from the Governor-General, the Dutch Government sent a Memorandum on 20 April 1890 to the British Government containing its counter-proposals. These were as follows:[31]

(a) The Netherlands Government accepted the principle of compromise that was reached at the delegates' conference.
(b) That the starting point of the boundary on the east coast of Borneo be fixed at a point called Broershoek, at the parallel 4°10′ north; the boundary line to be drawn westward and eastward from this point.
(c) The island of Sebatik should remain with the Netherlands.
(d) That the line of watershed of the River Simangaris and Soedang Sadong should divide the Netherlands' possessions from those of the BNBC, and the exact boundary line was to be traced on the spot by a mixed commission.
(e) The free navigation of the rivers in the disputed area should be upheld.

The British Government on its part submitted the Dutch counter-proposals to the Court of Directors of the BNBC for consultation. Based on the observations of the Court of Directors, the British Government in a dispatch dated 13 August 1890 made the following suggestions:[32]

(a) It accepted Broershoek as the starting point of the boundary on the east coast of Borneo where the parallel of 4°10′ north latitude met the sea.
(b) The BNBC was prepared to surrender all claims to any territories to the coast south of this point provided the Netherlands Government also agreed to surrender all claims to any territories to the north of that parallel including Batu Tinagat and any place which they may have occupied on the Tawau River.
(c) That, the Sebatik Island should belong to the BNBC or as a compromise the boundary line should run along the parallel of 4°10′ eastward as well as westward from Broershoek, so as to divide the island equally between the BNBC and the Netherlands Indian Government.
(d) The British Government was unwilling to accept the "watershed" argument for the line of demarcation as the rivers flowing into the St. Lucia Bay had their sources far north into North Borneo territory.

On 2 February 1891, the Dutch Government replied accepting most of the British counter-proposals, although it insisted that "the frontier should be formed by the watersheds of the rivers".[33] As far as the island of Sebatik was concerned, the Dutch Government was in favour of partitioning the island into two, and was thus willing to "cede ... without restrictions" to the BNBC that part of the island which was situated north of the latitude 4°10′N. The Dutch Government's decision concerning Sebatik Island was worded as follows:[34]

> As to the Island of Sebatik the Government of the Queen Regent is ready to continue negotiations on the basis of a compromise to arrive at a solution to meet the wishes of the British North Borneo Company, to cede to them without restrictions the part of that island situated north of 4.10 north latitude provided always that the British Government agrees to the present Dutch proposal for the boundary to the west of Broershoek.

3.3.3 The Anglo-Dutch Boundary Convention of 1891

As there was a general agreement on major points pertaining to the delimitation exercise, the two governments entered into another round of negotiations for the purpose of drafting a treaty to seal the issue. These negotiations started in February 1891 and culminated with the signing of a treaty called "Convention Between Great Britain and the Netherlands Defining Boundaries in Borneo, signed on 20 June 1891" (hereafter cited as the Boundary Convention of 1891).[35] As some of the articles of this treaty became major points of contention between the British and the Netherlands officials and later between Malaysia and Indonesia at The Hague, the important ones may be analysed in some detail here. By Article I, the two countries agreed that the boundary between the Netherlands possessions in Borneo and those of the British-protected States in the same island would start from 4°10′ north latitude on the east coast of Borneo. By Article II it was agreed that the boundary line would move westward following a west-north-west direction along 4°10′ north latitude generally. Some provisions or exceptions were made to the general line in cases where certain rivers flowed into the sea below or above this latitude. In such cases, the boundary line was permitted to be diverted at the watershed of a river within a radius of five geographical miles to allow the inclusion of "small portions or bends" of rivers within the Dutch territory (debouncing below 4°10′N) or the territory of the BNBC (debouncing above 4°10′N).

It must be noted here that the meaning of "geographical" miles, that is, whether they were "English" or "German" miles was not made clear. Later on, this point became a difficult issue to resolve when the actual demarcation of the boundary was undertaken in 1912.

Article IV is extremely important as its wording and intention became the focus of intense debate between Malaysia and Indonesia at The Hague. As such, it is necessary to reproduce the article in full before discussing some of its salient features. Article IV reads as follows:[36]

> From 4°10′ north latitude on the east coast the boundary-line shall be continued eastward along that parallel, across the Island of Sebittik [Sebatik]: that portion of the island situated to the north of that parallel shall belong unreservedly to the British North Borneo Company, and the portion south of the parallel to the Netherlands.

It was later argued by Indonesia that the boundary line was to *continue* eastward across the island of Sebatik into the sea following latitude 4°10′N. Malaysia, on the other hand, contended that the express purpose of the boundary line on Sebatik was to *divide* the island between the British and the Dutch.[37]

Article V of the treaty stipulated that the exact positions of the boundary would be determined at a suitable time in the future by mutual agreement by the two parties. By Article VIII, the Convention had to be ratified by both governments. An important prerequisite for the ratification to take place was obtaining the approval of the Netherland States-General.

3.3.4 The Ratification Process

As required by Article VIII of the Boundary Convention of 1891, the Dutch Government on 25 July 1891 submitted a Bill together with an Explanatory Memorandum and a Map to the country's States-General (parliament) for approval.[38] The Bill was passed by the said body on 8 March 1892. This map accompanying the Exploratory Memorandum (Figure 3.2) was drawn unilaterally by the Dutch Government and was not part of the Boundary Convention of 1891. For reasons known only to the creators of this map, the boundary line running along latitude 4°10′N on the northeast coast of Borneo on Sebatik Island extended about 50 miles into the sea and divided the islands in the area into Dutch and British spheres.[39] The Indonesian Government later relied heavily on this map to support their claim that the islands of Sipadan and Ligitan fell

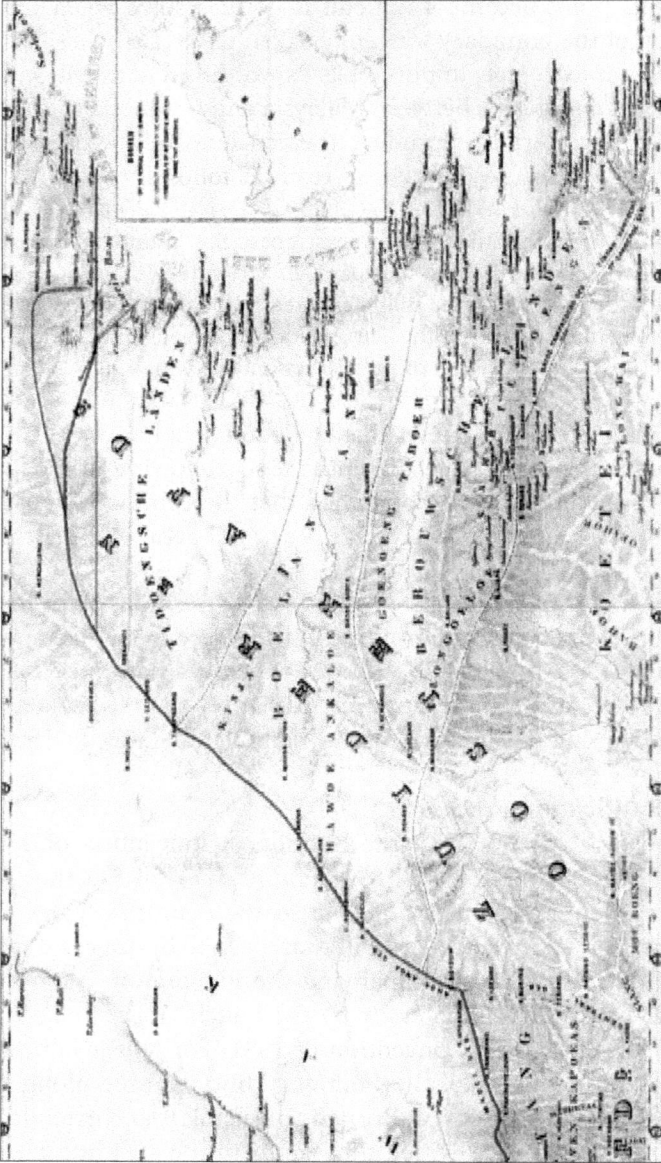

FIGURE 3.2
A Section of the Dutch Explanatory Memorandum Map of 1891

Legend: Blue Line: Boundary Claimed by the Netherlands
          Yellow Line: Boundary Claimed by the BNBC
          Green Line: Boundary Suggested by the British Government
          Red Line: Boundary Purported to have been agreed at the Boundary Convention of 1891

Source: ICJ, Memorial of Indonesia, vol. 1, 2 November 1999, Map 5.2.

below this line and therefore belonged to Indonesia. Two copies of the Explanatory Memorandum and the map were transmitted to the British Government by Sir Horace Rumbold, the British Government Minister at The Hague in a dispatch dated 26 January 1892. The map was also subsequently published in the Dutch Government's official journal. The British Government, however, did not see the necessity of protesting the inaccuracy of the map at the time. Rumbold, while submitting the map to Salisbury made the following comments:[40]

> [it, the map] has lately been published in the official Journal showing the
> boundary line as agreed upon under the late Convention, together with
> the boundaries which had been previously proposed... The map seems to
> be the only interesting feature of a document which does not otherwise
> call for special comment.

The Boundary Convention of 1891 was ratified by the Netherlands Government on 9 April 1892, and by the British Government on 30 April 1892. The exchange of ratifications took place on 11 May 1892 in London.[41]

3.3.5 The Process of Boundary Delimitation, 1891–1915
From 1891 to 1912, not much progress was made in terms of the actual demarcation of the boundary between North Borneo and Dutch Borneo. In 1901, a Commission comprising of Lieutenant Commander Dyne of H.M.S. *Waterwitch* and Captain Hovess together with the Officers of H.N.M.S. *Macasser* placed granite pillars for marking the boundary, one each on the eastern and western extremities of Sebatik Island and the third on the eastern side of Broershoek.[42] Further progress was however bogged down due to differing interpretations of some of the clauses of the Boundary Convention of 1891. In 1905, a conflict of opinion arose regarding the interpretation of Article II of the said Convention. The Netherlands raised the point as to:[43]

> whether the line starting from Broershoek at 4°10′ North Latitude should
> have a West North-Westerly direction from the actual point of departure
> to the point where the meridian of 117° longitude cuts the parallel 4°20′
> North Latitude, or whether according to the view of the British local
> authorities it should follow the parallel 4°10′ North for a certain distance
> from the point of departure on the coast before taking a West North-
> Westerly direction up to the above mentioned point of intersection.

Despite the contention of the BNBC that the second interpretation was correct, the Foreign Office supported the view taken by the Netherlands Government.[44] Matters such as these delayed the proceedings until 1910 when the Dutch Government broached the subject once again. In a Memorandum communicated to the British Government dated 6 December 1910, the Dutch lamented at the very little progress made concerning the actual demarcation of the boundary. All that had been achieved till 1910 had been the placing of the pillars of granite by the 1901 team.[45]

The Memorandum went on to express a very vital view concerning the importance of these granite pillars in relation to the boundary between the Netherlands' possessions in Borneo and the State of North Borneo, which was as follows:[46]

> Both Governments consider these poles as fixing the exact positions of the line of the frontier at the coast, as meant in article V of the Treaty.

In the same Memorandum, the Netherlands Government proposed a mixed commission to be appointed in order to finish up the delimitation of the frontier between North Borneo and Dutch Borneo.

3.3.6 The 1912–13 Land Boundary Delimitation Exercise

As a result of this proposal, a joint Anglo-Dutch Boundary Commission was set up in 1912.[47] The commission's aim was to survey and mark on the ground the boundary contemplated by Articles II and III of the Boundary Convention of 1891. The Netherlands Government appointed J.H.G. Schepers, Engineer of the Triangulation Brigade, Netherlands India, and E.A. Vreede, Second Lieutenant of the Netherlands Royal Navy as Joint Commissioners. The North Borneo Government appointed H.W.L Bunbury, a Civil Service Officer and G.V. Keddell, Civil Commissioner and Surveyor, respectively as representatives of the BNBC. They were instructed to demarcate on the spot the boundary between the Netherland possessions and the State of North Borneo.

The work of the Commission was once again hampered by conflicting interpretations of Article II of the Boundary Convention of 1891. One such point of controversy was the meaning to be attached to the word "geographical mile". Was it to be construed to be an "English" geographical mile, which was equal to three nautical miles, or a "German" geographical mile, which was equal to four nautical miles? There were other technical points which had to be cleared up as well, such as the meaning of "radius" and the length of the "deviation radius". The survey team asked for clarification.[48] The British Foreign Office, after careful consultation, accepted the usage of the English geographical mile.[49] The Dutch Government agreed to accept the views of the British Government on all the points of contention, and thus the matter was resolved.[50]

The team started its work in June 1912 and completed the job in January 1913. However, the Anglo-Dutch Boundary Commission of 1912 only undertook the survey and delimitation of the boundary on the mainland of Borneo. The demarcation of the boundary dividing the island of Sebatik was undertaken by a separate joint Anglo-Dutch team.

At the completion of the work assigned to the Anglo-Dutch Boundary Commission of 1912, a Protocol defining the boundary so demarcated was signed jointly by the Dutch and British members of the said commission on 17 February 1913.[51]

3.3.7 The Sebatik Island Boundary Delimitation Exercise, 1913–14

The job of demarcating the boundary on Sebatik Island was given to a team comprising of D.A.M.Q Boeje, First Lieutenant of the Netherlands Indian Army as the Netherlands Government's representative, and W.C. Moores Weedon, the District Officer of Tawau, North Borneo, and H.L. Fendall, the Assistant Surveyor of North Borneo as representatives of the North Borneo Government.

The survey which began in December 1913, was completed in May 1914.[52] The joint team, after having completed the demarcation of the boundary on Sebatik Island as provided for in Article IV of the Boundary Convention of 1891, made an important statement in their report of 1914 entitled "Boundary Delimitation between the Netherlands and British North Borneo Portion of Sebatik Island", which was as follows:[53]

> In accordance with instructions received from our respective Governments *we have taken as the boundary the straight line between the granite pillars in the East and West of Sebatik Island*, which were erected in 1901 by a Commission consisting of H.M. Macassar and H.M.S. "Waterwitch," and upon that line we have erected 16 concrete pillars. To the above we have all agreed and have appended our signatures at Tawao, British North Borneo, this 6th day of May, 1914. [author's emphasis]

It is crystal clear from this document that the easternmost terminal of the boundary was the granite pillar on the east coast of Sebatik Island which had been constructed since 1901. The boundary as determined by the joint Anglo-Dutch team of 1913–14 *did not go beyond* this eastern pillar on Sebatik Island into the sea. It is also abundantly evident that the team considered the boundary on Sebatik Island as the straight line drawn from the eastern pillar to the western pillar, upon which sixteen more concrete pillars were erected. The boundary demarcated on Sebatik Island, therefore, was designed to give practical effect to the British proposal of 13 August 1890 and subsequently agreed upon by the Dutch Government pertaining to Sebatik Island which reads as follows:[54]

> as a compromise, the boundary line should run along the parallel of 4°10′ ... *so as to divide the island equally between the BNBC and the Netherlands Indian Government.* [author's emphasis]

The purpose of the boundary on Sebatik Island was to divide the island equally between the two parties. This division was a compromise solution as both sides had claimed the island *in toto*. The correspondence between Britain and the Netherlands in 1890 and 1891 supports this view only. There is no evidence in the said correspondence which says that the boundary on Sebatik Island was to be drawn in such a manner as to divide the British and the Dutch sections of the surrounding sea as well.

3.3.8 The Anglo-Dutch Boundary Treaty of 1915

The Protocol or Commission Report of the 1912 Anglo-Dutch Boundary Commission together with the accompanying map which was signed at Tawau on 17 February 1913 was finally endorsed by a treaty signed between Britain and the Netherlands in London on 28 September 1915. The treaty, entitled "Agreement between the United Kingdom and the Netherlands Relating to the Boundary between the State of North Borneo and the Netherland Possessions in Borneo, 28 September 1915",[55] (hereafter cited as the Anglo-Dutch Boundary Treaty of 1915) reproduced the text of the 1913 Report *in toto*, describing the path of the boundary so demarcated.

The Anglo-Dutch Boundary Treaty of 1915 incorporated the work of the Sebatik boundary delimitation team and described the boundary on Sebatik Island in Article 3(i) as follows:[56]

> Traversing the island of Sibetik, the frontier line follows the parallel of 4°10′ north latitude, as already fixed by Article 4 of the Boundary Treaty [of 1891] and marked in the east and west by boundary pillars.

FIGURE 3.3
Copy of Map Attached to the Anglo-Dutch Boundary Treaty of 1915

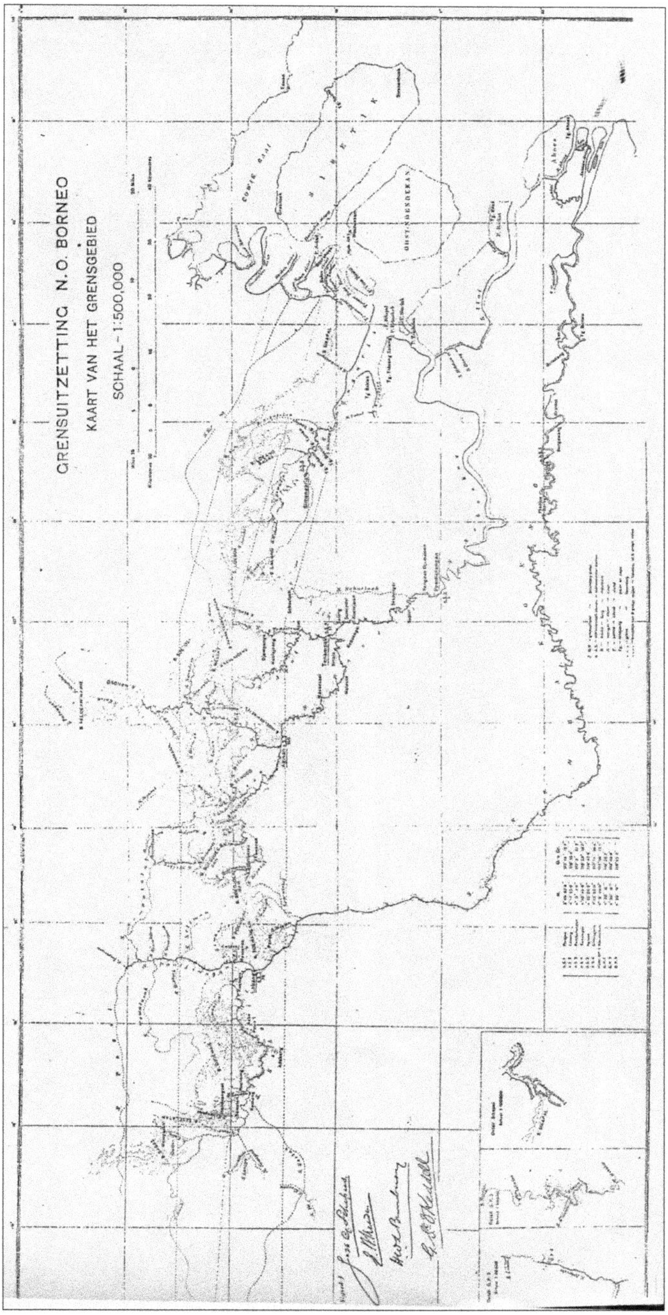

Source: ICJ, *Memorial of Malaysia*, vol. 2, 2 November 1999, p. 108.

FIGURE 3.4
Enlarged Section of the 1915 Boundary Map Showing the
Boundary Line on Sebatik Island

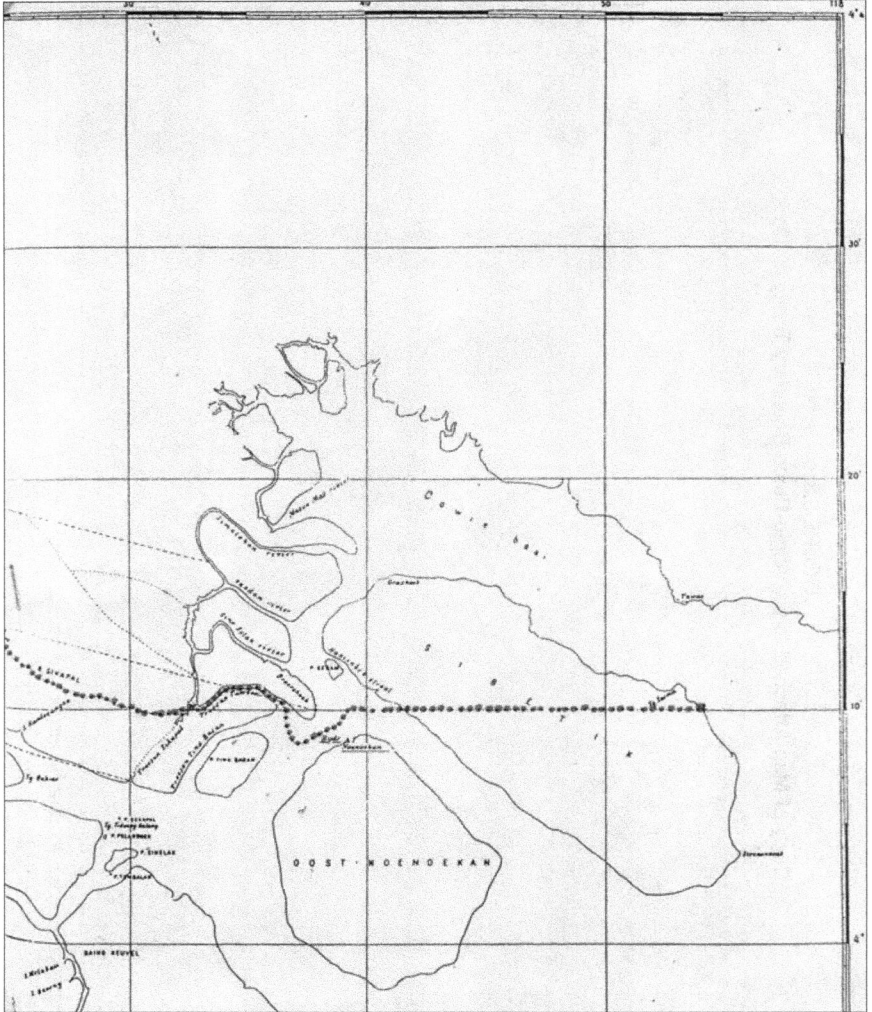

Source: ICJ, Memorial of Malaysia, vol. 2, 2 November 1999, p. 108.

As mentioned earlier, the Anglo-Dutch Boundary Treaty of 1915 was accompanied by a treaty map. Copies of this map pertaining to the boundary on the east coast and Sebatik Island are reproduced (see Figures 3.3 and 3.4). With the signing of this international agreement in 1915, the boundary issue which arose in the 1880s was largely settled.

Notes

1. For correspondence on this matter, see F.O. 12/86, ff. 298–306.
2. Acting Consul-General Treacher to the Marquis of Salisbury, 24 September 1878, Letter 128, *Papers Relating to the Affairs of Sulu and Borneo, Part 1 (Spain No. 1, 1882)*, F.O. 12/86, f. 290; and D.S. Ranjit Singh, *The Making of Sabah, 1865–1941: The Dynamics of Indigenous Society* (Kota Kinabalu: Government of Sabah, 2011), pp. 119–20.
3. K.G. Tregonning, *Under Chartered Company Rule (North Borneo 1881–1946)* (Singapore: University of Malaya Press, 1959), p. 18.
4. L.R. Wright, *The Origins of British Borneo* (Hong Kong: Hong Kong University Press, 1970), pp. 126–72.
5. For correspondence leading to the conclusion of the Madrid Protocol of 1885, see F.O. 12/86, ff. 312–15. For a copy of the Madrid Protocol of 1885, see J. de V. Allen, A.J. Stockwell and L.R. Wright, eds., *A Collection of Treaties and Other Documents Affecting the States of Malaysia, 1761–1963*, vol. 2 (London: Oceana Publications, 1981), pp. 465–68; and F.O. 71/18. Also see Appendix A.
6. See Allen, Stockwell and Wright, *A Collection of Treaties and Other Documents*, vol. 2, p. 465.
7. Ibid., p. 466.
8. For details of the Spanish-American War of 1898, see Pauline Maier et al., *Inventing America: A History of the United States* (New York: W.W. Norton and Company, 2003), pp. 664–70. Also see Chapter 4.
9. For a copy of this agreement, see "Treaty of Paris 10 December 1898", in *Treaties and Other International Agreements of the United States (1776–1949)*, by Charles I. Bevans, vol. 2 (Washington, D.C.: Department of State Publication, 1968), p. 616.
10. See Convention between the United States and Spain, 7 November 1900, *Papers Relating to the Foreign Relations of the United States for 1900*, vol. 1, pp. 1942–44.
11. Explanatory Memorandum No. 3, "Ratification of the Agreement made in London between the Netherlands and Great Britain and Ireland for the Fixing of the Boundaries between the Possessions of the Netherlands on the Island of Borneo and the States on that Island which are under British Protectorate", *Official Parliamentary Reports, The Netherlands, Session 1890–1891: 187.* (Hereafter cited as Explanatory Memorandum No. 3) Also see Earl Granville to Mr. Stuart (the British Ambassador in Holland), 6 January 1883, Item 6, C.O. 874/191.

12. Correspondence on this matter can be found in F.O. 12/86, ff. 328–349. See especially Mr. Stuart to Earl Granville, letter No. 10, 17 August 1880, F.O. 12/86, f. 336; and Earl Granville to Count de Bylandt, Letter No. 30, 7 January 1882, F.O. 12/86, f. 349. Also see Graham Irwin, *Nineteenth-Century Borneo: A Study in Diplomatic Rivalry* (Singapore: Donald Moore Books, 1965), p. 205.

13. Count de Bylandt to Earl Granville, 31 May 1882, Item 1, C.O. 874/191.

14. Earl Granville to Count de Bylandt, 31 August 1882, Item 4, C.O. 874/191. See Figure 3.1 for areas of overlapping Dutch and British claims in Borneo in the 1880s.

15. Earl Granville to Mr Stuart (the British Ambassador in Holland), 6 January 1883, Item 6, C.O. 874/191.

16. The Marquis of Salisbury to Sir Rumbold, 5 February 1889, Item 21, C.O. 874/191.

17. For a detailed account of Witti's career in North Borneo, his journeys of discovery and his final trip, see Josephine Boenisch Burrough, "Ference Xavier Witti; Two Narratives by G.C. Woolley and Owen Rutter", *Sabah Society Journal* 5, no. 3 (December 1971): 225–71. See also Treacher to Alfred Dent, 29 September 1881 and inclosures, C.O. 874/228, f. 193.

18. Sir Rutherford Alcock, Chairman BNBC, to Earl Granville, 26 February 1883 and inclosures, Item 7 and 10, C.O. 874/191.

19. Sir Rutherford Alcock, Chairman BNBC, to Earl Granville, 26 February 1883 and inclosures, Item 8 and 10, C.O. 874/191.

20. Earl Granville to Mr Stuart, 9 March 1883, and inclosures Item 10, C.O. 874/191.

21. Mr Stuart to Earl Granville, 27 March 1883, and inclosures Item 11, C.O. 874/191.

22. Count de Bylandt to Earl Granville, 6 April 1883 and inclosure entitled "Memorandum respecting the Boundary between the Netherlands and Soloh (Sulu) Possesions on the North-east Coast of Borneo", Item 12, C.O. 874/191.

23. The Marquis of Salisbury to Sir Rumbold, 5 February 1889, Item 21, C.O. 874/191.

24. Earl Granville to Count de Bylandt, 24 January 1884 and inclosures, Item 17, C.O. 874/191.

25. The Marquis of Salisbury to Sir H. Rumbold, 5 February 1889, Item 21, C.O. 874/191. A great deal of the evidence used by Salisbury to support his contentions was obtained from information supplied by the BNBC. See, for example, the extensive information contained in a memorandum prepared by the BNBC and submitted to the British Foreign Office in 1882. Sir R. Alcock to Earl Granville, 1 July 1882, and inclosures, Item 2, C.O. 874/191. Also see Count de Bylandt to Earl Granville, 6 April 1883 and inclosure entitled "Memorandum respecting the Boundary between the Netherlands and Soloh [Sulu] Possessions on the North-East Coast of Borneo", Item 12, C.O. 874/191; and M. Hartsen to Count de Bylandt, 19 March 1889, and inclosure, Item 44, C.O. 874/191.

26. The Marquis of Salisbury to Sir H. Rumbold, 5 February 1889 and Item 21, C.O. 874/191.

27. Proceedings of the Joint Commission appointed by the British and Netherland

Governments for considering the question of the Boundary between the Netherland Indian Possessions on the Island of Borneo and the Territory belonging to the British North Borneo Company, First, Second and Third Meetings held at the Foreign Office, London, 1889, Dutch Document Box A60, File 791, pp. 446–51. Also in F.O. 12/86 (hereafter cited as Proceedings of the Joint Commission).

28. Proceedings of the Joint Commission, First Meeting held at the Foreign Office, London, 16 July 1889.

29. Explanatory Memorandum No. 3, p. 5.

30. Proceedings of the Joint Commission, Third Meeting held at the Foreign Office, London, 27 July 1889.

31. Memorandum from Count de Bylandt to the Marquis of Salisbury, 20 April 1890, F.O. 12/86.

32. Despatch from the Marquis of Salisbury to Count de Bylandt, 13 August 1890, Dutch Document Box A60, File 791, pp. 212–23. Also in F.O. 12/86.

33. Despatch from Count de Bylandt to Lord Salisbary, 2 February 1891, F.O. 12/86.

34. Ibid.

35. For a copy of this treaty, see Convention Between Great Britain and the Netherlands Defining Boundaries in Borneo, 20 June 1891, C.O. 874/503, ff. 231–34. Also in F.O. 12/88, ff. 38–39. See also Appendix B.

36. Ibid.

37. Author's emphasis. For more details, see Chapters 5 and 6 below.

38. Explanatory Memorandum No. 3.

39. ICJ, *Case Concerning Sovereignty Over Pulau Ligitan and Pulau Sipadan (Indonesia/Malaysia), Memorial Submitted by the Government of the Republic of Indonesia*, vol. 1, 2 November 1999, Map 5.2. For the Indonesian case, see Chapter 5.

40. H. Rumbold to the Marquis of Salisbury, 26 January 1892, and inclosures, F.O. 12/90.

41. *Statute Book of the Kingdom of the Netherlands*, Netherlands, 1892.

42. See Notification 103 of 1901 in the *British North Borneo Herald*. Cited in C.O. 874/500.

43. Foreign Office London to the Secretary, British North Borneo Company, 24 March 1905, and inclosure, C.O. 874/499.

44. Foreign Office London to the Secretary, British North Borneo Company, 3 October 1905, and inclosure, C.O. 874/499.

45. Memorandum by the Netherlands Charge de Affairs to the Colonial Office, enclosure in Under Secretary of State, Colonial Office to the Secretary, British North Borneo Company, 6 December 1910, C.O. 874/449.

46. Ibid.

47. See Protocol Concerning Boundary Delimitation Between the Netherland Possessions and the State of North Borneo, 17 February 1913, C.O. 874/503, pp. 1–4.

48. For queries by the survey team see the following letters from H.W.H. Bunbury to the Government Secretary, North Borneo, 8 July 1912, enclosure in Fred N. Fraser,

Officer Administering the Government, North Borneo to Sir J. West Ridgeway, Chairman BNBC, 2 August 1912, C.O. 874/499; and Bunbury to Government Secretary North Borneo, 23 September 1912, enclosure in Fraser to Ridgeway, 12 October 1912, C.O. 874/499.

49. Secretary BNBC, to J. Scott Mason, Governor North Borneo 25 October 1912 and enclosures, C.O. 874/499.

50. The Under Secretary of State for the Colonial Office, London, H.I. Read to the Secretary, BNBC, 8 November 1912, C.O. 874/499.

51. See Protocol of 17 February 1913, C.O. 874/503, pp. 1–4.

52. Governor North Borneo to Chairman BNBC dated 9 July 1914 and enclosure from W.C. Moores Weedon entitled Boundary Delimitation between the Netherlands and British North Borneo Portion of Sebatik Island, C.O. 874/500.

53. Ibid.

54. See the British Government's proposals of 13 August 1890 and acceptance by the Dutch Government on 2 February 1891, above.

55. For a copy of the 1915 Boundary Treaty with the attached map, see *Agreement between the United Kingdom and the Netherlands Relating to the Boundary between the State of North Borneo and the Netherland Possessions in Borneo*, 28 September 1915. C.O. 874/503, ff. 251–53. See also Appendix C.

56. Ibid., f. 251.

4

Delimitation of the North Borneo–Philippines Sea Boundary and the Transfer of Sovereignty over Certain Islands to North Borneo, 1903–30

4.1 INTRODUCTION

In 1898, the United States became the new owner of the Philippine Islands. The territorial boundaries of the Philippines under its former master, Spain, were not accurately defined. Unlike Spain however, the United States was more meticulous, assertive and legalistic concerning the limits of its territorial control. The process of accurately identifying and confirming the territorial limits of its jurisdiction over the Philippines, especially in areas adjoining North Borneo, began in 1903. It was soon discovered that the State of North Borneo, under the British North Borneo Company (BNBC), was illegally administering twenty-six islands off the east coast of the state which in fact belonged to the Sultan of Sulu, and therefore rightly came under the US jurisdiction. From 1903 to 1930, the two sovereign powers in the region, Britain and the United States, were involved in resolving this issue of occupation and sovereignty. The United States was also keen to draw a permanent international boundary between possessions of North Borneo and the Philippine Islands, an endeavour which was completed in 1930. These two issues resulted in the forging of the Agreement of 1907 and the Boundary Convention of 1930 between Britain and the United States, which in turn decided the fate of a number of islands in the area, including Sipadan and Ligitan. This chapter explores the tangled nature of the issues involved and the resulting implications.

4.2 Contested Jurisdiction over Certain Islands off the East Coast of North Borneo

As has been discussed in Chapter 2, the BNBC acquired jurisdiction over the east coast of Sabah till the Sibuku River based on the Sulu Grants of 22 January 1878. According to the text of the documents, the extent of the Company's jurisdiction over the territorial waters was limited to nine nautical miles or three marine leagues from the coast.[1] In the vicinity of the sea near Sandakan and Tawau however, there were a group of islands numbering about twenty-six beyond the three marine leagues limit, but which the Company mistakenly thought belonged to it and thus brought them under its administration. See Figure 4.1. These islands[2] which included Sipadan and Ligitan, as well, became the centre of a dispute first as a result of the Sultan of Sulu claiming ownership over them beginning in 1899; and later as a result of the United States claiming sovereignty over the islands beginning in 1903. The circumstances of these developments may be surveyed in greater detail.

The dispute over the islands started in 1899 when the Sultan of Sulu, Haji Muhammad Jamalulkiram (r.1894–1936), met the Managing Director of the BNBC, W.C. Cowie, in Labuan and asked for the return of two islands named Baguan and Taganac. A letter containing this request was handed to Cowie.[3] Cowie's reply to the Sultan was that the Company was not in a position to entertain his request[4] whereupon the Sultan visited the Acting High Commissioner for the Malay States in Singapore, J.A. Swettenham on 4 May 1900 and pressed his claims. Swettenham wrote to the Governor of North Borneo stating the Sultan's case as follows:[5]

> [The Sultan] brought to my notice that the Company was collecting revenue on the islands of Taganac, and Baguan, which appear by your map to be some 15 miles off the coast near Sandakan Harbour. These islands the Sultan claims as part of his possessions which he has never alienated to the Company.

As these islands lay "outside" the three marine leagues zone off the coast, the limit of the Company's jurisdiction specified in the 1878 Grants by the Sultan of Sulu, Swettenham wished to know whether the Company claimed these islands, and if so by what title.

In a dispatch dated 7 June 1900, Hugh Clifford, the Governor of North Borneo, wrote to the Chairman of the BNBC, Richard B. Martin, explaining the issue and asking for advice. The Governor noted that he "failed to find

FIGURE 4.1
Map Showing the Three Marine Leagues Distance
from the Coast of North Borneo

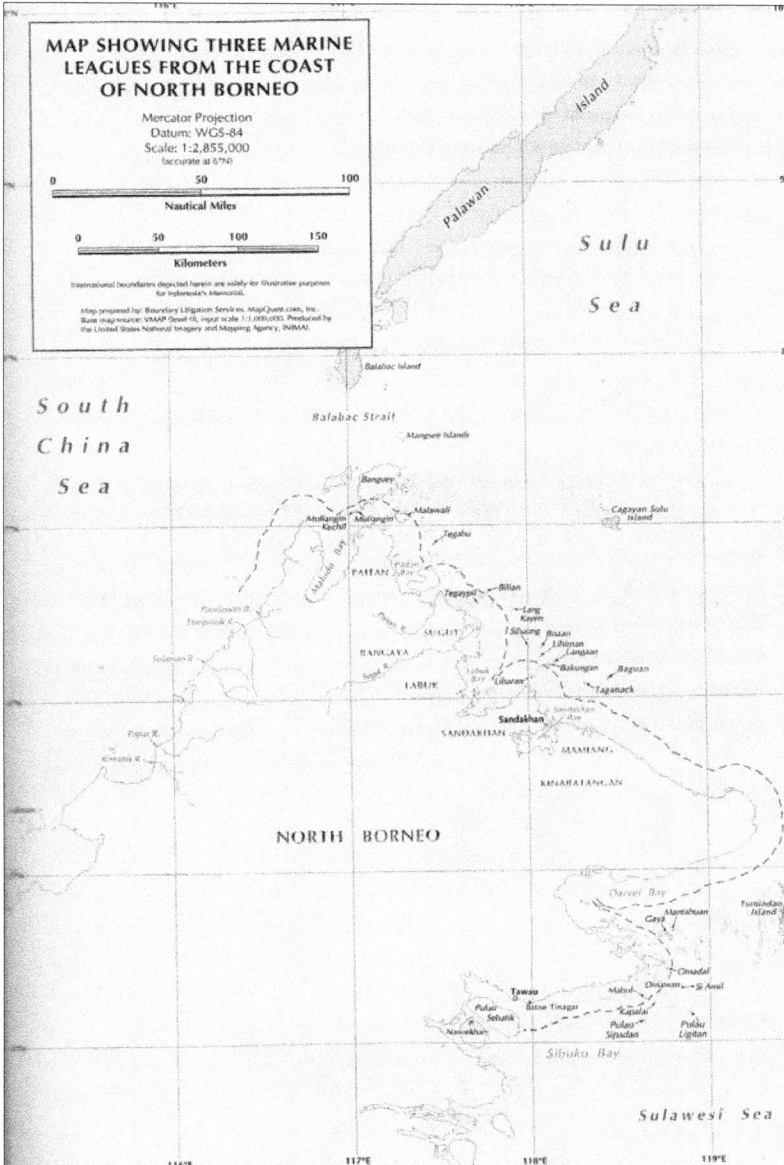

Source: ICJ, *Memorial of Indonesia*, vol. 1, 2 November 1999, Map 3.1.

anything to show that the islands in question were ever formally ceded to us," but defended the Company's jurisdiction over them on "undisturbed occupancy spreading over a long term of years".[6]

The Chairman of the BNBC concurred with the view that there had been no formal cession of these and many other islands off the east coast of North Borneo to the Company, but they "had always been regarded as an integral portion of the Company's Territory and had been administered as such". It was therefore to be construed that the Company held the islands by "prescriptive right". Under the circumstances, the Court of Directors could not entertain the Sultan's claim.[7]

The Company conveyed the various correspondences of the Sultan's claims to the Foreign Office. Lord Salisbury of the Foreign Office advised the Company to settle the matter by negotiation.[8] The Company, however, felt that negotiations would be detrimental to the interests of the British Empire and that of the Company.[9] Nevertheless, the Company had to abide by the Foreign Office ruling and consequently broached the subject with the Sultan of Sulu.

The Sultan showed a positive response and indicated he was willing to cede the islands to the Company "based on [a] fair and strong agreement".[10]

4.3 THE TAKEOVER OF THE PHILIPPINES BY THE UNITED STATES, 1898

Meanwhile, the United States obtained sovereignty over the Philippines as a result of the Treaty of Paris signed with Spain on 10 December 1898. The change in the ruling power happened as a result of the Spanish-American War of 1898.[11] This war broke out over Cuba which was a colony of Spain following a serious rebellion which had broken out on the island since 1868 demanding for independence. The United States considered Cuba of vital importance to its security and economy. Moreover, the United States was fast emerging as a world power, and just like other European powers, it needed colonial expansion for commercial and imperial needs. On 29 April 1898, America declared war on Spain to "save" Cuba. The American strategy was however not limited to Cuba.

The United States had plans to seize the Philippines as well, to serve as a base for the expansion of its commercial and imperial interests in China and Asia. Thus, even before a shot was fired in Cuba, a US naval fleet had already arrived in Manila Bay under the command of Admiral George Dewey on 30 April 1898. It immediately destroyed the Spanish fleet in the area. Manila fell on 13 August 1898 and negotiations began for the cession of the Philippines to the United States. The treaty ending the Spanish-American War was signed at Paris on 10 December 1898 and came to be known as the Treaty of Paris.[12] By this treaty, Spain ceded to the United States, the islands of Cuba, Puerto Rico and other islands under Spanish sovereignty in the West Indies. By Article III of the treaty, Spain also ceded the Philippine Islands to the United States in return for the payment of a sum of 20 million Spanish dollars by America. The same article fixed the limits of the territorial jurisdiction of the United States in the Philippine Islands.[13] See Figure 4.2.

However, it soon became apparent that the United States did not inherit all of the territorial domains in the Philippines over which Spain had exercised jurisdiction prior to the Treaty of Paris. This anomaly was pointed out to the US War Department, by the firm of the Matthews-Northrup Company which was engaged in the publication of maps of the Philippine Islands even during the Spanish period. In August 1899, the firm wrote to the War Department indicating that some important islands, which had been under Spanish jurisdiction, had been left out by Article III of the Treaty of Paris. The firm wished to ascertain whether they belonged to some other power. The most important of these islands were the Batan Islands, Kagayan-Sulu, and Sibutu.[14]

The US Government quickly moved to rectify the situation which resulted in the Convention of 7 November 1900 between the United States and Spain. By this Convention, the United States acquired the title to all islands and territories in the Philippines which had been left out by Article III of the Treaty of Paris of 1898. The relevant section of the sole article of the Convention of 1900 reads as follows:[15] See Figure 4.3.

> Spain relinquishes to the United States all title and claim of title, which she may have had at the time of the conclusion of the Treaty of Peace of Paris, to any and all islands belonging to the Philippine Archipelago, lying outside the lines described in Article III of that Treaty and particularly to the islands of Cagayan Sulu and Sibutu and their dependencies, and agrees that all such islands shall be comprehended in the cession of the Archipelago as fully as if they had been expressly included within those lines.

The BNBC was extremely alarmed, apprehensive, and jittery concerning the extent of jurisdiction acquired by the United States. At first, the BNBC

FIGURE 4.2
Map Showing the Line Described in the Treaty of Paris, 1898

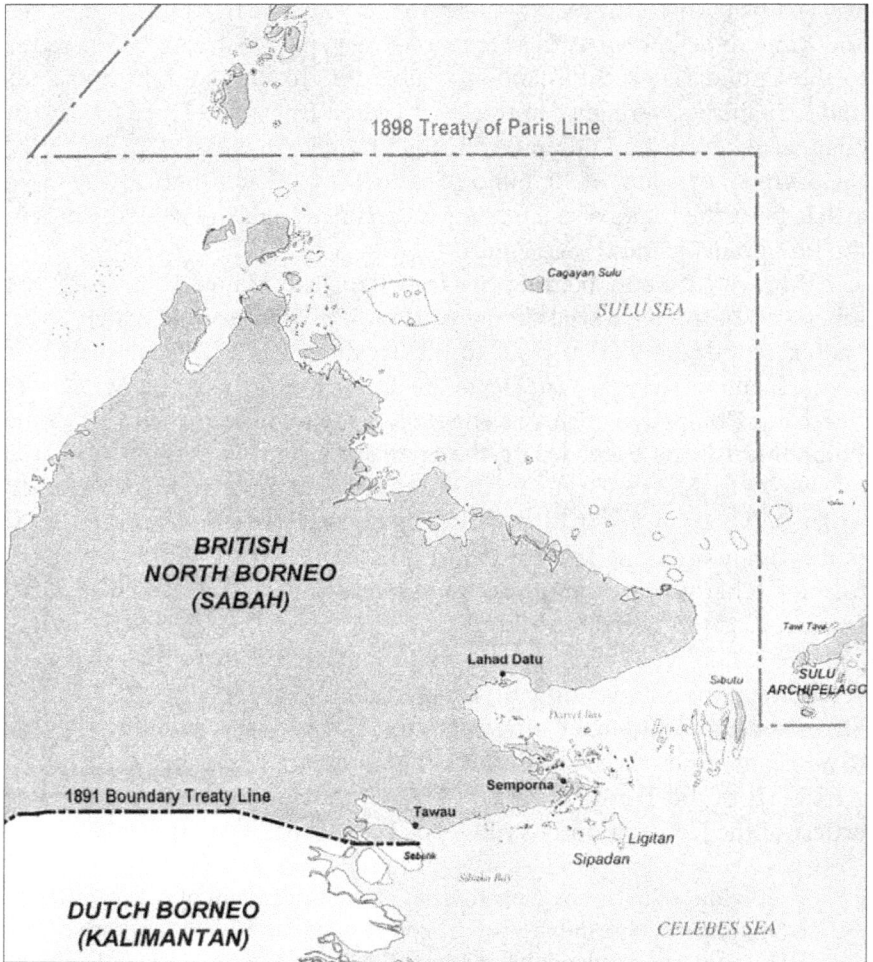

Source: ICJ, *Memorial of Malaysia*, vol. 1, 2 November 1999, p. 44.

thought that the Convention of 1900 included all the twenty-six or so islands administered by the Company since its inception but over which it had no clear title. However, on closer scrutiny of the Convention, it was discovered that these islands were not specifically mentioned. It is

FIGURE 4.3

Map Showing the Extent of the Philippines Territory as Defined by the Treaty of Paris, 1898 and the Convention of 1900

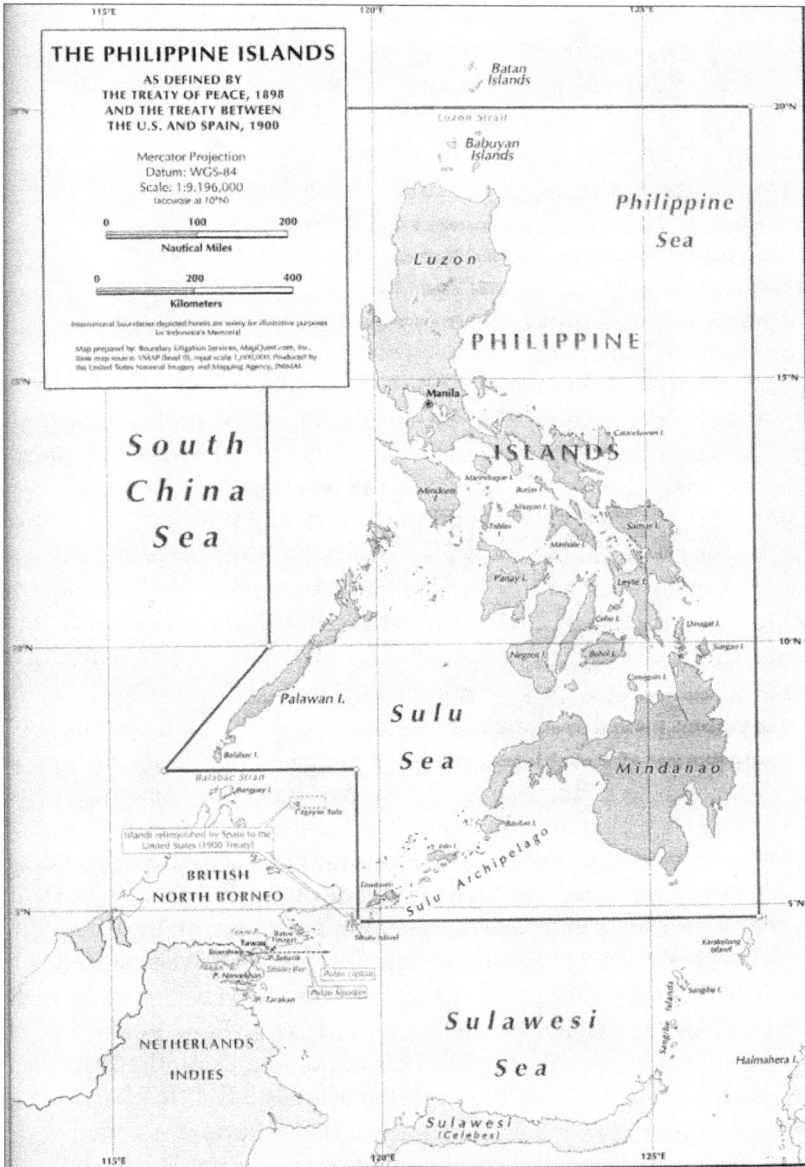

Source: ICJ, *Memorial of Indonesia*, vol. 1, 2 November 1999, Map 7.2.

extremely interesting to observe how W.C. Cowie, the Managing Director of the BNBC, reacted to these developments. In a letter dated 17 May 1901 marked "Strictly Private" to the new Governor of North Borneo E.W. Birch, Cowie remarked that since the Convention of 1900 was silent concerning the question of sovereignty over these islands, it was "decided to let sleeping dogs lie by not raising any question as to what comprised the Philippines and what belonged to North Borneo". To strengthen the Company's hold on these islands, however, he advised the Governor "without appearing do so" to plant the Company's flag on as many islands as possible. The planting of the flag was best done he wrote, "By giving the fishermen and turtle-egg collectors small flags to fly on the islands with instructions to keep them flying on the principal hut on each island. The great point is not to arouse suspicion in the matter and thus attract the attention of the Americans."[16]

The American authorities in the Philippines were themselves not certain as to the exact boundary line, especially in the southern extremity, with particular reference to certain groups of islands and reefs beyond the three marine leagues limit off the southeastern coast of North Borneo. The American Navy especially, started making active enquiries. In November 1902, Lieutenant E.L. Bisset, the Commanding Officer of the USS *Samar* made a cruise of the Sulu Archipelago and was alarmed that the Commanding Officer at Jolo had left out these regions from his administrative district. He immediately alerted his superior claiming that all of these islands and reefs were outside the limits of British North Borneo; that they had formerly belonged to the Spanish authorities; that the United States, having inherited all former Spanish possessions in the Philippines, should occupy them; and that if this was not done immediately, there was the danger of German intervention.[17] The Commander-in-Chief of the US Naval Force Asiatic Station, Rear Admiral R.D. Evans, strongly endorsed Bisset's views and urged the Civil Governor of the Philippines, W.H. Taft, and the Secretary of the Navy, to take immediate action to occupy these regions.[18] Both Commander Bisset and Admiral R.D. Evans visited North Borneo in November 1902 and April 1903 respectively and made known to the officials of the BNBC, including Governor E.W. Birch, that they were making enquiries about the status of the islands on the east coast of North Borneo outside the three marine leagues limit. They also wished to mark the three marine leagues line on their charts.[19]

Realizing the seriousness of the situation, Governor Birch advised the Court of Directors of the BNBC to request the Foreign Office to deal directly with the Americans instead of carrying on negotiations with the Sultan of Sulu. As the issue of conflicting sovereignty involved a number of islands and not just Taganac and Baguan, Birch opined as follows:[20]

> If a list were made of our islands and their sovereignty determined once for all, that which is now an unpleasant possibility would be set at rest and in my view there is no other way out of it for it is unwise any longer to deal with the Sultan of Sulu except through the Americans.

Cowie was alarmed by Birch's views and cautioned for immediate restraint. "The Court", he wrote, "wish you to understand that they prefer you to treat with the Sultan direct rather than through the American authorities".[21] Birch, however, was very perceptive of the reality of US jurisdiction over the Philippines and replied that he personally believed the Court was taking a wrong course for "if we can now get an agreement from the Sultan of Sulu they [the Americans] are quite likely to say that we had no right to deal with him except through them".[22]

Governor Birch had partially come to the view of the inevitability of American intervention as a consequence of learning of a statement made by the Sultan of Sulu Haji Mohammad Jamalulkiram to the American Official Interpreter at Jolo, Charles Schuck on 9 February 1903 concerning the status of the islands in dispute. In this statement, the Sultan declared that the cessions to the ODA in 1878 included only those islands within the three marine leagues limit from the Borneo coast and other islands such as Danawan, Pulau Gaya, and Omadal were "outside this line and not under the jurisdiction of the British North Borneo Government".[23]

4.4 Transfer of Some Islands by the Sultan of Sulu to BNBC, 1903

At the same time, however, the Sultan of Sulu Haji Muhammad Jamalulkiram was in touch with the BNBC's negotiator, A. Cook, who was ultimately able to work out a deal with the said ruler, for the cession of some islands on 22 April 1903. An Agreement called the "Confirmation of Cession of certain Islands off North Borneo" was concluded with the Sultan by which the latter ceded to the Government of North Borneo a number of islands for a sum of $300 a year.[24] These islands as named in the document were Langkayen, Boan (Boaan), Bakungan (Bakkungan Besar), Bakkungan Kechil, Libaran, Taganack (Taganac), Beguan (Baguan), Mantanbuan (Mantabuan), Gaya,

Omadal, Si Amil, Mabul, Kepalai, Dinawan (Danawan) and "all the other islands situated alongside, or round or between the islands that are above mentioned".[25]

Thus, it was not just the two islands of Taganac and Baguan over which the dispute had originally arisen which were transferred to North Borneo, but another twelve islands as well, and some smaller ones which were not named. The islands of Sipadan and Ligitan did not appear in the list, but the cession included all the "other islands" in the vicinity of the islands named in the 1903 Agreement. A closer look at the group of islands in the Semporna region would leave no doubt that the islands of Sipadan and Ligitan were included. (See Figure 1.5.)

4.5 THE UNITED STATES PROCLAIMED SOVEREIGNTY OVER 26 ISLANDS OFF THE COAST OF NORTH BORNEO, 1903

As anticipated by Governor Birch, the acquisition of these fourteen plus islands through negotiations with the Sultan of Sulu without reference to the United States landed the BNBC in serious complications. The Secretary of the US Navy took up the issues raised by Lieutenant E.L. Bisset and Rear Admiral R.D. Evans and wrote to the Secretary of State, John Hay on 14 March 1903 to obtain an authoritative interpretation of the extent of US jurisdiction in the Sulu Archipelago. John Hay studied the question meticulously in relation to the various treaties signed by the Sultan of Sulu with the Spanish Authorities; the Protocols of 1877; 1885 and 1897; the Treaty of Paris 1898; and the Convention of 1900, and came to the conclusion that the United States had:[26]

> sovereignty over the whole of the Sulu Archipelago up to three marine leagues of the mainland coasts of British North Borneo, with exception of the three named islands of Balambangan, Banguey and Malawali ...

Having obtained an authoritative view from the State Department, the Secretary of the Navy M.H. Moody, directed the Hydrographic Office to publish a chart on a scale sufficiently large to show all the islands, upon which was to be marked the boundary line as defined. He also instructed the War Department and the Civil Governor of the Philippines to take the necessary steps to assert the claim of the United States to all these islands and, if need be, to occupy them effectively. The Commander-in-Chief of the Asiatic Fleet was also given similar instructions.[27]

Following these directives, the Commander of the American gunboat, USS *Quiros*, Lieutenant Francis Boughter was instructed to proclaim US sovereignty over the islands in question. Lieutenant Boughter cruised to the Sulu Archipelago, and in June and July 1903 he proclaimed US sovereignty over a large number of islands by visiting them individually and planting US flags on them. Two cablegrams to the effect that such action was taken with names of the islands mentioned were sent to the Secretary of the Department of Navy in Washington.[28] A complete list of the islands off the coast of British North Borneo over which the United States proclaimed sovereignty in 1903 was also prepared. These islands numbered twenty-six including the islands of Sipadan and Ligitan which were clearly mentioned in the said list (Figure 4.4).[29] Lieutenant Boughter also sent a lengthy report on the islands he visited and over which US sovereignty was proclaimed. The report included hydrographic notes made by him. The islands of Sipadan and Ligitan were again specifically mentioned and described.[30]

The Hydrographic Office in Washington was instructed to prepare charts showing the boundary line incorporating all the islands over which the United States had proclaimed sovereignty in 1903. In preparing and drawing this boundary line pertaining to US sovereignty in the Sulu Archipelago and the islands off the coast of British North Borneo, the following charts were used:[31] H.O.C.2116; H.O.C.2117; H.O.C.2118; H.O.C.2119; H.O.C.1709; H.O.C.2121; and H.O.C.2122.

As the area was large and the charts were on a large scale, each chart covered a specific area. Chart 2117 covered the Sibuku Bay area, and as can be observed, the islands of Sipadan and Ligitan came within the US boundary line in the Sulu Archipelago as drawn by the Hydrographic Office in Washington in 1903 (see Figure 4.5).

4.6 THE ANGLO-AMERICAN AGREEMENT OF 1907: THE EXCHANGE OF NOTES

In June 1903, the Governor of North Borneo, E.W. Birch and the Resident of the East Coast, E.G. Barraut protested against Lieutenant Francis Boughter's act of proclaiming US sovereignty over the various islands off the east coast of North Borneo claiming that the BNBC had always administered these islands.[32] The Court of Directors instructed the governor not to take any action which would complicate matters as the whole issue was to be decided by the US and British Governments.[33] On 13 July 1903, Richard B. Martin, the Chairman of the BNBC, sent a lengthy memorandum to

FIGURE 4.4
List of Islands over Which Lieutenant Francis Boughter, Commander of the American Gunboat USS *Quiros* Proclaimed United States Sovereignty in 1903

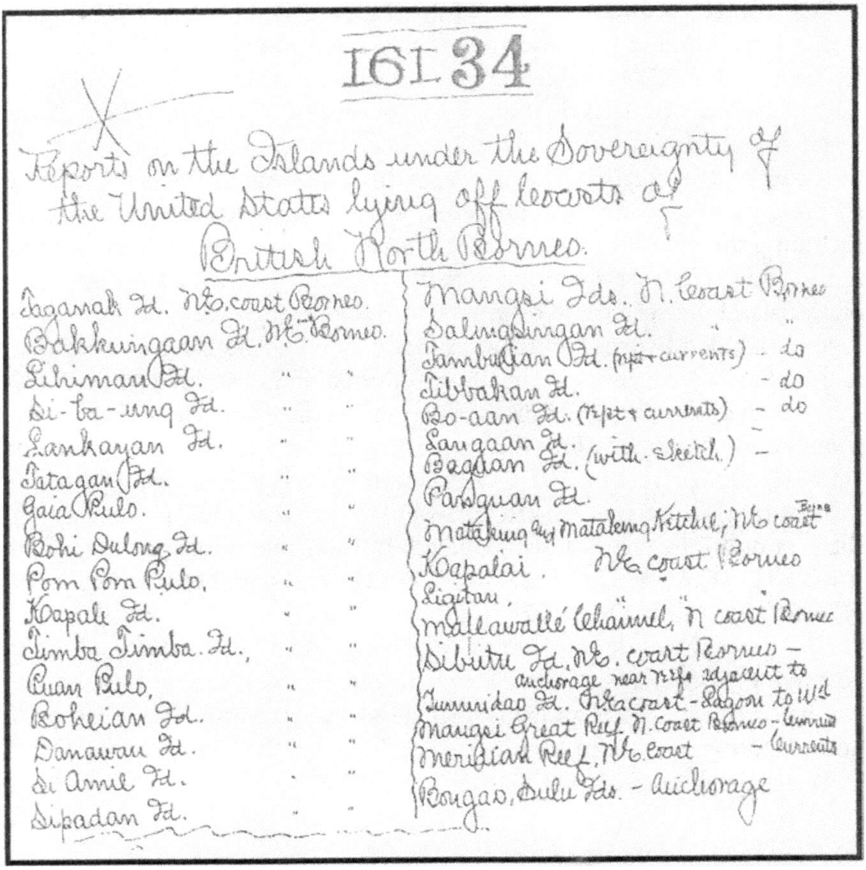
161.34

Reports on the Islands under the Sovereignty of the United States lying off coasts of British North Borneo.

Taganak Id. N.E. coast Borneo.	Mangsi Ids. N. Coast Borneo
Bakkungaan Id. N.E. Borneo.	Salingsingan Id. " "
Lihiman Id. " "	Tambulian Id. (reefs + currents) - do
Si-ba-ung Id. " "	Tibbakan Id. - do
Lankayan Id. " "	Bo-aan Id. (reefs + currents) - do
Tataganl Id. " "	Langaan Id. (with sketch) -
Gaia Pulo. " "	Bagaan Id.
Bohi Dulong Id. " "	Panguan Id.
Pom Pom Pulo. " "	Mataking or Mataking Kettle; N.E. coast Borneo
Kapali Id. " "	Kapalai. N.E. coast Borneo
Timba Timba Id., " "	Ligitan.
Buan Pulo. " "	Malawalle Channel, N coast Borneo
Boheian Id. " "	Sibutu Id. N.E. coast Borneo – anchorage near reefs adjacent to
Danawan Id. " "	Tumindao Id. N.E. coast – Lagoon to W'd
Si Amil Id. " "	Mangsi Great Reef N. Coast Borneo – currents
Sipadan Id. " "	Meridian Reef, N.E. Coast – currents
	Bongao, Sulu Ids. – Anchorage

Source: Hydrographic Office Survey Correspondence (U.S.A.), 1854–1907, R.G. 37, File 161.34, Box 9.

F.H. Villiers of the Foreign Office detailing the basis of the Company's occupation of the islands in dispute. Martin also attached a map, showing the "respective spheres of influence and control". According to Martin, all the islands and territory to the "east of the red line, have since our occupation of North Borneo, been under the suzerainty of Spain and the United States respectively; while those to the West of it have been administered by the

FIGURE 4.5

H.O.C. 2117 Showing Boundary Line Incorporating All the Islands in Sibuku Bay, North Borneo over Which the United States Proclaimed Sovereignty in 1903

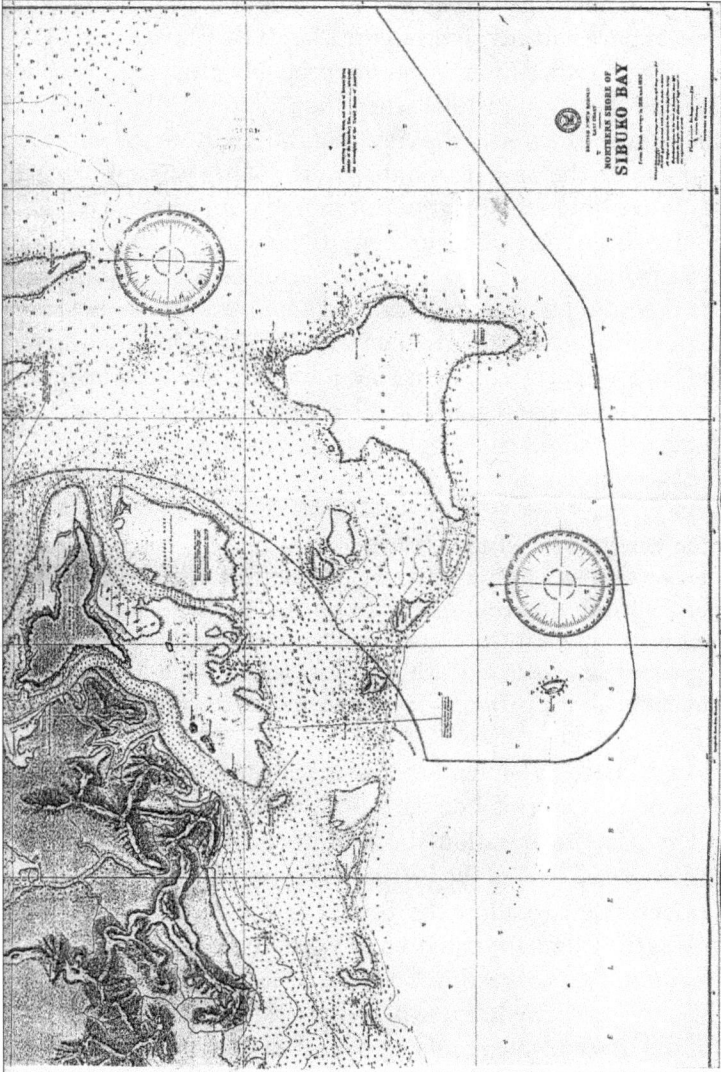

Source: Hydrographic Office Survey Correspondence (U.S.A.), 1854–1907, R.G. 37, File 563.49, Box 66.

Government of our State."[34] The British Foreign Office studied the basis of the Company's claims meticulously from all the arguments advanced by the Company and came to the conclusion recorded in a Memorandum dated March 1905 that "the Company's case falls at once to the ground, for they can never have had any rights to the islands they now claim". This eighteen-page Foreign Office Memorandum, probably prepared by Villiers, further concluded that even in 1903 when the Company advanced its claims, the British Government held the view that the "rights of the United States were indisputable". The only reason the United States was approached therefore was not to dispute their rights, but to find out "whether … they would be willing to forgo their rights to them [the islands] as an act of grace towards the company…".[35]

It is within this context that, negotiations were started in 1904 by the British Ambassador to the United States, Sir H.M. Durand with the Secretary of the State Department, John Hay. John Hay, however, favoured a general survey of the whole region for the purpose of drawing up a tentative sea boundary. Towards achieving this objective, he made the following proposal to the British Government in a note dated 10 December 1904:[36]

> the Government of the United States would be willing to come to an understanding with his Majesty's Government whereby a joint examination of the North Borneo neighbourhood shall be made by two experts, one on behalf of each Government, under instructions to agree if possible upon a tentative line which shall conveniently and fairly represent the intention of the parties to the Protocol of 1885…

In its reply dated 29 September 1905, the British Government indicated that it was not in favour of a demarcation exercise as there was "no intention" on their part "to question the title of the United States to the islands aforementioned". What the British Government desired was to request the US Government to allow the BNBC to continue administering the said islands as the Company had been doing so for many years, albeit mistakenly concerning their ownership.[37] W.C. Cowie, the Managing Director of the BNBC, was receptive to these proposals of the Foreign Office and minuted that if the United States could agree to "leave us in undisturbed possession of all the islands which have been controlled by us since the inception of the Company," the BNBC was prepared to recognize "their [United States] strictly legal rights". Cowie further proposed that the red line indicated on the map attached to Martin's memorandum to Villiers of the Foreign Office dated 13 July 1903 should be "recognized as defining the respective spheres of influence and control".[38] This proposal was conveyed to the American Government in January 1906.[39] Elihu Root, the new Secretary of State, was amenable to the new proposal and suggested that it might be carried out by an exchange of notes between the two governments. Before this could be executed, however, he requested the BNBC to furnish a chart of the region showing the line "which is recognized as dividing North Borneo territory from American territory".[40] The BNBC, however, disfavoured the proposal calling for the submission of the required chart as it would "necessitate the dispatch of a joint delimitation commission as originally suggested by the late Mr. Hay". The Company was of the opinion that such a mode of settlement would incur great expenses and require complicated legal procedures and therefore Cowie's simpler proposal was submitted to the Foreign Office.[41] The request was approved by the Foreign Office. The Company's proposals were incorporated in H.M. Durand's Memorandum of 23 June 1906 presented to Elihu Root. Attached to Durand's Memorandum was the 13 July 1903 Map with the red line "defining the respective spheres of influence and control".

Durand's Memorandum suggested a number of options, but the most important was the second proposal which was as follows:[42]

> The company would like to be left undisturbed in the administration of the islands without any detailed agreement, the United States Government simply waiving in favour of the company their right to administer ...

After weighing the merits of the different alternatives available, Elihu Root in an unofficial personal note to Durand dated 19 December 1906, concurred with the British view that there were great impediments for undertaking a boundary delimitation exercise leading to an international convention between the two countries. He was therefore in favour of adopting the second proposal contained in Durand's Memorandum that the Company be left in control of the islands for the time being with the following proviso:[43]

> It might be agreed that such an understanding shall be with the British Government, acting on behalf of the interests of British Subjects: *that it shall not carry with it territorial rights ... that the waiver shall cover the islands to the westward and southwestward of the line traced on the map which accompanied your memorandum of June 23 ...* [author's emphasis]

An exchange of Notes which were dated 3 July 1907 and 10 July 1907 respectively signified the formalization of the recently concluded agreement. The 3 July 1907 Note was from the new British Ambassador to the United States, James Bryce, to the US Secretary of State, Elihu Root. The Note conveyed the decision of the British Government formalizing the terms of the agreement and requested an assurance from the US Government concerning its adherence to and acceptance of the said terms. The terms were listed in the note. The Note of 10 July 1907 was a reply from the US Acting Secretary of State, Robert Bacon to James Bryce acknowledging the British note of 3 July 1907, and confirming US adherence to the agreement and the acceptance of the British note as sufficient ratification of the arrangements.[44]

A map which accompanied H.M. Durand's Memorandum of 23 June 1906 (originally attached to Martin's Memorandum of 13 July 1903) was annexed to the Notes and was deemed to form part of the said Notes.[45] Article 3 which is reproduced below, makes specific reference to this point. This line drawn on the map soon came to be known as the "Durand Line". See Figure 4.6.

By Article 1 of these Notes, the United States agreed to allow the BNBC to continue administering those islands outside the three marine leagues limit on the east coast of North Borneo which the Company had taken control since its inception. The existing status was to continue "indefinitely" at the pleasure of the United States and British Governments. Article 2 stressed the point that such a waiver did not "carry with it territorial rights" which meant that the United States was expressly reserving its sovereignty over the said islands. Article 3 referred to the islands which the United States was temporarily leaving under the administration of the BNBC, and this article is reproduced below:[46]

> Thirdly: That the temporary waiver of the right of administration on the part of the United States Government shall cover all the islands to the westward and southwestward of the line traced on the map which accompanied Sir H.M. Durand's memorandum of the 23rd of June 1906, and which is annexed to and to be deemed to form part of this note.

4.7 AMERICAN DESIRE TO TAKE OVER SEVEN TURTLE ISLANDS, 1918–28

From 1907 to 1918, the US Government did not actively show much interest in the jurisdiction of these islands, thus allowing the BNBC to carry on with

FIGURE 4.6
Map of North Borneo Annexed to the Notes of 3 July 1907 and 10 July 1907 Exchanged Between Britain and the United States, Showing the Durand Line

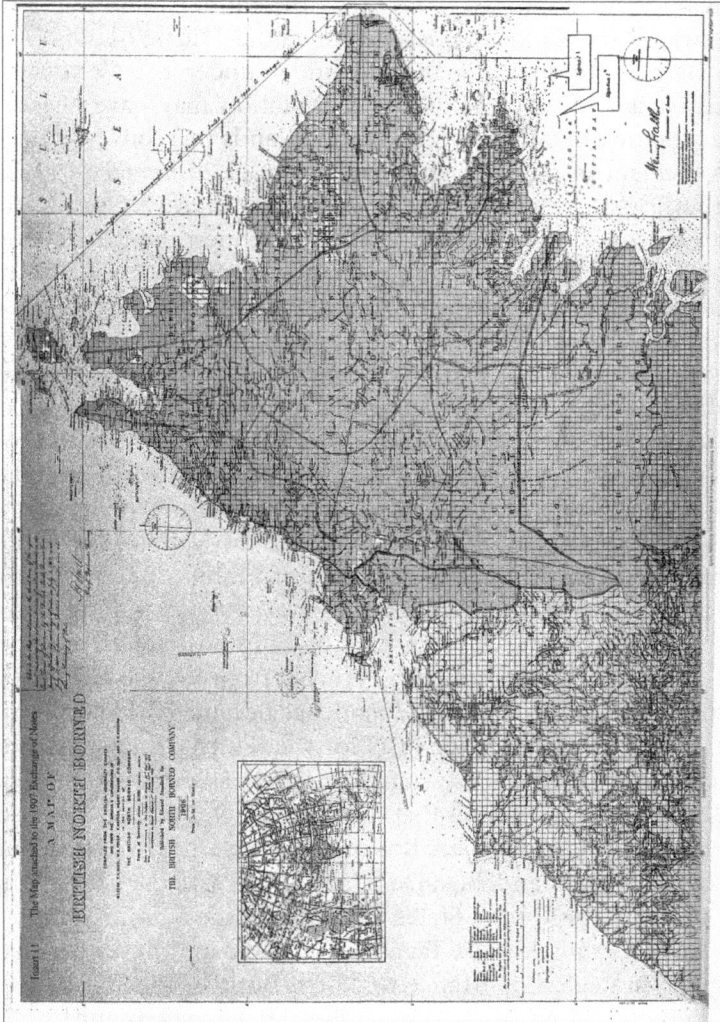

Source: ICJ, *Memorial of Malaysia*, vol. 1, 2 November 1999, opposite p. 55.

the administration undisturbed. In 1918, however, the Secretary of War requested that the limits of US jurisdiction in the vicinity of these islands be defined, as the Philippines Government wished to bring them under its control to consolidate its position in the region.[47] Initially, however, the US Government decided to take over the administration of only seven of the twenty-six islands in question called the "Turtle Islands Group" from the BNBC while leaving the remainder under the Company's control "until such time as a definitive delimitation may have been affected".[48] The intention of taking over the seven islands was conveyed to the British Government in a State Department Note of 29 January 1921 addressed to the British Ambassador at Washington, Sir A.C. Geddes. In the said Note, the US Government proceeded to request the British Government to enter into a fresh round of negotiations "with a view to affecting a new understanding between the two governments modifying the arrangement of 1907 ...".[49] A more specific reason given by Washington for wanting to affect a change in the 1907 Agreement was that the Government of the Philippines urgently wished to tighten its administrative control over some of the islands in the region, especially the island of Baguan to suppress smuggling of opium and Chinese persons from North Borneo into the southern Philippines.[50]

Another source, however, says that the United States created the border issue to deflect the demands of Filipino nationalists for quick independence as the United States was not yet willing to relinquish sovereignty over the Philippines. The Filipinos had already been given self-rule by the United States in 1916, but from 1919 to 1936, the demands of the nationalists for full independence became more vocal than before. The demands of the nationalists for the return of those islands was yet another reason for the US action.[51] It was ascertained subsequently in 1922 that the seven islands that the United States wished to take over from the BNBC included Baguan, Boaan, Lihiman, Langaan, Great Bakkungan, Little Bakkungan and Taganac.[52] The BNBC was particularly upset over the desire of the United States to take over the administration of two of the seven islands, that is Taganac and Baguan. These two islands were of great strategic importance to North Borneo, and the BNBC felt that the presence of an "American station [at Baguan Island] practically at the front door of our capital [Sandakan] will be a constant source of irritation, and the transfer of the island may convey a wrong impression to the native mind."[53] The island of Taganac was also of great strategic importance to North Borneo as it "commands the entrance to Sandakan

Bay". The BNBC was of the opinion that the United States was preparing the Philippines for independence in a short period of time and feared that in such an eventuality, islands like Taganac "would fall into the hands not of the United States Government but of a government which might in course of time became hostile ...".[54] The BNBC further strengthened its representations concerning the retention of Taganac Island by informing the Colonial Office that the Company had decided to build a lighthouse on the said island as the lack of such a facility had caused serious hindrance to navigation in Sandakan. With the rapid development of the Sandakan port, the installation of a lighthouse on Taganac had become a matter of urgency. The Company maintained that in fact lighting for the lighthouse had been purchased and was on its way to North Borneo. Governor A.C. Pearson of North Borneo summed up his concern about Taganac Island as follows:[55]

> The surrender of this island would therefore seriously prejudice the future of Sandakan commercially as well as strategically.

From 1922 to 1925, correspondence on the issue between both countries died down for a while. The United States was preoccupied with the issue of constitutional changes in the Philippines. From 1919 to 1934, Filipino nationalists demanding for independence led a number of missions to Washington. The United States was busy negotiating these demands. The outcome was the Tydings-McDuffie Act of 1934 which promised complete independence for the Philippines by 1946. (See Chapter 5.) The British Government, on the other hand, was busy trying to get an accurate picture concerning the status and importance of the "Turtle Islands" to North Borneo through correspondence with the BNBC, the Colonial Office, and the Admiralty. In the meantime, the BNBC went ahead with the erection of the lighthouse on Taganac Island in November 1922.[56]

The Admiralty was also asked to look into the matter of the "Turtle Islands" and the request by the United States to extend their survey of the Philippines into British territory in the affected area.[57] As a result of investigations by the Admiralty, it was established that two of the seven islands in question, that is Great Bakkungan and Little Bakkungan could well be within British North Borneo territorial waters of three marine leagues, thus giving the BNBC some grounds of claim to these two islands. Another issue that became crystal-clear was the British Government's stand that the BNBC had no grounds for contesting the US desire to repossess the seven islands.[58] On 21 April 1925, the US Secretary of State, Frank B. Kellogg took up the issue again and asked the British Government whether it had come to a decision concerning the matter.[59] Seeing the hopelessness of the situation, the BNBC in 1926 decided to accede to the demand of the US Government to take over the "Turtle Islands" and pressed merely for the right to maintain the lighthouse on Taganac after it was taken over by the United States in return for waiving all claims to Little Bakkungan and Great Bakkungan. Representations to this effect was made by the British Government to the American Government in a Note dated 21 April 1926 and was worded as follows:[60]

(1) H.M.G. accepted the fact that the BNBC had a good claim to Great Bakkungan and Little Bakkungan, the former being intersected by a line drawn 9 marine miles from the low watermark, while Little Bakkungan is within the line even if the said line is drawn from the high watermark.

(2) But H.M.G would agree to waive the claim to these two islands if the U.S. Government would undertake:-
  (a) to give the Chartered Co. full facilities for the maintenance of the Taganac Lighthouse which we had erected.
  (b) to give an assurance that an effective police post would be established on one of the islands.

(3) H.M.G. also asked for a definite statement from the U.S. Government, undertaking that any future transfer of the islands, to a third State should be subject to the restrictive provisions respecting fortifications under Article 19 of the Washington Naval Treaty.

4.8 NEGOTIATIONS FOR A DEFINITIVE NORTH BORNEO–PHILIPPINES BOUNDARY, 1926–28

The conditions contained in the British Government's Note of 21 April 1926 were communicated to the Governor General of the Philippines by the US authorities. The Governor General was not in favour of modifying the 1907 Agreement for the takeover of only seven islands. In fact, he recommended that the 1907 arrangement be abandoned completely and that a new treaty be concluded with Britain definitely defining the boundary between the Philippine Islands and North Borneo so that all the islands "found to belong to the United States be assumed by the Philippine Government".[61] The US Government concurred with the views of the Governor General of the Philippines. Subsequently, on 12 February 1927, the US State Department prepared a memorandum in which the issue of boundary delimitation was thoroughly outlined. It was proposed in this memorandum that "it would be better if the boundary were drawn farther from Borneo ... so that we would not mix into the affairs of Borneo unnecessarily."[62] In fact, the memorandum suggested the adoption of the "Durand Line" of 1906 except at certain places. The memorandum was accompanied by detailed notes on the new boundary line suggested. Two charts were also attached, and these indicated the 1903 three marine leagues line, the 1906 "Durand Line", and the new proposed boundary. These suggestions were approved by the State Department. The new boundary line and the "Durand Line" of 1906 were plotted on Charts No. 4707 and No. 4720 prepared by the US Coast and Geodetic Survey. The new proposals for a definitive delimitation of the boundary together with a detailed description of the intended boundary and a copy of Charts No. 4707 and 4720 were conveyed to the British Government in a dispatch from Frank B. Kellogg, the US Secretary of State, to Sir Esme Howard, the British Ambassador at Washington in a dispatch dated 20 August 1927.[63] Kellogg also invited the British Government to undertake negotiations with the US Government for the purpose of concluding a new treaty "definitely determining the boundary, in accordance with paragraph 5 of the Agreement of July 10, 1907". Referring to the new boundary line proposed by the United States, Kellogg commented as follows (see Figures 4.7 and 4.8):[64]

> It will be observed that the boundary now proposed by the United States lies farther from Borneo than does the "Durand Line", except in the vicinity of the Turtle Islands, and in the portion of the 119th meridian where the two lines coincide.

Concerning the BNBC's request to obtain a lease of an area on Taganac Island for the purpose of operating the lighthouse constructed there by the Company, Kellogg informed the British Government that the Philippine Government was prepared to take over the maintenance and operation of the said facility. The terms and conditions of the takeover would also form part of the negotiations of the new treaty.[65] The British Admiralty plotted the new boundary line and the "Durand Line" on their own charts and arrived at the view that the proposed definitive boundary was "not unduly favourable to United States interests", and in fact, it was more advantageous to North Borneo. North Borneo stood to gain more from the proposed boundary line as the United States would receive only Great Bakkungan,

FIGURE 4.7
Reconstructed Map Showing the Boundary Convention of 1930 Line
between North Borneo and the Philippines

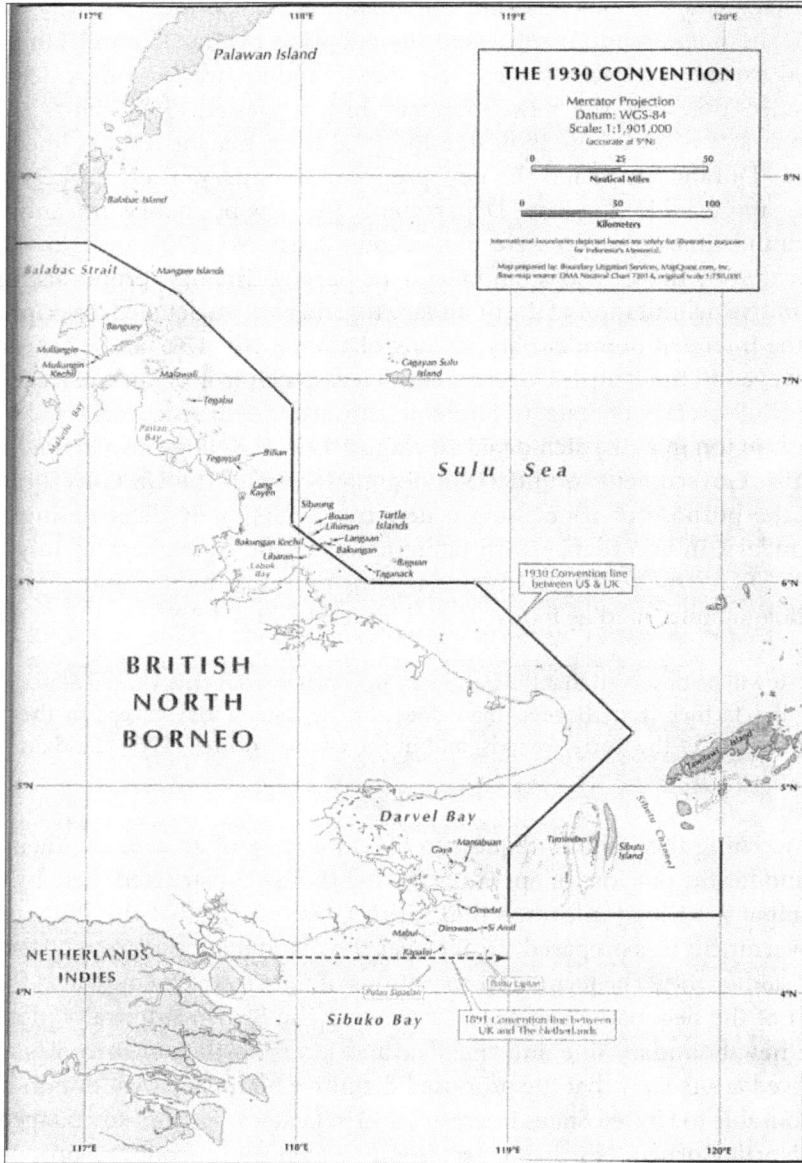

Source: ICJ, *Memorial of Indonesia*, vol. 1, 2 November 1999, Map 7.3.

FIGURE 4.8
Map Showing a Comparison of the 1898, 1907 and 1930 Treaty Lines

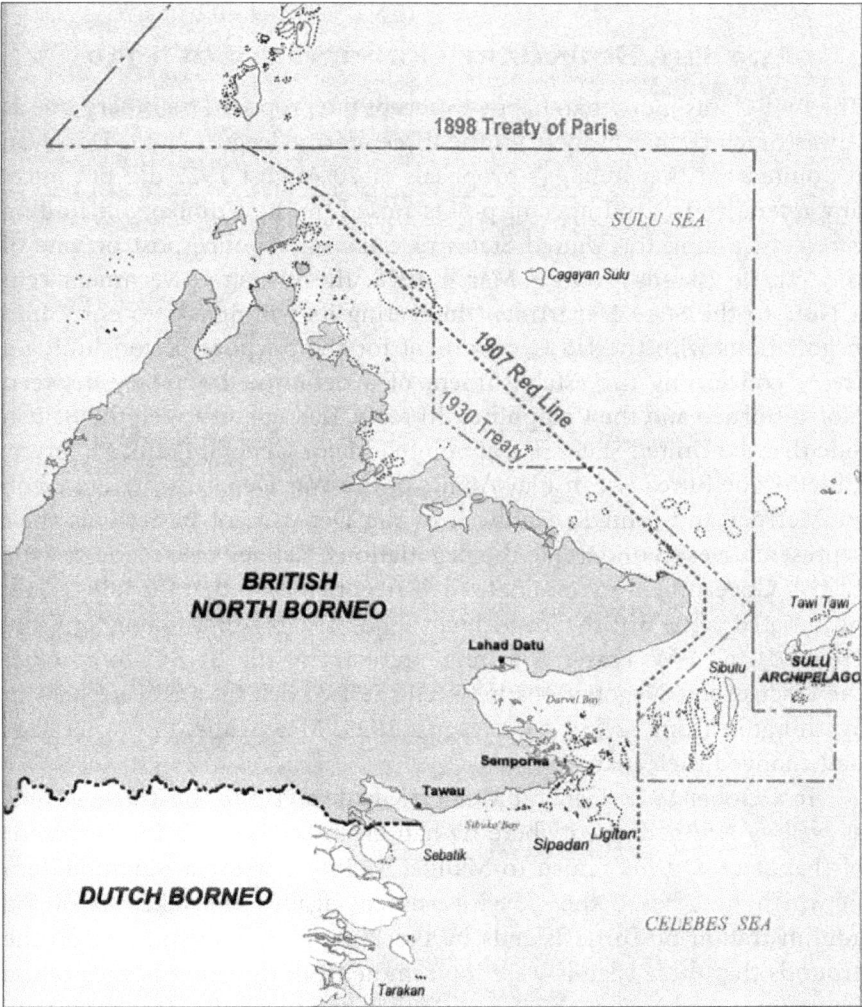

Source: ICJ, *Memorial of Malaysia*, vol. 1, 2 November 1999, p. 57.

dubiously claimed by North Borneo, but North Borneo would receive Buaning, Lankayan Mantabuan, Mataking and Ligitan Islands "to none of which she has any valid claim".[66] As such, the Admiralty supported the US proposals for the boundary delimitation in these words:[67]

It appears to Their Lordships, therefore, that there is nothing in the proposed settlement to which objection can reasonably be taken.

4.9 THE BOUNDARY CONVENTION OF 1930

The BNBC was more than happy to accept the proposed boundary line as it was much farther away from the three marine leagues limit. However, it pointed out that Kellogg's proposals of 20 August 1927 did not make any reference to a number of points raised by the Company, including a request asking the United States to establish a police post on one of the "Turtle Islands".[68] On 7 March 1928, the British Government sent a Note to the State Department indicating its willingness to enter into negotiations with the US Government for the purpose of concluding a treaty concerning the establishment of a definitive boundary between North Borneo and the Philippines. In reply, Kellogg informed the British side that the United States had appointed Major General Frank McIntyre, Chief of the Bureau of Insular Affairs of the War Department, and Jacob A. Metzger and John K. Caldwell of the Department of State as their representatives to undertake the negotiations. Kellogg also requested the British Government to nominate their negotiators so that the talks could be initiated.[69] The British Government appointed its Ambassador, Sir Esme Howard, and F.W. Fraser, a former Secretary of the BNBC, to conduct the discussions. Negotiations between the two delegations were held in Washington from 22 July to 2 August 1929. Meanwhile, the Americans had changed their plan.

In October 1928, General McIntyre made a visit to the Turtle Islands as well as North Borneo where he had an interview with the Governor of that state. On his return to Manila, McIntyre wrote a Memorandum in which he advised the US Government against the takeover of the administration of Turtle Islands by the Philippines Government on the grounds that these islands were too remote from the other islands of the Philippines Archipelago, but on the other hand were in close proximity to the coast of North Borneo. This issue was discussed by the American delegates before the arrival of the British team and in fact led to a radical change in the American proposal.

When the two teams met in Washington on 22 July 1929 for negotiations, the US side conveyed to the British delegates that they wanted the following:[70]

(a) A permanent delimitation of the boundary between the Philippines
     and North Borneo to resolve the issue.
(b) Confirmation of U.S. sovereignty over the seven Turtle Islands:
     [Nothing was said of the remaining nineteen islands. In 1903 and
     1907, the United States claimed sovereignty over twenty-six islands
     beyond the three marine leagues off the coast of North Borneo].
(c) The U.S. abandoned its plans to take over the administration of the
     7 Turtle Islands, thus leaving them under North Borneo rule until
     the U.S. decided otherwise. [This was a return to the status quo of
     1907.]

The British representatives were not given the reasons for this abrupt
change. The British Ambassador, Sir Esme Howard, tried to negotiate for
the sale or cession of these seven islands to Britain, but the United States
refused. The two delegations, therefore, concentrated on the business
of determining the outline of the boundary that had been prepared by
the United States. The line proposed was finally accepted by both sides,
and it was decided that two legal instruments were needed to conclude
the agreement. One was a formal treaty pertaining to the permanent
delimitation of the boundary and the other a concurrent exchange of
notes tantamounting to an informal agreement providing for a temporary
continued administration of the said seven islands by the BNBC. Drafts
of these two documents were prepared by the joint delegates on 2 August
1929. The British Ambassador subsequently submitted these drafts to the
British Foreign Office for approval.[71]

Both governments approved the drafts with minimal changes, and
the final boundary between the Philippines and North Borneo was
fixed by the Boundary Convention of 2 January 1930, signed by the two
powers at Washington. The exchange of Notes took place on 2 January
1930 and 6 July 1932. The Boundary Convention came into force on
13 December 1932.[72]

The treaty contained five Articles, but the most important were
Articles I, II and III. Article I of the Convention described the boundary
line separating the islands belonging to the Philippines and those to North
Borneo. The southernmost terminal of this boundary ended at a point where
the meridian of longitude 120 east intersected with the parallel 4°45′ north
latitude. Article II stated that the boundary line described in Article I was
indicated on Charts No. 4707 and 4720 published by the US Coast and
Geodetic Survey. These charts were attached to this treaty and were made

a part of it. Based on Article I, Article III confirmed that all islands to the north and east of the boundary line would belong to the Philippines and all islands to the southwest of the said line were to be owned by the State of North Borneo (see Figure 4.7 for the boundary line of 1930). Article III of the said treaty was worded as follows:[73]

Article III

All islands to the north and east of the said line and all islands and rocks traversed by the said line, should there be any such, shall belong to the Philippine Archipelago and all islands to the south and west of the said line shall belong to the State of North Borneo.

The Exchange of Notes specifically referred to a number of islands over which the United States reaffirmed its sovereignty but left their administration in the hands of the BNBC until it was decided otherwise. The names of these islands were as follows:[74]

(1) Sibaung, Boaan, Lihiman, Langaan, Great Bakkungan, Taganak, and Baguan in the group of islands known as the Turtle Islands.
(2) The Mangsee Islands.

Thus, ended the long uncertainty over the determination of the definitive boundary between the Philippines and North Borneo which began in 1903. Attempts to take over the seven Turtle Islands and the Mangsee Islands by the Filipino nationalists began as early as 1939.[75] After independence from the United States on 4 July 1946, Diosdado Macapagal became the chief proponent for resuming Philippine sovereignty over these seven islands. In 1946, the Philippines Government gave notice to Britain indicating its intention of taking over the administration of the Turtle and Mangsee Islands.[76]

The British Government replied that it was willing to hand over the administration of these islands as soon as both governments could set up a joint committee to "consider and report on the various questions relating to the administration" of the islands concerned.[77] Subsequently, two committees were established, one by each government. These two committees held their discussions at Sandakan. The Philippines committee was headed by Macapagal.[78] Based on the report of these committees, the Philippines Government took over final control of the Turtle and Mangsee Islands on 16 October 1947.[79]

4.10 Conclusion

It is evident, as shown by the documents, that the BNBC since 1882 was, mistakenly administering about twenty-six islands off the east coast of Borneo which did not belong to it as they were beyond the three marine leagues limit specified in the Sulu Grants of 1878. Immediately after the United States took over the Philippines from Spain in 1898, enquiries were made concerning the exact extent of the colony's territories. In 1903 especially, the United States became aware that the BNBC was administering a number of islands on the east coast of North Borneo beyond the three marine leagues limit of the territorial waters of that state. The United States was of the view that these islands, about twenty-six in number, were formerly owned by the Sultan of Sulu and therefore rightly belonged to the Philippines. To claim its legal rights, the United States proclaimed sovereignty over these twenty-six islands in 1903. The BNBC protested, but the British Government itself was of the view that the BNBC had no legal title to these islands. The American Government wanted to take over jurisdiction over these islands, but as a result of appeals by the BNBC, decided in favour of continued BNBC administration, while reserving unquestioned sovereignty over them. This arrangement was sealed in an exchange of Notes in 1907. The Notes were accompanied by a map showing basically the spheres of jurisdiction of the United States and Britain on the east coast of North Borneo. All the islands in question including Sipadan and Ligitan were recorded on this map. Unfortunately, they were not named in the Notes itself. This arrangement was to last until the United States decided otherwise. Starting from 1918, the United States began to seriously consider to undertake the delimitation of a permanent boundary between the Philippines and North Borneo. After protracted negotiations, the permanent boundary was finally fixed by the Boundary Convention of 1930. The boundary so drawn was much farther from the east coast of North Borneo as compared to the three marine leagues limit of 1878. The reason was that the United States wanted to retain sovereignty over seven islands only out of the twenty-six islands over which it had formally established ownership in 1903. It was also done in deference to the BNBC, as well as the fact that many of these islands were considered too remote for effective Philippines control. These seven islands, called the Turtle Islands were eventually taken over by the Philippines Government in 1947, but the rest, over nineteen in number, and including Sipadan and Ligitan, were effectively transferred to the State of North Borneo as specified by Article III of the Boundary Convention of 1930. A treaty map was attached to this Convention, and the names of all these nineteen islands are indicated. To my mind, there is clear documentary evidence and historical events to prove that Britain, and eventually Malaysia, had obtained legal title to nineteen islands in the region as a result of treaties and arrangements forged between the United States and Britain from 1907 to 1930. The only weakness of these bilateral treaties was that the names of these islands were not mentioned specifically in their texts. Notwithstanding this small legal oversight, I am of the view that Malaysia should have won the case on both the prerequisites: the possession of legal title and *effectivités*. However, as we shall see later in Chapter 7, the International Court of Justice (ICJ) chose to award sovereignty over Sipadan and Ligitan to Malaysia, not on the basis of possession of a legal title which Malaysia had emphasized, but rather on *effectivités*.

Notes

1. C.O. 874/54 Document 6.
2. A number of islands, about twenty-six, were beyond the three marine leagues limit fixed by the Sulu Grants of 1878 but were very close to the east coast of North Borneo. The BNBC mistakenly thought that these islands were included in the said grants. As such the Company continued to administer these islands since it took over the administration of North Borneo in 1882. These groups of islands were basically located in two areas, which is, off the Labuk Bay and the Sandakan Coast known as the Turtle Islands (ten in number) and another group consisting of about sixteen islands in Darvel Bay and off the Tawau Coast. The names of these islands as shown below, are based on the list of islands over which Lieutenant Francis Boughter of the American Navy proclaimed United States Sovereignty in 1903. See "Report on the Islands under the Sovereignty of the United States lying off the coast of British North Borneo, recently visited by the USS *Quiros* by Lieutenant Francis Boughter", July 1903 enclosure in R.F. Nicholson, Chief of the Bureau of Navigation, to The Assistant Secretary of Navy, 6 August 1903, Hydrographic Office Survey Correspondence (U.S.A.), 1854–1907, R.G 37, File 161.34, Box 9. Also, see Figure 4.4:
    (a) The Turtle Islands, off the Labuk Bay and the Sandakan Coast.
       (1) Sibalung
       (2) Boan
       (3) Lahiman
       (4) Bakkungan Besar (Great Bakkungan)
       (5) Langaan
       (6) Taganak (Taganac)

       (7) Baguan
       (8) Selingaan
       (9) Bakkungan Kecil
     (10) Guisaan
  (b) In Darvel Bay and off the Coast of Tawau.
       (1) Gaya Island
       (2) Bohaydulang
       (3) Mantabuan
       (4) Pandanan
       (5) Mataking
       (6) Pom Pom
       (7) Timba-Timba
       (8) Kalapuan
       (9) Bahayan
     (10) Si Amil
     (11) Danawan
     (12) Mabul
     (13) Kapalai
     (14) Ligitan
     (15) Sipadan
     (16) Omadal

3. Letter from Sultan of Sulu to W.C. Cowie, 15 January 1899, enclosure in Hugh Clifford, Governor North Borneo to Richard B. Martin, Chairman, BNBC, 7 June 1900, C.O. 874/1001.

4. W.C. Cowie, Managing Director, BNBC, to His Highness the Sultan of Sulu, 7 April 1899, enclosure in Hugh Clifford to Richard B. Martin, 7 June 1900, C.O. 874/1001.

5. J.A. Swettenham Acting High Commissioner, to Governor North Borneo, 8 May 1900, enclosure in Hugh Clifford to Richard B. Martin, 7 June 1900, C.O. 874/1001.

6. Hugh Clifford, Governor North Borneo to Richard B. Martin, Chairman BNBC, 7 June 1900 and enclosure, C.O. 874/1001.

7. Chairman, BNBC to Hugh Clifford, Governor North Borneo, 20 July 1900, C.O. 874/1001.

8. Sir Thomas Sanderson, Foreign Office to the Secretary BNBC, 11 August 1900, C.O. 874/1001.

9. Harington G. Forbes, Secretary BNBC to Richard B. Martin, Chairman BNBC, 12 September 1900, and enclosure, C.O. 874/1001.

10. The Sultan of Sulu to Governor Hugh Clifford, 27 November 1900, enclosure in E.W. Birch, Governor North Borneo to Richard B. Martin Chairman BNBC, 13 July 1901, C.O. 874/1001.

11. For details of the Spanish-American War of 1898, see Pauline Maier et al., *Inventing*

America: A History of the United States (New York: W.W. Norton and Company, 2003), pp. 664–70.

12. For a copy of the Treaty of Paris 10 December 1898, see Charles I. Bevans, *Treaties and Other International Agreements of the United States (1776–1949)*, vol. 2 (Washington, D.C.: Department of State Publication, 1968), p. 616.

13. Ibid.

14. The Matthews-Northrup Company to the War Department, U.S., 3 August 1899, Records of the Bureau of Insular Affairs Relating to the Philippine Islands, 1892–1935, R.G. 35, File 1907, Box 130–31.

15. See Convention between the United States and Spain, 7 November 1900, *Papers Relating to the Foreign Relations of the United States for 1900*, vol. 1, pp. 1942–44.

16. W.C. Cowie to E.W. Birch, 17 May 1901, C.O. 874/1001.

17. Lieutenant E.L. Bisset to the Commander-in-Chief, U.S. Naval Force, Asiatic Station, 4 November 1902, General Records of the Department of the Navy (U.S.A), 1900–1947, R.G. 80, File G.B. 424, 1900–1907, Box 122.

18. See letters from Rear Admiral R.D. Evans (a) to W.H. Taft, Civil Governor of the Philippines, 5 December 1902; (b) to the Secretary of the Navy, Navy Department, Washington, D.C., 5 December 1902; and (c) again to the Secretary of the Navy, Navy Department, Washington, D.C., 6 February 1903, General Records of the Department of the Navy (U.S.A), 1900–1947, R.G. 80, File G.B. 424, 1900–1907, Box 122; and Records of the Bureau of Insular Affairs Relating to the Philippine Islands 1898–1935, R.G. 350, File 907/10, Box 130–131.

19. Confidential report by A. Cook to Governor North Borneo, 28 November 1902, enclosure in Despatch No. 423 from E.W. Birch, Governor North Borneo to Richard B. Martin, Chairman BNBC, 24 December 1902, C.O. 874/1001; and Governor's Despatch No. 138/1903 from E.W. Birch, Governor North Borneo to Richard B. Martin, Chairman BNBC 16 April 1903 and enclosures, C.O. 874/1001.

20. Despatch 423 from E.W. Birch to Richard B. Martin, 24 December 1902, C.O. 874/1001.

21. Court's Despatch 67/1903 from W.C. Cowie, Managing Director BNBC, to E.W. Birch, Governor North Borneo, 20 February 1903, C.O. 874/1001.

22. Despatch No. 138/1903 from E.W. Birch, Governor North Borneo to Richard B. Martin, Chairman BNBC, 16 April 1903 and enclosures, C.O. 874/1001.

23. Translation of the Statement made by the Sultan of Sulu to the American Official Interpreter, Charles Schuck at Jolo on 9 February 1903, enclosure in Governor's Despatch No. 138/1903, C.O. 874/1001.

24. For the translated text of this document entitled "Confirmation of Cession of Certain Islands off North Borneo", dated 22 April 1903, see C.O. 874/53.

25. Ibid.

26. John Hay, Department of State, Washington to the Secretary of the Navy, 3 April

1903. General Records of the Department of the Navy (U.S.), 1900–1947, R.G. 80, File. G.B. 424, 1900–1907, Box 122.

27. M.H. Moody, Secretary, Navy Department, to the Secretary of War, 16 April 1903, Records of the Bureau of Insular Affairs Relating to the Philippines Islands 1893–1935, R.G. 350, File 907/19, Box 130–31.

28. See copies of the Cablegrams: Cablegram 1: General Records of the Department of the Navy (US) 1900–1947, R.G. 80, File G.B. 424, 1900–1907, Box 122. Cablegram 2: General Correspondence of the Office of the Secretary of the Navy, 1891–1926, R.G. 80 File 15826/7; Box 642.

29. See Hydrographic Office Survey Correspondence (US), 1854–1907, R.G. 37, File 161.34, Box 9. The islands over which Lieutenant Boughter established US sovereignty are listed on the front cover of this file, copy of which is reproduced as Figure 4.4.

30. Ibid.

31. See front cover, and Memorandum by Acting Hydrographer, Hydrographic Office., Washington, 8 August 1903 in Hydrographic Office Survey Correspondence, (US) 1854–1907, R.G. 37, File 563.49, Box 66.

32. E.H. Barraut, Resident East Coast to Lieutenant Boughter, 24 June 1903, enclosure in Despatch 235 from E.W. Birch, Governor North Borneo, to Richard B. Martin, Chairman, BNBC, 16 July 1903 and Despatch 213 from E.W. Birch, Governor North Borneo, to Richard B. Martin, Chairman, BNBC, 25 June 1903, C.O. 874/1001.

33. Court's Despatch 237/1903 from W.C. Cowie, Managing Director BNBC to E.W. Birch, Governor North Borneo, 26 June 1903, C.O. 874/1001.

34. Richard B. Martin, Chairman BNBC, to F.H. Villiers, Foreign Office, 13 July 1903, C.O. 874/1001. See Figure 4.6.

35. Foreign Office Memorandum dated March 1905, C.O. 874/1002.

36. John Hay, United States Secretary of State to. H.M. Durand, British Ambassador at Washington, 10 December 1904, enclosure in Durand to the Marques of Lansdowne, 12 December 1904, C.O. 874/1002.

37. H.M. Durand, British Ambassador to United States, to the US Secretary of State, 29 September 1905, C.O. 874/1002.

38. W.C. Cowie, Managing Director BNBC to Villiers, Foreign Office, 16 November 1905, enclosure in Under Secretary of State, Foreign Office, to the Secretary, BNBC, 2 February 1906, C.O. 874/1002.

39. H.M. Durand to the Secretary of State, 6 January 1906, C.O. 874/1002.

40. Elihu Root, US Secretary of State to H.M. Durand, British Ambassador to United States, 12 January 1906, enclosure, Foreign Office to the Secretary BNBC, 2 February 1906. C.O. 874/1002.

41. Harrington G. Forbes, Secretary BNBC, to the Under Secretary of State, Foreign Office, 10 May 1906, C.O. 874/1002.

42. See Memorandum and Map by H.M. Durand, British Ambassador to United States,

to the US Secretary of State, 23 June 1906, C.O. 874/1002. For the Memorandum, see Appendix D. For the map, see Figure 4.6.

43. Elihu Root, to Sir H.M. Durand, 19 December 1906, enclosure, in Letter No. 624 from Foreign Office to the Secretary BNBC, 9 January 1907, C.O. 874/1002. See Appendix E.

44. See Copy of Note from James Bryce, British Ambassador to the United States, to Elihu Root, Secretary of State, 3 July 1907 and copy of Note from Robert Bacon, Acting Secretary, US Department of State to James Bryce, 10 July 1907, enclosures in W. Langley, Foreign Office to the Secretary BNBC, 2 August 1907, C.O. 874/1002. Copy of the said Notes can also be found in *Papers Relating to the Foreign Relations of the United States for 1907*, vol. 1, pp. 542–49. See Appendixes F and G.

45. The map annexed to the Note of 3 July 1907 is reproduced as Figure 4.6. For correspondence pertaining to this map, see W. Langley, Foreign Office, Great Britain to the Secretary BNBC, 2 August 1907 and enclosure, C.O. 874/1002.

46. See Articles 1, 2 and 3 of the Notes, *Papers Relating to the Foreign Relations of the United States for 1907*, vol. 1, pp. 542–49. See Appendixes F and G.

47. Alvey A. Adee, US Department of State, to Mr Craigie, the British Charge, British Embassy Washington, 29 January 1921, enclosure in Sir A.C. Geddes, British Ambassador to the United States to the Marquis Curzon of Kedleston, British Foreign Office, 22 March 1922, C.O. 874/1002. Also in *Papers Relating to the Foreign Relations of the United States, 1927 and 1928*, vol. 2, pp. 724–986.

48. Ibid.

49. Ibid.

50. British Consulate General, Manila to the Governor of British North Borneo, 5 July 1922, C.O. 874/1002.

51. See Greg Poulgrain, *The Genesis of Konfrantasi: Malaysia, Brunei and Indonesia, 1945–1965* (Bathurst, NSW: Crawford House Publishing, 1998), p. 233. Also see Admiralty Memorandum of 4 July 1927, C.O. 874/1004.

52. A.C. Geddes, British Ambassador to United States to the Marquis Curzon of Kedleston, British Foreign Office, 27 September 1922, C.O. 874/1002. Also see Frank B. Kellogg, US Secretary of State to Sir Esme Howard, British Ambassador to the United States, 21 April 1925, *Papers Relating to the Foreign Relations of the United States, 1927 and 1928*, vol. 2, pp. 724–986.

53. A.C. Pearson, Governor North Borneo to the President BNBC, 22 July 1922, C.O. 874/1002.

54. Secretary BNBC to the Under Secretary of State, Colonial Office, 26 July 1922, C.O. 874/1002.

55. A.C. Pearson, Governor North Borneo to Forbes, Colonial Office, 6 November 1922, C.O. 874/1002. Also see Secretary BNBC to the Under Secretary of State, Colonial Office, 16 November 1922, C.O. 874/1002.

56. The Under Secretary of State, Colonial Office to the Secretary BNBC, 29 November 1922, C.O. 874/1002.

57. Admiralty Memorandum, 4 July 1927, 874/1004. Also in C.O. 531/20, ff. 30–43.
58. Ibid.
59. Frank B. Kellogg, US Secretary of State to Esme Howard, British Ambassador to the United States, 21 April 1925, *Papers Relating to the Foreign Relations of the United States, 1927 and 1928*, vol. 2, pp. 724–986.
60. See Foreign Office Memorandum of December 1927 entitled "Sovereignty of Islands off the East Coast of North Borneo", C.O. 874/1004.
61. Frank B. Kellogg, US Secretary of State to the US President, 18 June 1927, Records of the US Department of State, 1910–1929, R.G. 29, Micro 581, Roll 5.
62. Memorandum of the Division of Publications, US Department of State, 12 February 1927, Records of the Department of State, 1910–1929, R.G. 29, Micro 581, Roll 5.
63. Frank B. Kellog, US Secretary of State to Sir Esme Howard, British Ambassador to the United States, 20 August 1927 and enclosed Charts 4707 and 4720, C.O. 531/20, ff. 20–24.
64. Ibid.
65. Ibid.
66. Letter from the Admiralty to the Under Secretary of State, Foreign Office, 23 November 1927, enclosure in Admiralty to the Under Secretary of State, Colonial Office, 23 November 1927, C.O. 531/20 ff. 12–14.
67. Ibid.
68. Letter from the Under Secretary BNBC to the Under Secretary of State, Colonial Office, 28 November 1927, C.O. 874/1004.
69. Frank B. Kellogg, US Secretary of State to the British Charge (Chilton), 21 September 1928, *Papers Relating to the Foreign Relations of the United States, 1927 and 1928*, vol. 2, pp. 724–986.
70. J.P. Cotter Acting Secretary to State Under Secretary, to Charles G. Dawes, American Ambassador to Britain, 13 August 1929, Records of the US Department of State, 1910–1929, R.G. 29 Micro 581, Roll 5.
71. Ibid. Also see Draft Copies of these documents in C.O. 531/21, ff. 44–51.
72. Boundary Convention Between Great Britain and the United States, 2 January 1930, Charles Bevans, *Treaties And Other International Agreements of The United States, (1776–1949)*, vol. 2, pp. 473–81. Also in C.O. 531/22, ff. 25–26. Appendix H.
73. See Article III of Boundary Convention Between Great Britain and the United States, 2 January 1930.
74. See Exchange of Notes, From the British Ambassador to the Secretary of State, 2 January 1930, Boundary Convention Between the Great Britain and the United States, 2 January 1930.
75. See S. Wyatt Smith, British Consulate-General, Manila to the Right Honourable Anthony Eden, MP, 21 January 1941, and enclosures, C.O. 874/1006.

76. Note from the Vice-President of the Republic of the Philippines to His Majesty's Charge' d'Affairs at Manila, 19 September 1946, in *A Collection of Treaties and Other Documents Affecting The States of Malaysia, 1761–1963*, edited by J. de V. Allen, A.J. Stockwell and L.R. Wright, vol. 2 (London: Oceana Publications, 1981), pp. 554–55.
77. See Note from His Majesty's Minister at Manila to the Acting Secretary for Foreign Affairs of the Republic of the Philippines, 7 July 1947, ibid., pp. 556–57.
78. Poulgrain, *The Genesis of Konfrontasi*, pp. 231–33.
79. See Note from the Vice-President of the Republic of the Philippines to His Majesty's Minister at Manila, 16 December 1947; and Note from His Majesty's Minister at Manila to the Vice-President of the Republic of the Philippines, 20 April 1948, in *A Collection of Treaties and Other Documents*, by Allen et al., pp. 561–62.

5

The Emergence of Successor States to Colonial Regimes and the Phenomena of Expansionist Nationalisms in Maritime Southeast Asia

5.1 Introduction

The dispute over the ownership of the islands of Sipadan and Ligitan developed between Indonesia and Malaysia in 1969. The Philippines has an ongoing claim over Sabah since 1962. In order to understand how these three nations became embroiled in these territorial disputes, it is imperative to understand the process of how they became legal successor states to the colonial regimes in the region; how they inherited some of the unresolved territorial problems of the colonial era; and how expansionist nationalisms clashed over British Borneo.

5.2 The Emergence of the Philippines as Legal Successsor to Spain and the United States

When Spain occupied the Philippines in the late sixteenth century, it inherited a territory which was fragmented and lacked any experience of an organized central government. Although Spanish rule was often harsh and oppressive, Spain unified the islands under a relatively organized central administration, introduced Western education and more importantly brought Christianity to the Filipinos. Consequently, the three hundred years of Spanish rule from 1571 to 1898 made the Philippines the only Asian country with a Christian majority and the highest degree of Western influence.[1] The Philippines also became the first country in Southeast Asia to launch an anticolonial movement against its colonial masters and achieve independence. The spark of nationalism was ignited in the 1880s and 1890s by a middle-class Filipino intellectual and medical doctor named Jose Rizal who agitated for reforms by calling upon the Spanish authorities to give the Filipinos their just rights, liberty, and representation in the Spanish Parliament. His very moderate demands were unheeded by the government which in fact deported him to Mindanao in 1892 to curtail his influence. Whereupon, the nationalist movement passed into the hands of revolutionaries and went underground. In 1892, these revolutionaries, headed by Andres Bonifacio formed a secret society called Katipunan which sought to achieve independence from Spanish rule through armed rebellion. The Katipunan gained widespread support from Filipinos to the extent that it was able to arouse a nationwide insurrection in 1896. The Spaniards reacted with severe repression. Jose Rizal was executed on charges of rebellion and sedition, and the insurrection was mercilessly crushed. The leadership of the revolutionaries passed into the hands of another leader, Emilio Aguinaldo who carried on the rebellion, but found the Spanish too strong to defeat. Nevertheless, the revolutionaries declared the Philippines an independent republic in March 1897 and elected Aquinaldo as its President.[2] Aguinaldo, however, was unable to dislodge the Spaniards by force and decided to negotiate. Both sides finally struck the Pact of Biacnabato in 1897, by which the revolutionary leaders agreed to go into voluntary exile to Hong Kong. Spain on its part agreed to pay them a sum of 800,000 pesos as compensation. Spain also agreed to undertake reforms for the upliftment of the Filipinos. Both sides did not honour the pact. Aguinaldo used the money paid by Spain (half of 800,000 pesos) to buy arms in Hong Kong with the aim of coming back to launch a fresh assault on the Spaniards.[3] In all this, the United States which was at war with Spain over Cuba in the Caribbean, also wanted to acquire the Philippines for strategic and commercial reasons. Consequently, US personnel in Hong Kong, including Commodore George Dewey, the head of the US fleet in the region, were asked to make contacts with Aguinaldo and his group of revolutionaries. A pact was struck between the Americans and Aguinaldo by which Dewey promised to help the revolutionaries expel the Spanish from the Philippines. In reality, this was a ruse by the United States to take over the Philippines from the Spaniards. Aguinaldo, who had been brought back to the Philippines by the US Navy, organized a remarkable resistance, but Dewey ignored his success and in fact entered into a secret deal with the Spanish. As discussed in Chapter 4, Spain ceded the Philippines to the United States through the Treaty of Paris in 1898 for the sum of 20 million Spanish dollars.[4]

5.2.1 The US Era, 1898–1946

The Treaty of Paris had left out some islands in the southern Philippines from the jurisdiction of the United States. The most important of these islands were the Batam Islands, Kagayan-Sulu, and Sibutu. To consolidate its control over the kingdom of Sulu, the United States signed an agreement with the ruling Sultan of Sulu, Muhammad Jamalulkiram II (r.1894–1936) in August 1899 called the Bates Treaty. By this treaty, the sultanate surrendered partial sovereignty to the United States.[5] In 1900, through a convention between the United States and Spain, the territories, including Sulu, which had been left out from the 1898 treaty, were officially incorporated into the cession.[6] Relations between the US authorities and the Filipino revolutionaries culminated in a bitter war of attrition from 1899 to 1902. The United States soon realized the futility of continued hostility with the Filipinos and quickly embarked on a policy of political reforms. In 1901, a civilian government took over from military rule and the Philippines was divided into an administrative structure based on provinces and municipalities in which Filipinos were given full participation.[7] This system of administration was extended to Sulu in 1903 when a Moro Province was created.[8] The United States also speeded up its programme of preparing the Philippines for early independence. Towards this end, an elected assembly of eighty Filipinos was created in 1907 to act as the state's legislature. In 1912, the new Governor-General, Francis Burton Harrison (1912–20), accelerated the process of granting self-government to the Filipinos. His initiative resulted in the Jones Law of 1916 which gave the Filipinos complete control over their own internal affairs.[9] Jones Law also stated that the United States would grant independence as soon as a stable government could be established in the Philippines. A modern constitution for the Philippines was also created. A number of Filipino leaders began to emerge on the political stage at this time; some of the most prominent being Sergio Osmena, Manuel L. Quezon, and Manuel Roxas, who were capable of establishing a solid and stable goverment.[10] As the Filipinos were moving rapidly towards self-rule and modern democracy, they felt that monarchial systems, such as the Sulu

Sultanate, were archaic and inconsistent with democratic ideas. Sultan Muhammad Jamalulkiram was thus prevailed upon to formally give up all his political and civil powers in 1915. In this case, the Governor of the Department of Mindanao and Sulu, Frank W. Carpenter, was authorized by the Governor-General of the Philippines to persuade the Sultan to give up his temporal sovereignty to the United States while retaining his position as "titular spiritual head" of the Sulu people. This agreement was signed by the two parties on 22 March 1915 at Zamboanga and was called the "Carpenter Agreement". By this agreement, the Sultan lost all his political powers to the United States which also obtained absolute sovereignty over the Sultanate and its dependencies. The US authorities of the Philippines were of the opinion that with the conclusion of the Carpenter Agreement of 1915, the Sulu Sultanate was terminated.[11] After having attained self-government in 1916, the Filipinos began to demand independence immediately. In the 1920s however, the United States began to have second thoughts about its pledge of 1916 and began to stall the progress towards granting independence to the Philippines. As a result, reactionary policies set in, led mainly by the new Governor-General, Leonard Wood (1921–27). To deflect the demands of Filipino nationalism, the United States, in 1922 revived the border issue with North Borneo pertaining to the takeover of the Turtle Islands.[12] The Filipinos, however, persisted in their demands and led by leaders such as Manuel Roxas and Manuel L. Quezon they undertook a number of missions to Washington between 1919 and 1934 to negotiate for independence. These efforts resulted in the 1934 Tydings-McDuffie Act which created the self-governing Commonwealth of the Philippines. The Commonwealth came into being in 1935, and Manuel L. Quezon was elected as the country's first president. The emergence of the Commonwealth Government of Filipino nationalists had serious consequences for the future of the Sulu Sultanate. The Filipino nationalists considered the existence of the Sultanate a contradiction to the unitary structure of the Commonwealth. Therefore, when Sultan Muhammad Jamalulkiram II died in 1936, the new Philippine Government decided not to recognize any special status of the Sultan of Sulu, nor to pay him any pension as had been agreed in the Carpenter Agreement of the 1915.[13] The Tydings-MacDuffie Act also provided for the granting of full independence to the Philippines after a period of ten years from the formation of the Philippines Commonwealth. Independence was achieved on 4 July 1946 with Manuel Roxas as the new president.[14]

5.3 THE EMERGENCE OF THE REPUBLIC OF INDONESIA AS A LEGAL SUCCESSOR TO THE DUTCH

As discussed in Chapter 2, the Dutch East India Company (DEIC) was abolished by the Batavian Republic in 1799. By the Convention of London of 1814, Britain returned to the Dutch all colonies in the East Indies occupied during the Napoleonic Wars. The actual transfer took place only in 1816, and this time it was the Dutch Government which took over control of the administration. However, as usual, the Dutch began to impose their jurisdiction with great speed and assertiveness, reintroducing the DEIC's monopolistic policies. As the people of the East Indies had seen a great deal of free trade during the absence of the Dutch in the period of the Napoleonic Wars, there was great opposition to the reimposition of Dutch rule with its commercial restrictions. As a result, revolts broke out in the Celebes, Moluccas, and Borneo. Worst still, a devastating rebellion broke out in Java called the Java War from 1825 to 1830. The Java War was a costly affair, and together with a host of other factors, including the Belgium Revolt at home in 1830, it brought the Netherlands to the brink of bankruptcy.[15] One of the consequences of Holland's preoccupation with the debacle in Java was the lack of Dutch expansion into Borneo till the 1840s when the establishment of James Brooke in the Brunei Empire shook them into action.[16] To save the Netherlands from total economic and financial ruin, the Culture System was introduced in Java from 1830 to 1870.[17] This system was based on the compulsory production of cash crops by the Javanese peasant for the government on one-fifth of his farmland or alternatively, the contribution of his services for sixty-six days in a year. The system eventually not only saved the Netherlands from bankruptcy but, it in fact brought untold prosperity and riches to the mother country and the Dutch business community. However, in the later stages, excessive exploitation and abuse impoverished the Javanese farmers causing untold misery and famine. When the horrors of the Culture System finally dawned upon the Dutch Government, it took measures to abolish the practice in 1870, and replace it with the Ethical Policy (1901–20), in an attempt to make amends and repay a "debt of honour" to the Indonesian people.[18]

The riches brought about by the Culture System initiated a policy of Dutch political expansion into the Outer Islands in the 1840s. As a result of this policy, Bali, Banka and the major ports of Celebes were brought under Dutch control from 1840 to 1860. The "intrusion" of James Brooke into the region of the Brunei Empire, that is, Old Sarawak in 1841, gave further impetus to the Dutch to consolidate their political hold over the southern and eastern parts of Borneo. Dutch imperialism reached its zenith in the 1870s when they embarked upon a campaign to subdue the strong and independent kingdom of Acheh. The venture turned out to be a costly affair as it led to a disastrous war of attrition with Acheh from 1873 to 1903 before the stubborn kingdom could be conquered.

Meanwhile, the Ethical Policy, launched in 1901, sought to bring about a limited measure of emancipation to the Indonesians by the introduction of policies such as decentralization, the improvement of social services, the implementation of elementary Western education and the incorporation of the educated Indonesians into the civil service. It was in this atmosphere that the seeds of nationalism began to germinate in Indonesia in the early decades of the twentieth century.[19] The earliest organization to emerge that sought to create some degree of identity and cultural consciousness among the Indonesians was the Budi Utomo (High Endeavour) based in Java. A group of Western-educated elites founded this organization in 1908. Its aims were mainly social in nature including the spread of education and cultural revivalism. It did not enjoy much appeal except in Java. In 1912 another organization called the Sarekat Islam (SI) was formed by a group of Indonesian batik traders who resented the Chinese domination of the batik industry. Its objectives included protecting its members against Chinese competition and protecting Islam against the activities of Christian missionaries. SI began to have political aims when it began demanding self-government. The Sarekat gained mass support and in 1919 was reported to have a following of two million members. The most radical organization to emerge in Indonesia was the Communist Party of Indonesia (PKI) which was formed in 1920. In 1926, the PKI launched an armed uprising aimed at overthrowing the Dutch but failed to garner popular support and was crushed. In 1927, a group of young Western-educated Indonesians led by a fiery and charismatic figure named Sukarno formed the Persarekatan National Indonesia (PNI).[20] This political group with a strong nationalist agenda became so popular that the Dutch became alarmed. In 1930, the Dutch arrested the leaders, including Sukarno, and outlawed the party. Most of the powerful nationalist leaders such as Sukarno, Mohammad Hatta, and Sutan Syahrir remained in prison till the Japanese freed them in 1942.

Constitutionally, the Dutch made some concessions to the more moderate nationalists. In this respect, a Peoples Council or Volksraad was created in 1918. In 1925, elected Indonesians were given a majority position in the council. The body was however purely advisory in capacity with no legislative powers. In 1936, the Volksraad requested for the formation of an imperial conference to discuss the granting of self-government to the Indonesians. The Dutch, however, did not respond till the Second World War.

The Japanese invaded and defeated the Dutch in Java in January 1942. They released the imprisoned nationalist leaders and in 1943 set up a puppet government under Sukarno with Mohammad Hatta as his deputy.[21] Although the Japanese did not make any concessions to the nationalists, the latter cooperated with them with the aim of preparing for independence. The Japanese also created and formed an Indonesian army of more than a million soldiers to help them in maintaining law and order. This army later became the backbone of resistance to the Japanese themselves and later the Dutch upon their return in 1945. On 15 August 1945, Japan surrendered to the allies.[22] This news was not announced in Java. While the Japanese were still in Java, Sukarno proclaimed independence on 17 August 1945, thereby establishing the Republic of Indonesia.[23]

On 29 September 1945, British troops arrived in Java to liberate Indonesia from the Javanese. The Dutch soon followed. The Dutch claimed sovereignty over the whole of Indonesia and refused to recognize the Republic. The Dutch had underestimated the strength of the Republic and soon realized the benefit of negotiations. The Dutch proposed a partnership with Indonesia in a Commonwealth where the Netherlands would have ultimate sovereignty. The Republican Government's position was that the Netherlands must recognize its sovereignty as a starting point for negotiations. As these terms were not acceptable to both sides, negotiations broke down, and hostilities started. Further negotiations led to the Linggajati Agreement signed in November 1946.[24] The Dutch recognized the Republican Government's control over Java and Sumatra, and both sides agreed to form the United States of Indonesia. The agreement was however soon broken and the Dutch, having consolidated their position, launched what came to be known as "police action" by which force was used to attack the Republican Government where its leaders were detained. The Dutch action of resorting to oppressive measures brought about world outrage and condemnation. The Indian Prime Minister at that time, Jawaharlal Nehru organized the Asia Conference on Indonesia to put pressure on the Dutch. The Conference urged the Security Council to intervene in the dispute. The Security Council soon took action and ordered a ceasefire, the release of political prisoners by the Dutch and the reinstatement of the Republican Government. The United States also applied pressure on the Netherlands to grant independence to Indonesia. The Dutch finally transferred sovereignty to the Republic of the United States of Indonesia on 27 December 1949.[25] On 28 December, Sukarno entered Jakarta as the President of the new nation. In 1950, Indonesia abandoned the federal structure in favour of a unitary state. However, 17 August 1945 is still celebrated as Independence Day.

5.4 THE EMERGENCE OF MALAYSIA AS LEGAL SUCCESSOR TO THE BRITISH

5.4.1 Introduction

Unlike the Philippines and Indonesia, where colonial regimes were concentrated in the authority of the mother country or a state-supported company like the DEIC as in the case of the East Indies, Malaysia's experience was very different. Different parts of the area now called Malaysia were governed by different colonial agencies/authorities at different times. It was the English East India Company (EEIC) which established the first British outposts in the Malaysian region. These outposts were Balambangan, which lasted only from 1773 to 1775, Penang (1786), Singapore (1819) and Malacca (1824). In 1841, a British adventurer, James Brooke, established himself as the governor of Old Sarawak under the jurisdiction of the Sultan of Brunei. From 1846 to 1946, the Brookes functioned as independent rulers or "White Rajahs" of the new state of modern Sarawak which they created out of the embers of the decaying Brunei Empire.[26] In the Malay Peninsula, the EEIC organized the three ports of Penang, Malacca and Singapore into an administrative unit called the Straits Settlements in 1826.[27] The British Government, on the other hand, generally abstained from active interference in the affairs of the Malay States as they were quite content with obtaining paramountcy in the Malay Peninsula as a result of the Anglo-Dutch Treaty of 1824. The only territory directly acquired by the British Government was the island of Labuan in 1846. Labuan was obtained from the Sultan of Brunei principally to serve as a naval base for safeguarding British strategic and commercial interests in relation to the newly acquired base of Hong Kong.[28] Meanwhile, the EEIC was abolished in 1858 after the devastating Indian Mutiny of 1857.[29] Britain took direct control of India, but the Straits Settlements remained under the jurisdiction of the new Indian Government till 1867 when the Colonial

Office took over its administration and turned it into a Crown Colony.[30] In 1874, Britain also decided to take direct control of the western Malay States because of the emergence of New Imperialism which made Britain fearful of German expansion and also because of the disorders prevailing in these states due to the rise in tin mining activities and the entry of large-scale Chinese tin miners into the region.[31] On 11 January 1874, the British concluded the Pangkor Agreement with the major chiefs of Perak resulting in the introduction of the Residential System in the state. This system was subsequently extended to Selangor, Negeri Sembilan, and Pahang. In 1896, these four states were grouped into a federation called the Federated Malay States. British protection was extended to Johor in 1885. Britain also later acquired the four northern states of Kedah, Perlis, Kelantan and Terengganu from Thailand through the Anglo-Siamese Treaty of 1909. British control over the Malay Peninsula was thus completed by 1909.[32] In Borneo, Britain had acquired Labuan from the Sultan of Brunei in 1846, and had also established paramountcy over the territories of the Brunei Empire through the Anglo-Brunei treaty of 1847. As mentioned earlier, the Brookes carved out the modern state of Sarawak from the crumbling Brunei Empire. In the north, various speculators became interested in the Sabah area which finally fell into the hands of the British North Borneo Company (BNBC). This company, from 1882 to 1946, forged the diverse territories acquired into another new state called North Borneo, now Sabah.[33]

5.4.2 The British Dominion Scheme

For a brief period, from 1942 to 1945, all of Southeast Asia, except Thailand, came under the Japanese Occupation. The speed with which the British colonial possessions in Southeast Asia fell to the Japanese made the British determined to unite all these different units, except Burma, into one administrative unit called the British Dominion of Southeast Asia after the war.[34] In addition to defence considerations, administrative uniformity and economic development, such a merger was to be a prelude to preparing the region for self-government, an objective which became one of the cornerstones of the postwar British policy in Southeast Asia. This postwar planning was undertaken in 1943. To pave the way for the realization of the dominion idea, which was essentially the precursor of the later Malaysia scheme proposed by Malaya's first Prime Minister Tunku Abdul Rahman in 1961, the British Government planned to take over North Borneo from the BNBC and Sarawak from the anachronistic dynasty of the White Rajahs. In this move, they were assisted by the fact that the BNBC had become bankrupt and that the last Rajah of Sarawak, Charles Vyner Brooke wished to secede Sarawak to the British Crown. Both North Borneo and Sarawak were thus taken over by the British Government in 1946 and designated as Crown Colonies. North Borneo become a Crown Colony on 15 July 1946 and Sarawak, on 1 July 1946.[35] The much-reduced kingdom of Brunei remained under British Protection, which was initiated in 1888; while a British Resident was appointed in 1906.[36] Events on the ground, however, made the British realize that it was not possible to implement the dominion idea at one go as local regional problems in the Malay Peninsula and British Borneo were themselves insurmountable. The British therefore were forced to deal with these regional problems first before pursuing the broader union scheme. In Malaya, the British were confronted with two major unresolved problems. One was the failure to unify the many different administrative units within Malaya itself, despite some feeble attempts to do so in the early twentieth century. British Malaya in fact consisted of seven different political entities. These were the Straits Settlements as one unit, the four Federated Malay States as one unit, and the Unfederated Malay States as five independent entities under British Protection. The British Government realized that it was paramount to unify Malaya itself first before proceeding with the larger dominion scheme. The second intractable problem was the question of what to do with the large Chinese population which had settled in Malaya over the years, basically in response to labour demand in the burgeoning tin mining industry. This may be called the "Chinese Problem". By the 1940s, the migrant Chinese and Indian settlers had outnumbered the native Malay population. In 1911, the population of the Malay States and Straits Settlements was as follows: Malays, 1,437,000; Chinese, 916,000; and Indians, 267,000. In 1941, the Malay population was 2,278,000, but the Chinese population had increased to 2,379,000, thus overtaking the Malay population. The Indian population stood at 744,000.[37] The arrival of Indian migrants to work on the rubber estates assumed importance after 1910. The result was that the native Malay population was marginalized, and a plural society emerged in Malaya. In addition, the Malayan Chinese population played an important role in leading an anti-Japanese guerilla movement in the jungles of Malaya from 1942 to 1945. The anti-Japanese movement was led by an organization called the Malayan Peoples Anti-Japanese Army (MPAJA) mainly composed of Malayan Chinese fighters belonging to the Malayan Communist Party (MCP) which had been formed in 1930. The British collaborated with the MPAJA by supplying them with arms, food, training, and advice through a special unit which was air-dropped into the jungles of Malaya in 1943, called Force 136. When the war was over, the MPAJA was disarmed, although not all weapons were surrendered to the British authorities.[38] Because of the important role played by the Chinese community in the economic development of Malaya, as well as the organization of the anti-Japanese guerilla warfare during the period of the Japanese Occupation, the British felt greatly indebted to the Malayan Chinese. In this context, therefore, the British wished to create a permanent solution to their status and position in the new land of their adoption, which as yet, was totally unclear or defined. The solution to both these problems was the Malayan Union scheme which was forced upon the throats of the Malay rulers in 1946. The Malayan Union which lasted only two years—1946 to 1948—forcibly merged all the Malay States into a unitary state, thus effectively destroying the existence of the native states and reducing the Malay monarchies to virtual oblivion. To solve the "Chinese Problem", the Malayan Union offered extremely liberal citizenship rights to the Chinese, thus making them in effect equal in status to the native Malays.[39]

Although nationalist feelings in Malaya were quite dormant before the war, except for a mild Malay ethnic awakening, the introduction of the Malayan Union brought a sudden outburst of organized opposition by the Malays spearheaded by the formation of the United Malays National Organization (UMNO) in 1946. UMNO opposed the Malayan Union which was seen as symbolizing the death of the Malay *Negeri* (States), the Malay Rulers and Malay claims to their homeland. The British were taken aback by this unexpected turn of events. They quickly backtracked their policies, abandoned the pro-Chinese stance, made a 360 degrees turn by adopting a pro-Malay policy, and replaced the Malayan Union with the Federation of Malaya in 1948. The Federation of Malaya created a central government but retained the structure of the Malay States and the status of the Malay Rulers. It also made the granting of citizenship to non-Malays much more difficult.[40] The British however achieved one of the pillars of their policy in the Malay Peninsula, that is, the merger of all the Malay States into a federation.

Now going back to the dominion plan. The merger between the Malayan Federation and Singapore, which had been kept separate since 1946, failed to materialize. British Borneo had its own set of difficulties. In Sarawak, the British had to grapple with a crippling agitation from the natives, especially the Sarawak Malays, who opposed cession on the grounds that Sarawak, as a semi-independent state, was reduced to a colony. Known as the Anti-Cession Movement, it sapped the energies of the British Colonial

Government from 1946 to 1951 when it finally petered out.[41] Realizing that integration within the two separate Malayan and Bornean blocs was not progressing well, the British Government decided in 1949 to try to achieve the broader dominion idea at one go. Towards implementing this strategy, the post of the British Commissioner-General for Southeast Asia was created to coordinate the integration process between all the different political units. Despite great efforts made by the Commissioner General, in this case, Malcolm MacDonald, the "Grand Scheme" failed to materialize. Events in the Malay Peninsula and Singapore precluded a merger between the two, while constitutional and political differences between the Malayan bloc and the Borneo bloc were too wide for the scheme to take off.[42] In Malaya, the Chinese, mainly supported by the MCP, felt betrayed by the British turnabout. To the Chinese, the Federation of Malaya Agreement meant that their community had no stake in the country. So, the MCP, with the aim of redressing the Chinese Question, and also to advance the Komintern agenda of spreading the Communist revolution, started an armed revolt in Malaya in 1948. The MCP aimed to overthrow the colonial regime and establish a Communist Republic aligned to China.[43] The Colonial Government reacted by declaring a State of Emergency on the whole country on 18 June 1948. This Emergency lasted till 1960, but the Communist insurgency was a prolonged affair. In 1968, a second insurgency started, which ended only on 2 December 1989 when a tripartite agreement to end the conflict was concluded between the Malaysian Government, the Thai Government, and the MCP.[44]

Meanwhile, especially from 1949 to 1953, the insurgency created a great deal of bloodshed, as well as social turmoil and economic disruption. Paradoxically, however, it speeded up the independence of Malaya. The British, making every effort to contain and crush the Communist revolt, decided to make political concessions to the Chinese community. In this context, the Malayan Chinese Association (MCA) was formed in 1949 under British auspices to erode Chinese support for the MCP. More importantly, the British promised to speed up independence for Malaya if the Malays, Chinese and Indians could display political solidarity, although the colonial masters' idea of early independence meant a few decades away.[45] The social, economic and security debacle in Malaya alienated Singapore which did not want to be merged with a poorer, unstable neighbour. The Chinese population in Singapore also feared the championing of special Malay rights by UMNO in Malaya.[46] In the Federation itself, political developments began to take fundamental decision-making out of the hands of the colonial masters. The formation in 1954 of the Alliance Party composed of UMNO, MCA and the Malayan Indian Congress (MIC) (formed in 1946) and its resounding victory in the 1955 elections to the Federal Council effectively placed Malayan leaders in charge of their own destiny. Under the dynamic leadership of Tunku Abdul Rahman, Malaya thus began to move towards independence at a pace far ahead of the British timetable. In this context, the views of Tunku Abdul Rahman and UMNO concerning the Malaya-Singapore merger and the wider Colonial Malaysia Scheme became decisive.

Although eventually there grew a strong body of opinion in Singapore in 1954 and 1955 advocating merger with the Federation of Malaya, Tunku and UMNO strongly opposed such a union. They feared that the Malays would be outnumbered by the addition of over a million Chinese; that the Malays would lose political dominance; and that Malaya's security would be seriously threatened. The British, taking stock of the situation could not countenance merger in the face of UMNO's rejection.

As far as the Colonial Malaysia Scheme was concerned, Tunku Abdul Rahman in fact lent support to the idea in 1955 and 1956, but the form for him was to be "Greater Malaya" which was to be established in the future after Singapore, Sarawak, Brunei and North Borneo had achieved independence. For the moment, however, in 1956, Tunku was more concerned with immediately winning independence for Malaya and did not want any scheme of merger or territorial expansion to derail this supreme objective. "At this stage," he declared in 1956, "it is wise to be prudent like Kamal Ataturk who resolutely opposed territorial expansion in favour of improving Turkey itself first."[47] Thus when Malaya achieved independence in 1957, ahead of the colonial timetable and ahead of Singapore, the British Grand Design was rendered untenable and therefore remained unfulfilled. The idea of Malaysia, however, remained alive both in the minds of the British and Tunku Abdul Rahman and finally came to fruition in 1963 as a culmination of the combined forces of decolonization and expansionist Southeast Asian nationalisms.

5.4.3 Tunku's Malaysia

After achieving independence for Malaya in 1957, Tunku Abdul Rahman again broached the subject of forming Malaysia on 27 May 1961. Speaking at a luncheon in Singapore given by the Foreign Correspondents Association of Southeast Asia at the Adelphi Hotel, the Tunku made his famous speech on that fateful day as follows:[48]

> Malaya today as a nation realizes that she cannot stand alone and in
> isolation ... Sooner or later she should have an understanding with
> Britain and the peoples of the territories of Singapore, North Borneo,
> Brunei and Sarawak. It is premature for me to say now how this closer
> understanding can be brought about, but it is inevitable that we should
> look ahead to this objective and think of a plan whereby these territories
> can be brought closer together in political and economic cooperation.

Various theories have been advanced explaining Tunku's consideration for
the formation of Malaysia. Noordin Sopiee postulates two theories. One
is the "expansion theory", and the other the "security theory". According
to the expansion theory, Tunku first conceived of the idea around 1955,
and later in 1957, when British officials in Borneo were contemplating the
formation of a northern Borneo federation. The Tunku asked the British
Government to bring about the incorporation of British Borneo into a
Malaysia federation, but the British Government wanted the inclusion of
Singapore as well. The Tunku, however, was unwilling to do this because of
the fear of Chinese domination. In its extreme form, the expansion theory
postulates that Singapore was only brought into the Malaysia plan as a
means to incorporate the Borneo territories into the Federation.

The security theory, on the other hand, contends that Tunku's main
consideration was the danger of Singapore turning communist in 1961.
This would pose a security threat to Malaya, and therefore, he wanted
Singapore's incorporation into the Federation for security reasons. The
Borneo territories were only desired to counterbalance the predominantly
Chinese population of Singapore.[49]

5.4.4 The Decolonization Theory

This work, however, is supporting the view that it was the broader theories
of decolonization and expansionist nationalisms that became the foundation
of Tunku's Malaysia. In this context, it may be noted that a major impulse
that drove Tunku to announce the Malaysia Scheme in 1961 was the desire
to help complete the unfinished British Grand Design of decolonization
which had been derailed as a result of Malaya's unexpected independence
in 1957. When this Grand Design had to be aborted in 1957, Britain
began to face an intractable dilemma of finding a workable solution for
decolonizing the rest of her colonial possessions in the region. The British
found it unfeasible to grant independence separately to Singapore, North
Borneo, Sarawak and Brunei as they were too small or too weak politically,

economically and in security terms to survive alone. They were also extremely vulnerable to the forces of expanding communism, a situation the British colonial masters wished to avoid for the preservation of their own interests in the region. In the Borneo region, the British tried to find a workable solution by fostering the formation of a North Borneo federation from 1957 to 1960. The attempt, however, failed miserably due to the opposition of the Sultan of Brunei; the rise of Party Rakyat Brunei (PRB) which wanted to establish a Negara Kalimantan Utara linked to Indonesia; and the rising tide of communism in Sarawak, spearheaded by the Sarawak Communist Clandestine Organization. The Singapore problem became even more alarming with the stark possibility of a communist take-over of the government in 1961. In these dire circumstances, the British began to look to Malaya and Tunku Abdul Rahman to help solve their decolonization problem.[50] Tunku was quite ready to do the colonial job for the British but had another motive as well for the creation of Malaysia. This second orientation was the desire for territorial expansion, an impulse very much consistent with the phenomena of expansionist nationalisms of the time, especially in insular Southeast Asia.

5.4.5 Expansionist Nationalisms of Southeast Asia and the Contest for British Borneo

Paradoxically, the rise of nationalism in the Philippines, Indonesia, Brunei and the Federation of Malaya, also produced a desire among the leaders of these countries for territorial expansion in the region for various reasons. This phenomena may be termed expansionist nationalisms. In the Philippines, the main architect of this nationalist expansion was Diosdado Macapagal, who since the achievement of independence by the Philippines in 1946, began to campaign for the recovery of North Borneo by his country. He was extremely disturbed by the "annexation" of North Borneo by the British Government from the BNBC and its conversion to a Crown Colony in 1946. Macapagal had always entertained the notion that North Borneo was a lease made by the Sultan of Sulu in 1878 and that one day, the Philippines Government, as successor to the Sulu Sultanate, would be able to retake North Borneo from the BNBC. Now that North Borneo had become a British Crown Colony, the urgency for such a move became even more pronounced. Moreover, the descendants of Sultan Muhammad Jamaluladzam of Sulu who had originally granted the Borneo territories to the Overbeck-Dent Association (ODA) in 1878, were unhappy with the British Government which had stopped the payment of the annual lease monies to them since 1946. They had subsequently formed the Kiram Corporation to fight for their rights. Different lawyers fought their cases, including Nicasio Osmena who took over as their attorney in 1958. However, the issue of the annual lease cession monies was not resolved. Meanwhile, Sukarno in Indonesia wanted to resurrect the Majapahit Empire and laid claim to all former Dutch colonies in the region, including West New Guinea (West Irian) which was not handed over by the Dutch to the Indonesia Republic in 1949. Indonesia also had designs over British Borneo, over which it was casting "covetous eyes" as early as 1953. In the 1950s, therefore, there was a real possibility of a clash developing between the Philippines and Indonesia in the Borneo region.[51] The scenario suddenly took on a new turn when Tunku Abdul Rahman announced his Malaysia Scheme on 27 May 1961.

Tunku's Malaysia Scheme also smacked of expansionist aims. Tunku basically wanted North Borneo, Sarawak and Brunei as part of a Greater Malaya. Tunku was willing to bring in Singapore only if the British Borneo territories were brought in first. His proposal, announced on 27 May 1961 as Tunku recorded, took everyone by "storm".[52] The year 1961 was also election year in the Philippines. Macapagal, who was vying for the presidency, made the issue of taking back North Borneo a central theme of his campaign. Macapagal eventually won the election and became President of the Philippines on 30 December 1961. From henceforth, he began to pursue the retrieval of North Borneo with greater vehemence. Meanwhile, the Kiram Corporation, unable to make any headway on their own, handed over their case to the jurisdiction of the Philippine Government. Armed with this authority, the Philippines Government officially laid claim to North Borneo on 22 June 1962.[53]

The possibility of a clash between the Philippines and Indonesia over the Borneo region deflected to opposition by these two countries to the Malaysia Scheme. While the Philippines laid an official claim to Sabah, Indonesia began to accuse Malaysia of being a neocolonialist plot and vowed to crush the new entity. It soon launched an undeclared war called Confrontation (*Konfrontasi*) (1963–66), which ended with the downfall of Sukarno. In Brunei, the PRB led by A.M. Azahari was seriously advocating the revival of the former Brunei Empire in the form of Negara Kalimantan Utara in the years 1956–62.[54] These expansionist nationalisms overlapped in the territorial milieu of British Borneo, which became the main theatre of contest between these nationalisms. The concepts of Greater Malaya, Greater Brunei, Greater Indonesia and Greater Philippines were totally irreconcilable and thus produced political turmoil in the region.

5.4.5 The Realization of the Malaysia Scheme, 1963

Despite the serious opposition from the Philippines, Indonesia, and the PRB, Malaysia was nevertheless formed on 16 September 1963, minus Brunei. It must, however, be pointed out here that Malaya's expansionist nationalism was to a large extent blunted by the exercise of self-determination by the population of Sabah and Sarawak who also obtained a number of safeguards for their states before agreeing to form the new federation of Malaysia. In fact, most of the leaders of Sabah and Sarawak initially rejected Tunku's Malaysia proposal in favour of forming their own federation in British Borneo consisting of Sabah, Sarawak and Brunei,[55] although the British had toyed with such a scheme from 1958 to 1960 and given up the idea mainly due to lack of support from the Sultan of Brunei. Meanwhile, Malaya launched a strong diplomatic initiative to win over the leaders of Sabah and Sarawak. Towards this end, it formed the Malaysia Solidarity Consultative Committee (MSCC) in July 1961 consisting of political leaders from Sabah, Sarawak, Singapore and Malaya (Brunei did not participate) to thrash out doubts concerning the new proposed federation. By the time the fourth and final meeting of the MSCC was held in Singapore from 1 to 3 February 1962, most of the Sabah and Sarawak leaders had become strong supporters of the new federation.[56] To give a semblance of legitimacy to the idea that the new federation was not forced upon the people of Sabah and Sarawak by their colonial masters and Malaya, the British Government formed a fact-finding commission on 17 January 1962. Known as the Cobbold Commission, this body held its sessions in Sabah and Sarawak from February to April 1962. It finally reported as follows:[57]

> About one-third of the population in each territory strongly favours early realization of Malaysia without too much concern about terms and conditions. Another third, many of them favourable to the Malaysia project, ask, with varying degrees of emphasis, for conditions and safeguards varying in nature and extent … The remaining third is divided between those who insist on independence before Malaysia is considered and those who would strongly prefer to see British rule continue for some time to come.

Based on the findings of the Cobbold Commission, the British Government believed that there was enough support for going ahead with the new federation. A separate commission was appointed for Brunei. The Brunei Commission discovered that the majority of the people of that state rejected Malaysia.[58] To work out the constitutional arrangements for Sabah's and

Sarawak's participation in the new federation, the Inter-Governmental Committee (IGC) headed by Lord Landsdowne, the British Minister of State for Colonial Affairs, was formed in August 1962. Political parties from Sabah and Sarawak submitted separate lists of safeguards for their individual states. These later came to be known as the "20 Points". The IGC deliberated on these 20 Points. They were not accepted *in toto* but were modified, and some were even rejected. The IGC completed its report on 27 February 1963.[59]

Meanwhile, the contest for British Borneo was indeed heating up. As mentioned earlier, the Philippines laid official claim to Sabah on 22 June 1962. In Brunei, the PRB launched an armed revolt on 8 December 1962, with the aim of preventing the formation of Malaysia and forming their own Negara Kalimantan Utara aligned to Indonesia. These threats to British Borneo had the effect of further pushing the majority of the people of Sabah and Sarawak to support the Malaysia alternative. It was therefore not surprising that when the IGC report was presented to the Legislative Councils of both of the states, it was quickly approved and passed. Following the acceptance of the IGC report by the legislatures of these two states, and also the Malayan Parliament, representatives from all the parties concerned met in London and concluded the Malaysia Agreement on 9 July 1963. Brunei decided to remain out. Interestingly, both Sabah and Sarawak tasted self-government for a brief period of time before Malaysia was formed. Sarawak was granted self-government by Britain on 22 July 1963, and Sabah on 31 August 1963.[60] It is no wonder that both Sabah and Sarawak have always insisted that they "formed" Malaysia, but did not "join" Malaysia; and that the new federation was formed between four equal partners, that is, Malaya, Singapore, Sabah and Sarawak. Echoing this sentiment, a prominent politician of Sarawak, James Wong Kim Min wrote in 1995 as follows:[61]

> We did not enter Malaysia, but we formed Malaysia together with North Borneo (now Sabah), Singapore and Malaya.

5.5 CONCLUSION

Thus, the Philippines, the Republic of Indonesia and Malaysia, together with Brunei and Singapore became the successor states to the Spanish (and later American), Dutch, and British spheres of colonial control in the region. They consequently inherited the problem of undefined borders and conflicting territorial claims from the colonial and precolonial eras. Expansionist nationalisms of a number of these successor states created a fierce contest for British Borneo which came to a head in the 1960s, in the form of the Philippines' claim to Sabah, the "Greater Malaya" scheme, the PRB's Negara Kalimantan Utara and Indonesia's Confrontation (1963–66). To some extent, the British Borneo question was settled with the realization of Malaysia in 1963, the end of Confrontation in 1966, the formation of the Association of Southeast Asian Nations (ASEAN) in 1967, and the emergence of Brunei as an independent state in 1984. However, many more areas of territorial disputes remain. The Philippines has not given up its claim over Sabah. The 1958 United Nations Continental Shelf Convention and the 1982 United Nations Convention on the Law of the Sea have produced more areas of contest. The Sipadan and Ligitan case was one product of these historical developments.

Notes

1. D.R. SarDesai, *Southeast Asia: Past and Present* (Basingstoke: Macmillan, 1989), pp. 67–68.
2. Ibid., pp. 142–50.
3. D.G.E. Hall, *A History of South-East Asia* (Basingstoke: Macmillan, 1994), pp. 760–64.
4. For a copy of the Treaty of Paris 1898, see Charles I. Bevans, *Treaties and Other International Agreements of the United States (1776–1949)*, vol. 2 (Washington, D.C.: Department of State Publication, 1968), p. 616.
5. "The Bates Treaty of 1899. Conditional Agreement Between Brig-General John C. Bates, Representing the United States and the Sultan of Jolo (Sulu), August 20, 1899", Filipino.biz.ph – Philippine Culture, http://filipino.biz.ph/culture/.
6. See Chapter 4.
7. Hall, *A History of South-East Asia*, p. 809.
8. K.G. Tregonning, *Under Chartered Company Rule (North Borneo 1881–1946)* (Singapore: University of Malaya Press, 1959), p. 195.
9. Hall, *A History of South-East Asia*, pp. 809–11.
10. Nicholas Tarling, ed., *The Cambridge History of Southeast Asia, Volume Two, The Nineteenth and Twentieth Centuries* (Cambridge: Cambridge University Press, 1992), pp. 262–63.
11. R. Haller-Trost, *The Contested Maritime and Territorial Boundaries of Malaysia: An International Law Perspective* (London: Kluwer Law International, 1998), p. 158. See also http://www.gov.ph/1915/03/22/memorandum-carpenter-agreement-march-22-1915/.
12. See Admiralty Memorandum of July 1927, C.O. 874/1004 and Greg Poulgrain, *The Genesis of Konfrontasi: Malaysia, Brunei and Indonesia, 1945–1965* (Bathurst,

NSW; Crawford House Publishing, 1998), p. 233. See Chapter 4 for details concerning the boundary issue with North Borneo and the sovereignty over the Turtle Islands.

13. Haller-Trost, *Contested Maritime and Territorial Boundaries of Malaysia*, pp. 158–59.

14. Tarling, *The Cambridge History of Southeast Asia, Volume Two*, pp. 262–64 and 349.

15. SarDesai, *Southeast Asia*, pp. 89–90.

16. See Chapter 2.

17. B.H.M. Vlekke, *Nusantara: A History of the East India Archipelago* (Cambridge, Mass.: Harvard University Press, 1943), pp. 265–76.

18. John F. Cady, *Southeast Asia: Its Historical Development* (New York: McGraw-Hill Book Company, 1964), pp. 371 and 529.

19. Ibid., pp. 368–69 and 529.

20. Tarling, *The Cambridge History of Southeast Asia, Volume Two*, p. 302.

21. Hall, *A History of South-East Asia*, p. 863.

22. John Funston, ed., *Government and Politics in Southeast Asia* (Singapore: Institute of Southeast Asian Studies, 2001), p. 78.

23. Hall, *A History of South-East Asia*, p. 890.

24. Tarling, *The Cambridge History of Southeast Asia, Volume Two*, p. 357.

25. Funston, *Government and Politics in Southeast Asia*, p. 78.

26. Some good works on the history of the "White Rajahs" of Sarawak, include: S. Runciman, *The White Rajahs, A History of Sarawak from 1841 to 1946* (Cambridge: Cambridge University Press, 1960); and R.H.W. Reece, *The Name of Brooke: End of White Rajah Rule in Sarawak* (Kuala Lumpur: Oxford University Press, 1982).

27. K.G. Tregonning, *A History of Modern Malaya* (Singapore: Eastern Universities Press, 1964), p. 106.

28. See Graham Irwin, *Nineteenth-Century Borneo: A Study in Diplomatic Rivalry* (Singapore: Donald Moore Books, 1955), pp. 115–24; and D.S. Ranjit Singh et al., "Kajian Sejarah Labuan, 1800–1984", Unit Perundingan Universiti Malaya, Kuala Lumpur, 2006, pp. 16–20.

29. Percival Spear, *A History of India*, vol. 2 (Harmondsworth: Penguin Books, 1975), pp. 139–49.

30. SarDesai, *Southeast Asia*, p. 95.

31. C.D. Cowan, *Nineteenth Century Malaya: The Origins of British Political Control* (London: Oxford University Press, 1961), pp. 99, 144 and 212; and C.N. Parkinson, *British Intervention In Malaya, 1867–77* (Singapore: University of Malaya Press, 1959), pp. 82–114.

32. Cady, *Southeast Asia*, pp. 435 and 445.

33. For more details, see Chapter 2.

34. D.S. Ranjit Singh, "A Dominion of Southeast Asia", *Journal of the Malaysian Branch of the Royal Asiatic Society (JMBRAS)* 71, Part 1 (1998): 27–40.

35. Tregonning, *Under Chartered Company Rule*, p. 222. Also see Reece, *The Name of Brooke.*

36. See D.S. Ranjit Singh, *Brunei 1839-1983: The Problems of Political Survival* (Singapore: Oxford University Press, 1991), pp. 67–101.

37. See Hall, *A History of South-East Asia*, p. 836.

38. Cheah Boon Kheng, *Red Star over Malaya: Resistance and Social Conflict During and After the Japanese Occupation of Malaya, 1941–1946* (Singapore: Singapore University Press, 1983), pp. 56–75; and Edgar O'Ballance, *Malaya: The Communist Insurgent War, 1948–60* (London: Faber and Faber, 1966), pp. 34–59.

39. There are a number of excellent works on the Malayan Union, chief among them being: J. de V. Allen, *The Malayan Union* (New Haven: Yale University Southeast Asia Studies, 1967); A.J. Stockwell, *British Policy and Malay Politics During the Malayan Union Experiment 1942-1948*, Monograph No. 8 (Kuala Lumpur: Malayan Branch of the Royal Asiatic Society, 1979); and Albert Lau, *The Malayan Union Controversy, 1942-1948* (Singapore: Oxford University Press, 1991).

40. Barbara Watson Andaya and Leonard Y. Andaya, *A History of Malaysia* (Basingstoke: Macmillan Press, 1982), pp. 254–57.

41. See Reece, *The Name of Brooke*, and Sanib Said, "Anti-Cession Movement, 1946 to 1951: The Birth of Nationalism in Sarawak", Graduation Exercise, Department of History, University of Malaya, Kuala Lumpur, 1976.

42. Ranjit Singh, "A Dominion of Southeast Asia", pp. 30–40.

43. See Richard Stubbs, *Hearts and Minds in Guerrilla Warfare: The Malayan Emergency 1948-1960* (Singapore: Eastern Universities Press, 2004), pp. 30–32 and 42–61.

44. The Emergency period, 1948 to 1960, is well covered by some excellent works including: Anthony Short, *The Communist Insurrection in Malaya, 1948–1960* (London: Frederick Muller, 1975); and Stubbs, *Hearts and Minds*. The second Communist insurgency from 1968 to 1989 is not well researched by scholars. However, there is an interesting account of VAT 69, an elite force established in 1969 which fought the second insurgency. See A. Navaratnam, *The Spear and the Kerambit: The Exploits of VAT 69, Malaysia's Elite Fighting Force 1968-1989* (Kuala Lumpur: Utusan Publications & Distributors, 2001). For the tripartite agreement between the governments of Thailand and Malaysia, and the MCP signed on 2 December 1989 ending the hostilities, see ibid, pp. 189–90.

45. See Stubbs, *Hearts and Minds*, pp. 206–18; R.W. Komer, *The Malayan Emergency In Retrospect: Organization of A Successful Counterinsurgency Effort* (Santa Monica, California: The Rand Corporation, 1972), pp. 64–66; and Joseph M. Fernando, *The Making of the Malayan Constitution*, Monograph No. 31 (Kuala Lumpur: Malaysian Branch of the Royal Asiatic Society, 2002), pp. 9–33.

46. See Ranjit Singh, "A Dominion of Southeast Asia", pp. 32–40, and Funston, *Government and Politics in Southeast Asia*, p. 163.

47. Mohamed Noordin Sopiee, *From Malayan Union to Singapore Separation: Political*

Unification in the Malaysian Region 1945–1965 (Kuala Lumpur: Penerbit Universiti Malaya, 1976), pp. 103–10 and 129–30.

48. Department of Information Malaya, Kuala Lumpur, 1962.

49. Noordin Sopiee, *From Malayan Union to Singapore Separation*, pp. 125–27.

50. Nicholas Tarling, *Southeast Asia: A Modern History* (South Melbourne: Oxford University Press, Australia. 2001), pp. 132–35; Poulgrain, *The Genesis of Konfrontasi*, pp. 252–53; and G.M. Kahin, ed., *Governments and Politics of Southeast Asia* (New York: Cornell University Press, 1967), pp. 304–5.

51. Poulgrain, *The Genesis of Konfrontasi*, pp. 185–89; Hall, *A History of South-East Asia*, pp. 930–32; and Tarling, *Southeast Asia*, pp. 134–35.

52. T.P. Abdul Rahman, *Looking Back: Monday Musings and Memories* (Kuala Lumpur: Pustaka Press, 1977), p. 82.

53. M.O. Ariff, *The Philippines Claim to Sabah: Its Historical, Legal and Political Implications* (Singapore: Oxford University Press, 1970); and Poulgrain, *The Genesis of Konfrontasi*, pp. 231–32 and 240.

54. J.A.C. Mackie, *Konfrontasi: The Indonesia-Malaysia Dispute 1963–1966* (Kuala Lumpur: Oxford University Press, 1974), and Ranjit Singh, *Brunei, 1839–1983*, pp. 172–77.

55. See J.P. Ongkili, *The Borneo Response to Malaysia, 1961–1963* (Singapore: Donald Moore Press, 1967), p. 22.

56. Noordin Sopiee, *From Malayan Union to Singapore Separation*, pp. 146–55.

57. See para. 144 of the Report of the Commission of Enquiry, North Borneo and Sarawak, 1962, reproduced in Datuk Amar James Wong Kim Min, *The Birth of Malaysia* (Kuching: 1995), pp. 55–56.

58. Ranjit Singh, *Brunei 1839–1983*, pp. 167–69.

59. For a very comprehensive study of the proceedings of the IGC and an excellent discussion on the "20 Points", see Datuk Dr Herman J. Luping, *Sabah's Dilemma: The Political History of Sabah (1960–1994)* (Kuala Lumpur: Magnus Books, 1994), pp. 47–95. Also see *Government of Malaysia, Report of the Inter-Governmental Committee 1962* (Kuala Lumpur: Government Printer, 1963).

60. *New Straits Times*, 16 September 2013.

61. James Wong Kim Min, *The Birth of Malaysia*, p. 5.

6

The Bases of Indonesia's Claim

6.1 Introduction

Indonesia advanced its claim to Pulau Sipadan and Pulau Ligitan based on a number of arguments. The linchpin of its submissions was that it held a legal title over these two islands as a result of historical circumstances; the Anglo-Dutch Boundary Convention of 1891; and the process of ratification of the said Convention which involved proceedings in the Dutch Parliament, especially those pertaining to the Explanatory Memorandum Map of 1891. To Indonesia, possession of a legal title was paramount, and no amount of subsequent *effectivités* could displace such a title; they could only enhance it. Indonesia built its case on four major bases as stated below:

1. A grand argument that Indonesia possessed legal title over Sipadan and Ligitan;
2. a supporting argument based on State Practice or *Effectivités*;
3. map evidence; and
4. activities of colonial powers in the region.

6.2 Indonesia's Case Based on the Possession of a Legal Title

6.2.1 Legal Title Derived From Historical Developments

In its written Memorial, Indonesia went to great lengths to explain the uncertain nature of the traditional territorial boundaries in the northeastern region of Borneo in the nineteenth century.[1] The explanation was necessary as the native rulers paid more attention to control over people rather than territory. As such, territorial concessions made by local rulers to European powers in the region in the nineteenth century often overlapped so much so "that this lack of precision in determining territorial possessions in the area was the source of confusion among the colonial powers themselves".[2] The *Memorial of Indonesia*, vol. 1 proceeded to explain that the Sultan of Bulungan had jurisdiction over territories as far as Batu Tinagat, situated at parallel 4°19′ north on the northeast coast of Borneo. The Sultan of Bulungan, Muhammad Khahar-Oedien had signed a Contract of Vassalage with the Netherlands Indies Government on 12 November 1850, by which he acknowledged submission to Dutch overlordship as far back as 1834. Indonesia claimed that Article II of the 1850 Contract of Vassalage contained definitive evidence that the islands of Sipadan and Ligitan belonged to the Sultan of Bulungan.[3] The particular section of this Article pertaining to the above matter was quoted as follows:[4]

> The following islands shall belong to Boeloengan: Terakkan, Nenoekkan and Sebittikh, *with the small islands belonging thereto.*

Indonesia contended that Pulau Sipadan and Pulau Ligitan were part of the group of "small islands" stated in this Article. As discussed in Chapter 3, the Sultan of Sulu, on the other hand, laid claim to territory as far south as the Sibuku River, and thus claimed ownership over the two contested islands as well.[5] During the Oral Pleadings, Sir Arthur Watts, Q.C., leading Consul for Indonesia, again explained the tangled nature of these overlapping claims by the two Sultanates but emphasized that Bulungan had a better claim. He submitted as follows:[6]

> The claims of the two Sultans overlapped: the Sultan of Sulu at times appeared to claim lands as far south as the "Sibuko River", while the Sultan of Boeloengan claimed lands—and indeed, exercised territorial control—at least as far north as Batoe Tinagat and the Tawau River.

Thus, on historical grounds, Indonesia contended that its predecessor in title, the Dutch, had overlordship since 1834 over the Sultanate of Bulungan which possessed the two islands of Sipadan and Ligitan. To make their case stronger, Indonesia emphasized that the 1850 Contract of Vassalage was reaffirmed by a new contract between the Sultan of Bulungan and the Dutch on 2 June 1878.[7]

6.2.2 Legal Title Obtained as a Result of the Anglo-Dutch Boundary Convention of 20 June 1891

At the heart of the Indonesian case was the Boundary Convention of 1891 between Britain and the Netherlands (hereafter cited as the Boundary Convention of 1891) which defined the boundary between their respective possessions in Borneo. Indonesia claimed that the Boundary Convention of 1891 gave it definitive title over Pulau Sipadan and Pulau Ligitan.

Advancing this argument, Chapter V of the *Memorial of Indonesia*, vol. 1 went on to explain that when Britain and the Netherlands established control over their respective colonial possessions in Borneo in the nineteenth century, the uncertainties concerning boundary lines were "brought to an end" by the conclusion of the Boundary Convention of 1891 between the two powers. The *Memorial of Indonesia*, vol. 1 contended that the terms of the Boundary Convention of 1891, and its "contemporaneous" interpretation by the parties concerned, "leave no doubt as to the inclusion of both Ligitan and Sipadan within the colonial domains of the Netherlands".[8]

In the oral submissions, Watts further elaborated that Indonesia's title in the area was derived from the previous title of the Netherlands as Indonesia's colonial predecessor; and that the Dutch title was "confirmed" by the provisions of the Boundary Convention of 1891.[9]

The *Memorial of Indonesia*, vol. 1 went to great lengths to "prove" that the negotiations between the British and the Netherlands Governments leading to the Boundary Convention of 1891, and the various articles of the Convention itself "confirmed" the Dutch (and subsequently Indonesian) title to the two islands in dispute. One point clarified by the *Memorial of Indonesia*, vol. 1 was that the Anglo-Dutch Joint Commission which was set up to negotiate the delineation of the boundary in Borneo had agreed in 1889 that the place chosen as the starting point of the said boundary was "Broershoek", which was situated on the east coast "where the parallel of 4°10′ north latitude meets the sea".[10] Then quoting Article IV of the Boundary Convention of 1891, the *Memorial of Indonesia*, vol. 1 argued strongly that the said article stated clearly that the boundary line emanating from the starting point on the east coast of Borneo "shall be continued eastward" across the island of Sebatik out to sea. The words "continued eastward", Indonesia contended "does not embrace a line of only limited extent with a nearby terminal point, but rather a line of indeterminate extent".[11] Indonesia further argued that since the main purpose of the Anglo-Dutch negotiations and the Boundary Convention of 1891 was to "settle definitely the whole problem of the limits of the British and

Dutch possessions in the area", and since the two islands in contention belonged to the Dutch by virtue of the Sultan of Bulungan's ownership over them, the eastward boundary line was meant to cut across the island of Sebatik and run out to sea "as far as necessary to divide islands or territories whose attribution might be problematical and was therefore to be determined".[12]

During the Oral Pleadings, Watts again drew attention to the importance of Article IV of the Boundary Convention of 1891. He submitted as follows:[13]

> Directly in issue, however are provisions of Article IV, prescribing the eastward prolongation of the boundary ... the starting point is screened from the open sea to the east by the island of Sebatik. Article IV thus provided that the boundary, beginning at the agreed starting point on the coast at parallel $4°10'$ N "shall be continued eastward along that parallel, across the island of Sebatik."

Indonesia submitted that this provision of Article IV was intended to provide, and was properly to be interpreted as providing, a line of division between *all* Dutch and British territories in the area. As such, the line was to extend out to sea so far as necessary to separate Dutch and British offshore territories in the region.

6.2.3 Legal Title Obtained as a Result of the Process of Ratification and the Explanatory Memorandum Map of 1891

Article VIII of the Boundary Convention of 1891 provided for ratification of the treaty after it had received approval of the Netherlands States-General. On 25 July 1891, the Dutch Government submitted a Bill together with an Explanatory Memorandum to the States-General seeking its approval for the acceptance of the Boundary Convention of 1891. The Explanatory Memorandum outlined the reasons behind the Dutch Government's negotiations with the British pertaining to the boundary in Borneo and how the Boundary Convention of 1891 benefited the Dutch. A map which the *Memorial of Indonesia*, vol. 1 called the Explanatory Memorandum Map, was attached to the Memorandum.[14] Among other things, this map showed, a red line which Indonesia claimed was the boundary line agreed in the Boundary Convention of 1891. This red line, which cut across the island of Sebatik and proceeded out to sea, ended somewhere to the south of Pulau Mabul.[15] Indonesia paid particular emphasis to the importance of this map and the whole process of ratification to strengthen its case. The

Memorial of Indonesia, vol. 1 gave the following exposition concerning the Explanatory Memorandum Map of 1891:[16]

> The Explanatory Memorandum map, and in particular the red line drawn on it, shows that the boundary line as agreed followed the parallel of latitude 4°10´ N starting at the eastern coast of Borneo, crossing the … Island of Sebatik, and then *continuing eastwards beyond that island* and out to sea north of Pulau Sipadan and Pulau Ligitan. It thus clearly shows that Pulau Sipadan and Pulau Ligitan fall on the Dutch side of the boundary line agreed in the Convention.

A closer look at this 1891 map, however, reveals that Pulau Ligitan and Pulau Sipadan were not marked on the map. The quotation above which contends that the red line "clearly" showed that these two islands fell on the Dutch side was therefore presumptuous. It is highly plausible that neither party paid any particular attention to these two islands in 1891.

To correct the earlier faulty contention and to make the argument more plausible, Sir Arthur Watts explained in the Oral Pleadings that the purpose of submitting the Explanatory Memorandum Map of 1891 to the States-General was to "illustrate … the general effect of the Convention", and therefore there was no need for "abundant cartographical detail". He framed his argument in more detail as follows:[17]

> Moreover, so far as concerns the small offshore islands, their precise location was at that time, and for that purpose, somewhat beside the point. What mattered was the course followed by the line of attribution at the sea: islands south of that line were Dutch, and islands to the north were British—without any need to identify them.

Since there was no map appended to the Boundary Convention of 1891, it would be natural to ask whether in fact the Dutch Explanatory Memorandum Map accurately represented agreements reached in the negotiations leading to the conclusion of the treaty in 1891. Indonesia advanced a few arguments to support the contention that in fact the Explanatory Memoranda Map of 1891, not only accurately represented the agreements reached during the negotiations, but that the map was part of the ratification process and therefore had a legal standing. Some of the arguments advanced by Indonesia in support of the above claim are outlined below.

The legality of the map and its binding nature was explained within the context of the process of ratification. The Boundary Convention of

1891 (Article VIII) expressly required the approval of the Convention by the Dutch States-General. Indonesia argued that the map was "an integral part of the process of ratification of the Convention".[18] Watts, in his oral submissions, laid great emphasis on the importance of this process of ratification. He submitted as follows:[19]

> The ratification process with which it [the map] was associated is in any event an important act in relation to the treaty being ratified ... This is particularly so where ratification is expressly stipulated in the treaty to be dependent upon the approval of that party's legislature.

Another important point advanced was that the map represented the contemporary understanding of the Netherlands Government concerning Article IV of the Boundary Convention of 1891. It was submitted to the States-General together with the Explanatory Memorandum just one month after the Boundary Convention of 1891 was concluded. The fact that the issue was debated and the relevant bill passed strengthened the view that the map, therefore represented a contemporary interpretation of Article IV of the Boundary Convention of 1891.

Moreover, it was not just the view of the Dutch Government then. The British Government, Indonesia alleged, gave its assent to this contemporary interpretation by virtue of the fact that, despite having complete knowledge of the proceedings in the Dutch Parliament and having also acquired copies of the Explanatory Memorandum and the Map, it made no dissent or protest.[20] In this context, it must be noted that Sir Horace Rumbold, the British Ambassador at The Hague at the time, sent two copies of the Explanatory Memorandum together with the attached map to the British Foreign Office in a despatch dated 26 January 1892. As noted earlier in Chapter 3, Rumbold made the following remarks concerning the said map:[21]

> [it, the map] has lately been published in the official Journal showing the boundary line as agreed upon under the late Convention, together with the boundaries which had been previously proposed. The map seems to be the only interesting feature of a document which does not otherwise call for special comment.

There was, however, no response from the British Government on the matter. Indonesia also alleged that Rumbold subsequently sent to his government a full translation of the debate in the States-General after the said body had passed the bill on 8 March 1892 approving the Boundary Convention of 1891. The Treaty was ratified in London on 22 May 1892.[22]

Watts, in his submissions, further postulated that this knowledge and the lack of dissent on the part of the British Government "necessarily implies Great Britain's concurrence with the content of the map". He strongly concluded the argument as follows:[23]

> That in turn involves irrefutable acquiescence in the depiction of the Convention line, such that all islands to the south of that line ... and thus in particular the islands of Sipadan and Ligitan ... belong to the Netherlands.

Bearing all these factors in mind, Indonesia was emphatic in claiming that the parties concerned in fact adopted the map as part of their treaty settlement.[24]

In summing up Indonesia's arguments pertaining to its possession of a legal title to the two disputed islands, we find that it was bent upon advancing the view that a legal title was superior to state practice, especially when such a title was based on a treaty. Reinforcing this stand, Watts put forth a forceful argument, which was as follows:[25]

> A treaty-based title is entitled to overwhelming respect, particularly when it is opposed by only limited State practice in a contrary sense, and even more so when that practice is itself contradictory.

Indonesia declared that in the present case it had a clear treaty-based title which was "settled in favour of the Netherlands, and now (by way of succession) in favour of Indonesia, by virtue of the treaty settlement embodied in the 1891 Convention".[26]

6.3 INDONESIA'S CASE BASED ON STATE PRACTICE OR *EFFECTIVITÉS*

Indonesia argued that the legal title to Pulau Sipadan and Pulau Ligitan acquired by the Netherlands by the Boundary Convention of 1891 was subsequently confirmed by *effectivités* undertaken by the Dutch and later, the Indonesian Government.

6.3.1 Dutch *Effectivités*

The main activity highlighted by Indonesia in terms of state action relating to the two islands during the Dutch colonial period was the expedition of the Dutch destroyer, the *Lynx* in November and December 1921. The said destroyer was sent to the vicinity of the two islands to check for piracy. Indonesia maintained that the destroyer confined its operations within the territorial seas of Pulau Sipadan and Pulau Ligitan and that the commander of the *Lynx* scrupulously kept out of the territorial waters of Pulau Si Amil which was within the three marine leagues zone of North Borneo. On 26 November 1921, a landing of armed Dutch personnel was made on Pulau Sipadan. The destroyer also made a naval patrol close to the island of Ligitan. These actions, Indonesia claimed "constituted acts *par excellence* of the exercise of governmental authority with respect to the islands", thus confirming Dutch sovereignty over the islands.[27]

6.3.2 Indonesian Naval Patrols to the Islands Before 1969

Between 1965 and 1968, Indonesian naval personnel made a number of visits to the islands of Sipadan and Ligitan. These patrols were limited to islands situated south of latitude 4°10′ N. Reports submitted by these patrols clearly indicated that both islands were uninhabited. These visits, Indonesia claimed, demonstrated that Indonesia had sovereignty over them.[28]

6.3.3 Traditional Fishing Activities

Indonesia also claimed that its fishermen often conducted traditional fishing activities on and around the islands. They sometimes stayed overnight at Pulau Sipadan.[29]

6.3.4 Oil Concessions by Indonesia and Malaysia

The general tenor of the Indonesian argument concerning the granting of offshore oil prospecting licences to foreign concerns in the 1960s till the year of the dispute, 1969, was that both parties scrupulously adhered to the 4°10′ N latitude as the dividing line for granting such concessions. One such Malaysian concession protruded eastwards into the sea beyond the two disputed islands, but its southern limit was carefully fixed at 4°10′30″ N latitude, that is, 30 seconds short of the 4°10′ N.[30]

6.4 MAP EVIDENCE

The Indonesian side, quoting judicial precedents, emphasized the importance of maps, as they represented the "physical expressions of the will of the

State or the States concerned". They were important in other ways too as they "may have corroborative or confirmatory character".[31]

In the present case, Indonesia admitted that no map formed an integrated part of the Boundary Convention of 1891. It also admitted that maps produced by the parties concerned in interpreting the boundary line "do not have the same character as maps forming part of such a treaty". Nevertheless, Indonesia was of the opinion that the non-treaty maps pertaining to the boundary demarcation had their own relevance as they were "instrumental in revealing the intention of the parties".[32]

In support of its case, Indonesia referred to various maps, including the Dutch Explanatory Memorandum Map of 1891; the British North Borneo Company's (BNBC) maps; and the Malaysian Government maps.

6.4.1 The Explanatory Memorandum Map of 1891
Indonesia once again gave a great deal of attention to the 1891 Explanatory Memorandum Map of 1891. As the arguments pertaining to the significance of this map have already been discussed in some detail above, it is redundant to go into its merits once again.

6.4.2 The 1903 BNBC Map
Another map produced by Indonesia as evidence that the British viewed the Boundary Convention of 1891 line as extending offshore, leaving Pulau Sipadan and Pulau Ligitan on the Dutch side of the sea boundary was a map entitled "Borneo" published by Stanford in 1903. Stanford was the official cartographer for the BNBC. Commenting on this 1903 map, the *Memorial of Indonesia*, vol. 1 reads as follows:[33]

> The 1903 Stanford map thus represented the contemporaneous view of what the BNBC itself considered to be the limits of its territorial possessions. The map clearly shows that the BNBC recognized that the southern limits of its territory east of the island of Sebatik coincided with prolongation of the 4°10′ N parallel of latitude established by the 1891 Convention to a point lying well to the east of Pulau Ligitan and Pulau Sipadan. Both islands were clearly recognised as belonging to Dutch Borneo.

6.4.3 Other Maps
Indonesia also tended as evidence a few more maps mainly published by the British and Malaysian Governments. Some of these were the "Colony of North Borneo" map of 1953; the 1964 and 1965 maps published by the

Survey Department of the British Ministry of Defence; the 1964, 1967 and 1972 maps published by the Malaysian Directorate of National Mapping, entitled "Malaysia Timor, Sabah", and the 1968 map published by Malaysia's Ministry of Lands and Mines.[34]

The *Memorial of Indonesia*, vol. 1 contended that as even these Malaysian official maps "consistently depicted the extension of the 4°10′ N line of latitude out to the sea as the southern limit of Malaysia's territorial possessions in the area", it meant that Sipadan and Ligitan were south of this line, and therefore were in Dutch, and later Indonesian territory.[35]

6.5 INDONESIA'S CLAIM BASED ON ACTIVITIES OF COLONIAL POWERS IN THE REGION

Indonesia claimed that a review of the conduct of the Colonial powers who had jurisdiction in the region, that is, Britain, Spain and the United States, confirmed that Indonesia possessed sovereignty over the disputed islands.

6.5.1 The Position of Great Britain

Indonesia's basic argument concerning Britain's position in the region was that the offshore limit of the concessions obtained by the Overbeck-Dent Association (ODA) from the Brunei and Sulu Sultanates, which were later inherited by the BNBC in 1882, was three marine leagues from the coast. As such, these concessions did not include Pulau Sipadan and Pulau Ligitan which were much farther out to sea.

On 22 April 1903, the BNBC signed a document with the Sultan of Sulu by which a number of islands lying beyond the three marine leagues limit from the coast of North Borneo were transferred to the jurisdiction of the Company.[36] Indonesia argued that all these islands mentioned in the 1903 Confirmation of Cession document lay to the north of the 4°10′ N line of latitude "established by the 1891 Boundary Convention as the boundary between the territorial possessions of the Netherlands and Great Britain". The islands of Sipadan and Ligitan were not included in the Confirmation deed. In fact, they were located to the south of the demarcation line. The 1903 BNBC map further confirmed these facts. Indonesia claimed that all this evidence showed, that both the British Government and the BNBC did not consider Pulau Sipadan and Pulau Ligitan as falling within their territorial waters.[37]

6.5.2 The Position of Spain

The *Memorial of Indonesia*, vol. 1 examined in detail the area of jurisdictions of both Spain and the Sulu Sultanate in the region in the nineteenth century and argued that Pulau Sipadan and Pulau Ligitan did not form part of their domains. A similar view was expressed concerning the 1885 Protocol between Spain, Great Britain, and Germany.[38]

6.5.3 The Position of the United States

In dealing with the jurisdiction of the United States, Indonesia examined Article III of the 1898 Treaty of Paris and the sole Article of the Convention of 1900 between the United States and Spain. These articles refer to the limit of the Philippines Archipelago ceded by Spain to the United States after the conclusion of the Spanish-American War in 1898. The Indonesian contention was that the definition of the Philippine Archipelago in both these treaties did not include the two disputed islands.[39]

6.5.4 Anglo-American Agreements Regarding Certain Islands Off the Coast of North Borneo, 1903–30

Indonesia then examined the events which led to the United States claiming sovereignty over certain groups of islands lying more than the three marine leagues line from the coast of North Borneo in 1903. These claims caused the BNBC to protest against the United States' action as the Company had been administering these islands from its inception in 1882. The dispute led to the 1907 Exchange of Notes between Britain and the United States. The final settlement of the territorial possessions of Britain and the United States in the Borneo region was concluded with the signing of the Boundary Convention of 1930 between the two powers.[40] The Indonesian contention was that all these negotiations and agreements from 1903 to 1930 between Britain and the United States did not concern Pulau Sipadan and Pulau Ligitan. The Boundary Convention of 1930 fixed the southern limits of the Philippines sea boundary at 4°23′ N, well to the north of the two islands in dispute.[41]

6.6 Conclusion

As discussed in this chapter, Indonesia emphasized the paramountcy of possessing a legal title, especially when such a title was based on a treaty. To Indonesia, a treaty-based title was supreme and could not be displaced or taken over by any amount of state practice or *effectivités*. Indonesia, therefore, concentrated on proving that it held a treaty-based legal title to the islands of Sipadan and Ligitan, and consequently neglected somewhat, or did not have enough evidence, in laying more emphasis on *effectivités*. To prove possession of a legal title, Indonesia depended on two major historical events. One was the Anglo-Dutch Boundary Convention of 20 June 1891, and the second was the process of ratification of the said Convention in the Dutch Parliament on 25 July 1891. As far as the Anglo-Dutch Boundary Convention of 1891 was concerned, Indonesia relied heavily on Article IV, saying that its contents provided for the extension of the boundary line eastwards from the starting point at Broershoek across Sebatik Island out to sea as far as necessary so as to divide all the colonial possessions of the British and the Dutch in the area, including the islands of Sipadan and Ligitan. As the boundary line was located at 4°10′ N, and if it was meant to extend out to sea to an "indeterminate extent" as claimed by Indonesia, then the islands of Sipadan and Ligitan would fall to the south of this "dividing" line, and so come into the Dutch sphere of jurisdiction. Indonesia also claimed that even before the Boundary Convention of 1891 was signed, the negotiations that preceded it were conducted with the primary objective of settling "definitely the whole problem of the limits of British and Dutch possessions in the area", including the islands of Sipadan and Ligitan.[42] The question that arises is, was this the intention of the two parties behind the conclusion of the Boundary Convention of 1891? Before reviewing Indonesia's stand on Article IV of the Anglo-Dutch Boundary Convention of 1891, it may be useful to scrutinize the terms of reference of the Joint Anglo-Dutch Commission set up in early 1889 to examine the question of the disputed boundary between the two powers in Borneo. It is crystal clear from this document that the boundary to be considered was an inland boundary and not a boundary that extended into the sea to divide offshore islands. The relevant wording of point three of the terms of reference of the Commission reads as follows:[43]

> the British and Netherland Governments will proceed without delay to define ... *the inland boundary-lines* which separate the Netherland possessions in Borneo from the territories belonging to ... the British North Borneo Company respectively. [author's emphasis]

Moreover, the islands of Sipadan and Ligitan were not an issue of dispute at the time; neither were they mentioned at all either during the negotiations or in the articles of the 1891 boundary treaty. It is also highly doubtful whether the two contending powers even knew of their existence at the material time. Now turning to Article IV of the Boundary Convention of 1891. The wording of this article, especially the one which provided that the boundary line "shall be continued eastwards along that parallel [4°10′ N] across the island of Sebatik" was hotly debated by both Indonesia and Malaysia. Indonesia was of the view that the line was meant to cut across the island of Sebatik and run out to sea for an indefinite distance, so as to divide islands in the area into the Dutch and British spheres of control. The Malaysian Government's view was that the boundary line was meant to divide the island of Sebatik only, into the Dutch and British sections, and had nothing to do with a sea boundary. This question of interpretation was resolved by the International Court of Justice (ICJ) in Malaysia's favour.[44] However, leaving aside the grammatical aspects of the words discussed above, what was the intention of the Joint Anglo-Dutch Commission of 1889 and their respective governments pertaining to this article? As discussed in Chapter 3, it is clear from the various proposals and counter-proposals that were exchanged by both the British and Dutch sides during the process of negotiations from 1889 to 1891, that the issue of contention was the Sebatik Island itself. Both sides wanted to retain the whole island for themselves, until the British made their counter-proposals in a despatch to the Dutch Government dated 13 August 1890. In these proposals, the British indicated their desire again to retain Sebatik Island but were willing to come to a compromise along the following lines:[45]

> ... the Sebatik island should belong to the BNBC or as a compromise the boundary line should run along the parallel of 4°10′ eastwards as well as westwards from Broershoek, so as to divide the island equally between the BNBC and the Netherlands Indian Government.

On 2 February 1891, the Dutch Government replied, accepting this compromise on the division of Sebatik Island into two halves by the eastward extension of the boundary line from Broershoek.[46] It is abundantly clear therefore that Article IV specifically referred to the division of Sebatik Island between the two powers, and had nothing to do with the allocation of offshore islands, east of Sebatik.

The process of ratification of the 1891 treaty is a bit trickier. Article VIII of the Boundary Convention of 1891 made ratification by both parties mandatory before the treaty could come into force. The said article also specified that the approval of the Dutch parliament was required before ratification could take place. This particular section of Article VIII is worded as follows:[47]

> The present Convention shall be ratified ... after the said Convention shall have received the approval of the Netherland States-General.

In this context, Indonesia's assertion that the ratification process was an integral part of the 1891 treaty is valid. The problem that arises from this act is the validity of the map attached to the Explanatory Memorandum presented to the States-General by the Dutch Government. This map showed the boundary line running along latitude 4°10′ N cutting across Sebatik Island and extending into the sea on the northeast coast of Borneo for about 50 miles. The Boundary Convention of 1891 itself had no map attached to it, so it is uncertain whether the Dutch Memorandum Map represented an accurate version of the boundary discussions leading to the signing of the treaty. The Indonesian side claimed the map indeed represented a contemporary interpretation of Article IV of the Boundary Convention of 1891, an interpretation which Indonesia alleged was also accepted by the British Government as it made no dissent or protest. This contention was somewhat supported by Sir Horace Rumbold's remarks on the map which he said showed "the boundary line as agreed upon under the late Convention".[48] It is also mystifying why the British Government did not protest at the time if indeed the map was a misrepresentation of what transpired during the discussions between the two parties from 1889 to 1891.

There is not much controversy about Dutch *effectivités*. The map evidence also does not require much comment. The section on activities of colonial powers in the region deserves some attention. In outlining the activities or state action of the United States in the region, Indonesia limited its arguments to the 1898 Treaty of Paris and the Convention of 1900. Citing these two treaties, Indonesia contended that the territorial possessions of the United States in the Philippines did not include the islands of Sipadan and Ligitan. The 1903 action of the United States whereby it proclaimed its sovereignty over a number of islands, about twenty-six in number, and including Sipadan and Ligitan mentioned by name, was not cited by the Indonesian side.[49] However, this is understandable. All in all, a strong bid was made by Indonesia to prove possession of a treaty-based legal title to the two disputed islands. Chapter 8 will analyse the ICJ's views on the evidence presented by Indonesia.

Notes

1. International Court of Justice (ICJ), *Case Concerning Sovereignty over Pulau Ligitan and Pulau Sipadan (Indonesia/Malaysia), Memorial Submitted by the Government of the Republic of Indonesia*, vol. 1, 2 November 1999, pp. 55–60 (hereafter cited as the *Memorial of Indonesia*, vol. 1). Also see ICJ, *Verbatim Record in the Case Concerning Sovereignty over Pulau Ligitan and Pulau Sipadan (Indonesia/Malaysia)*, 3 June 2002, 10.00 a.m., pp. 26–37 (hereafter cited as *Verbatim Record*).

2. *Memorial of Indonesia*, vol. 1, para. 4.44, p. 51.

3. See Chapter 2 above.

4. *Memorial of Indonesia*, vol. 1, para. 3.21, p. 15. A translated version of this contract can be found in M. Hartsen to Count de Bylandt, 19 March 1889, Item 44, C.O. 874/191.

5. For details on the extent of Dutch and Sulu jurisdiction on the north east coast of Borneo see "Memorandum respecting the Boundary between the Netherlands and Soloh [Sulu] Possessions on the North-east Coast of Borneo", in Count de Bylandt to Earl of Granville, 6 April 1883, Item 12, C.O. 874/191. Also see Chapter 3.

6. *Verbatim Record*, 3 June 2002, 10.00 a.m., para. 16, p. 21.

7. *Memorial of Indonesia*, vol. 1, para. 4.63, p. 57. For more details on this subject, see "Memorandum respecting the Boundary between the Netherlands and Soloh [Sulu] Possessions on the North-east Coast of Borneo", in Count de Bylandt to Earl of Granville, 6 April 1883, Item 12, C.O. 874/191.

8. *Memorial of Indonesia*, vol. 1, para. 5.1, p. 61. For the negotiations between the British and Dutch Governments which led to the Boundary Convention of 1891 which defined the boundaries between the colonial possessions of the two powers in Borneo, see Chapter 3.

9. *Verbatim Record*, 3 June 2002, 10.00 a.m., para. 14, p. 21.

10. *Memorial of Indonesia*, vol. 1, para. 5.27, p. 75.

11. Ibid., para. 5.43, p. 83.

12. Ibid., pp. 79–86. For a copy of the Boundary Convention of 1891, see C.O. 874/503, ff. 232–34. Appendix B.

13. *Verbatim Record*, 3 June 2002, 10.00 a.m., para. 21, p. 22.

14. *Memorial of Indonesia*, vol. 1, p. 87; *Verbatim Record*, 3 June 2002, 10.00 a.m., para. 52, p. 20. For more details, see *Explanatory Memorandum No. 3, Ratification of the Agreement Made in London between the Netherlands and Great Britain and Ireland for the Fixing of the Boundaries between the Possessions of the Netherlands on the Island of Borneo and the States on that Island Which Are under British Protectorate, Official Parliamentary Reports the Netherlands, Session of 1890–1891*: 187.

15. See Figure 3.2.

16. *Memorial of Indonesia*, vol. 1, para. 5.50, p. 88.

17. *Verbatim Record*, 3 June 2002, 10.00 a.m., para. 58, p. 21.

18. *Memorial of Indonesia*, vol. 1, para. 5.51, p. 88.

19. *Verbatim Record*, 3 June 2002, 10.00 a.m., para. 60, p. 22.

20. *Memorial of Indonesia*, vol. 1, para. 5.63, pp. 95–96.

21. H. Rumbold to the Marquis of Salisbury, 2 January 1892, and inclosures, F.O. 12/90.

22. *Memorial of Indonesia*, vol. 1, para. 5.63, pp. 88–95.

23. *Verbatim Record*, 3 June 2002, 10.00 a.m., para. 66, p. 23.

24. *Memorial of Indonesia*, vol. 1, para. 5.63, pp. 95–96; and *Verbatim Record*, 3 June 2002, 3.00 p.m., para. 66, p. 23.

25. *Verbatim Record*, 3 June 2002, 10.00 a.m., para. 29, p. 24.

26. *Memorial of Indonesia*, vol. 1, para. 5.69 and 5.70, pp. 98–99.

27. *Memorial of Indonesia*, vol. 1, pp. 101–3.

28. Ibid., p. 104.

29. Ibid., para. 6.9, p. 104.

30. For more details, see ibid., pp. 104–9.

31. Ibid., para. 6.32 and 6.34, pp. 110–11.

32. Ibid., para. 6.39, p. 113.

33. Ibid., para. 6.56, p. 119.

34. Ibid., pp. 121–27.

35. Ibid., para. 6.74, p. 125.

36. For a copy of this document, see Translation of Agreement between the Sultan of Sulu and the BNBC dated 22 April 1903, enclosure in E.W. Birch, Governor North Borneo to Chairman BNBC, 29 April 1903, C.O. 874/1001. For the circumstances leading to the conclusion of this agreement between the BNBC and the Sultan of Sulu, see Chapter 4 above.

37. *Memorial of Indonesia*, vol. 1, pp. 129–35.

38. Ibid., pp. 135–39.

39. *Memorial of Indonesia*, vol. 1, pp. 139–40. For the contents of the *Treaty of Paris, 1898* and *the Convention of 1900 between the United States and Spain*, see Charles I. Bevans, *Treaties and Other International Agreements of the United States, 1776–1949*, vol. 2 (Washington, D.C.: Department of State Publication, 1968), p. 616; and *Paper Relating to the Foreign Relations of the United States for 1900*, pp. 1942–44. Also see Chapter 4 above.

40. For more details of these events, see Chapter 4.

41. *Memorial of Indonesia*, vol. 1, pp. 139–42.

42. See section 6.2.2 above.

43. See Proceedings of the Joint Commission appointed by the British and Netherland Governments for considering the question of the Boundary between the Netherland Indian Possessions on the Island of Borneo and the Territory Belonging to the British North Borneo Company, First Meeting held at the Foreign Office, London, 16 July 1889, Dutch Document Box A60, File 791, pp. 446–51. Also in F.O. 12/86.

44. See Chapter 8.

45. Despatch from Marquis of Salisbury to Count de Bylandt, 13 August 1890, Dutch Document Box A60, File 791, pp. 212–23. Also in F.O. 12/86.
46. Despatch from Count de Bylandt to Lord Salisbury, 2 February 1891, F.O. 12/86.
47. See Article VIII, Convention Between Great Britain and the Netherlands Defining Boundaries in Borneo, 20 June 1891, C.O. 874/503, f. 232.
48. See above, the section 6.2.3 on Ratification.
49. See Chapter 4.

7

The Bases of Malaysia's Claim

7.1 INTRODUCTION

The gist of Malaysia's case was that Pulau Sipadan and Pulau Ligitan had been under the possession and administration of its predecessors in title, the British North Borneo Company (BNBC) and Great Britain and itself, in an uninterrupted manner for a long time, since 1878 in fact. In addition, Malaysia claimed that it had acquired sovereignty over the two islands as a result of a series of treaties and engagements made since 1878 with various States and Parties who had jurisdiction in the area. The Netherlands did not challenge or contest these transactions which were open and public at the material time. In fact, the Indonesian claim to the islands which arose in 1969, was never advanced by the Netherlands.

Malaysia then went on to stress the point that even if the issue of transactions with other powers in the region was removed from its arguments, the long and uninterrupted possession and administration of the two islands in question would be sufficient enough to prove its sovereignty over them. The *Memorial of Malaysia*, vol. 1 elaborated this point as follows:[1]

> But in any event, even if—hypothetically—those transactions had never occurred, the fact of long and peaceful possession and administration dating as long ago as 1878 and unchallenged by any opposing conduct of Indonesia or its predecessor in title, the Netherlands, must be decisive. That fact, even if it stood alone, would be quite sufficient basis for upholding Malaysia's sovereignty over the islands as against Indonesia.

Indonesia's claim, on the other hand, Malaysia contended, relied almost entirely on the interpretation of Article IV of the Boundary Convention of 1891 and an internal map published in the same year after the conclusion of the said Convention. Malaysia rejected the interpretation advanced by Indonesia pertaining to Article IV of the Boundary Convention of 1891 and the arguments relating to the internal Dutch Map (the Explanatory Memorandum Map of 1891). Under the circumstances, Malaysia submitted that there were only two issues for the International Court of Justice (ICJ) to consider which were as follows:[2]

i. The confirmation of Malaysia's sovereignty over the two islands based upon long and effective possession and administration, and on treaties with other interested States [Spain and the United States]; and
ii. The rejection of Indonesia's claim based upon its interpretation of the Boundary Convention of 1891 and the internal Dutch Map.

It is clear from the beginning that Malaysia was banking more on *effectivités* than the possession of a legal title. However, it presented a comprehensive case built on an array of bases which can be listed as follows:

1. Acquisition of sovereignty through international Acts and Treaties.
2. Continuous peaceful possession and administration of the islands since 1878.
3. Inactivity of the Netherlands and Indonesia in relation to the islands of Sipadan and Ligitan.
4. Rejection of Indonesia's contention that the Boundary Convention of 1891 supported its claim.
5. Confirmation of Malaysia's Sovereignty by the implementation of The Boundary Convention of 1891 and The Boundary Demarcation Agreement, 1915 (The Boundary Treaty of 1915).
6. Map Evidence.

7.2 Acquisition of Sovereignty through International Acts and Treaties

7.2.1 Historical Evidence Showing that Pulau Sipadan and Pulau Ligitan Belonged to Sulu in the Nineteenth Century

In outlining the long chain of events by which it purportedly acquired sovereignty over Sipadan and Ligitan, Malaysia at first produced historical evidence to show that the two islands in dispute, in fact, belonged to the Sultanate of Sulu in the nineteenth century. Two important documents cited by Malaysia may be highlighted here. One is a description of the domains of the Sultan of Sulu by James Hunt in his work published in 1837 entitled "Some Particulars relating to Sulo, in the Archipelago of Felicia". Hunt mentioned two of the southernmost dependencies of Sulu on the northeast coast of Borneo as Mangindora and Tirum. The island of *Separan* (Sipadan) was mentioned as being part of the province of Mangindora. In describing Tirum, "the last province on Borneo belonging to Sulo", Hunt mentioned the Sibuku River as well as other rivers along the coast before arriving at the Kingdom of Bulungan. The *General Atlas of the Netherlands Indies* published in Leiden in 1870 with the approval of the Dutch Government was another important piece of historical evidence produced to show that the disputed islands belonged to Sulu. In this Atlas, the map of the east coast of Borneo showed the area of the Domains of Sulu which included a cluster of islands around Darvel Bay "including specifically 'P.Siparan' (Sipadan) and 'P.Legetan' (Ligitan)".[3]

7.2.2 The Sulu Grants of 1878
Malaysia then went on to cite various agreements and engagements which finally led to the transfer of the two islands to its jurisdiction in the course of time. In this context, it first referred to the 1878 Grants by the Sultan of Sulu by which the said ruler transferred his territorial rights in North Borneo to the Overbeck-Dent Association (ODA). This territory stretched from the Pandasan River on the west coast of Sabah to the Sibuku River on the east coast, including all the islands along the coast up to a distance of three marine leagues.[4]

7.2.3 The Madrid Protocol of 1885
Malaysia then moved on to discuss the importance of the Madrid Protocol of 1885 between Britain, Spain, and Germany. Reference was made to the Protocol to highlight the point that any controversy arising out of the interpretation of the 1878 Sulu Grants concerning the issue of sovereignty was completely resolved by the 1885 Protocol. By the terms of the said Protocol, Britain and Germany clearly recognized Spain's sovereignty over the whole of the Sulu Archipelago. In return, Spain relinquished "as far as regards the British Government, all claims of sovereignty" over territory covered by the 1878 Sulu Grants (Article III of the 1885 Protocol). Thus, the question of British sovereignty over the territories granted by Sulu

Sultan in 1878 was given international recognition by the 1885 Protocol. Malaysia stressed the point that even though the islands of Sipadan and Ligitan were not covered by the 1878 Grants, the BNBC was of the view that it had authority over these islands and thus started administering them right from 1878 [1882].[5]

7.2.4 The Anglo-Dutch Boundary Convention of 1891

The Anglo-Dutch Boundary Convention of 1891 was the next treaty cited. Malaysia contended that the Boundary Convention of 1891 did not refer to Pulau Sipadan and Pulau Ligitan at all. The *Memorial of Malaysia*, vol. 1 recorded the argument on this point as follows:[6]

> The Treaty [the Boundary Convention of 1891] did not refer to Ligitan or Sipadan. The Netherlands made no claim to those islands, nor did it ever subsequently assert any title to those or any other islands off the coast of North Borneo.

7.2.5 Treaties with the United States

Here, the events leading to the American takeover of the Philippines from Spain were related. By the Treaty of Paris, 1898 and the Convention of 1900, the United States acquired sovereignty over the whole of the Philippines and the Sulu Archipelago. The United States, however, felt that some of the islands outside the three marine leagues limit off the east coast of North Borneo which belonged to Sulu were administered by the BNBC. In 1903, the United States specifically claimed sovereignty over these islands, including Pulau Sipadan and Pulau Ligitan. The BNBC protested, claiming it had always regarded these islands [twenty-six of them] as belonging to North Borneo. The dispute led to the 1907 Exchange of Notes between Great Britain and the United States. In a nutshell, the *Memorial of Malaysia*, vol. 1 outlined the significance and legal effect of the 1907 agreement as follows:[7]

> In the 1907 Exchange of Notes, Great Britain thus recognised the continuing sovereignty of the United States, as successor to Spain, over the islands beyond the 3 marine league line. On the other hand the United States accepted that these islands had been in fact administered by the British North Borneo Company and agreed to allow that situation to continue, subject to termination on 12 months' notice.

> It is clear from all relevant sources that the islands covered by the 1907 Exchange of Notes included all those adjacent to the North Borneo

coast beyond the three marine league line. These sources include: (a) the correspondence associated with the voyage of the *USS Quiros*; (b) the Sultan's certificate of 1903; (c) the map attached to the 1907 Exchange of Notes. These sources are fully consistent with each other, and it is clear that they covered, *inter alia*, Ligitan and Sipadan.

Malaysia then narrated how in 1930 a precise sea boundary was drawn between the US possessions in the Philippines Archipelago and the possessions of British North Borneo on the east coast. The sea boundary was agreed upon by the two relevant powers, Britain and the United States in the Boundary Treaty of 1930. By the terms of this treaty, the United States transferred sovereignty over some of the islands administered by the BNBC under the 1907 Exchange of Notes to the latter. These islands included Pulau Sipadan and Pulau Ligitan.[8]

7.2.6 Transfer of North Borneo to the British Government
The next stage in the chain of sovereignty transfers came in 1946. On 26 June 1946, the BNBC transferred all its rights over North Borneo to the British Government. North Borneo became designated as a Crown Colony.

7.2.7 Malaysia Acquired Sovereignty over North Borneo in 1963
With the formation of Malaysia on 16 September 1963, the Colony of North Borneo became a member of the new federation under the name of Sabah. Malaysia thus acquired sovereignty over all territories formerly belonging to the Colony of North Borneo. The chain of sovereignty transfers was thus completed. In concluding this section, Malaysia stressed the point that none of the states in the region contested the various agreements and treaties between Britain and the United States pertaining to sovereignty and continuous administration of the two islands concerned. The *Memorial of Malaysia*, vol. 1 ended this section with these words:[9]

> These transactions show beyond a shadow of doubt that none of the States in the region contested this *status quo*, whether in terms of peaceful administration or sovereignty. There is absolutely no indication that any of those States ever entertained the idea that the unexpressed effect of the 1891 Boundary Treaty was as Indonesia now, belatedly argues … to transfer Ligitan and Sipadan to the Netherlands.

7.3 Continuous Peaceful Possession and Adminstration of the Islands since 1878

The linchpin in Malaysia's case was that it and its predecessors in title, the BNBC and then the British Government, had a long and undisputed possession and administration of the two islands since 1878. This fact alone was sufficient to support its title to the islands concerned. Malaysia's *effectivités* over the two islands were instituted by such state activities as legislation; administrative activities; the extension of judicial and police jurisdiction; the construction and maintenance of navigational aids and lights; the reaction to foreign incursions; the absence of *effectivités* by rival claimants; and map evidence.

In providing evidence to support its claim of long and undisturbed occupation and administration since 1878, Malaysia cited a number of state acts pertaining to jurisdiction over the two islands. These are discussed below.

7.3.1 The Regulation and Control of the Collection of Turtle Eggs on Sipadan and Ligitan

Since the 1878 Sulu Grants, the BNBC had always assumed that the islands lying off the coast of Tawau and Semporna, including the two islands in dispute, were under its jurisdiction. This assumption was translated into state practice. In 1887, the Company established an administrative station at Semporna. In 1903, it appointed Panglima Udang, a Bajau, as the Native Magistrate of Darvel Bay, based at Semporna. Matters concerning administration and jurisdiction over the islands in Darvel Bay, including Sipadan and Ligitan were always a matter for the British authorities (BNBC Officers) in the East Coast Residency at Tawau, or more locally, the District Officer at Semporna.

Concrete examples of the *effectivités* of the BNBC pertaining to Sipadan can be traced back to 1910 when a dispute concerning the right to collect turtle eggs on Sipadan between two local chiefs was settled by the District Officer of the BNBC at Semporna. In 1913, the Resident of the East Coast issued a licence for the collection of turtle eggs on Sipadan Island to two of the Company's chiefs of Danawan Island. Further evidence of the Company's official involvement in the affairs of Sipadan appeared in 1916 when the Acting Resident of the East Coast, G.C. Irving, issued a Notification Letter (*Surat Katrangan*) confirming the customary rights of two local chiefs of

Danawan Island named Panglima Abu Sari and Maharaja Mahmud and their heirs to collect turtle eggs from Sipadan. In 1918, the Company's Native Chief of Semporna, Panglima Udang, finally settled the respective shares of turtle egg collection rights of these two licence holders and their heirs. G.C. Irving endorsed the agreement in the same year.

The year 1917 was especially important in terms of North Borneo's official *effectivités* on the island of Sipadan. In that year, the Government of North Borneo passed what was known as the Turtle Preservation Ordinance. The Ordinance gave the Governor of North Borneo the power to declare certain territories of the State of North Borneo, including its territorial waters, as native reserves for the collection of turtle eggs. In the absence of an area specified as such, the collection of turtle eggs was therefore deemed an offence under the Ordinance. This legislation became significant to Sipadan in 1919 when that island was officially declared as a native reserve for the collection of turtle eggs pursuant to section 3 of the said Ordinance.

From 1919 onwards, there was a continuous enforcement of the Turtle Preservation Ordinance of 1917 on Sipadan. On 28 April 1954, for example, the District Officer at Tawau issued a licence under the provisions of this Ordinance to the Borneo Abaca Company permitting its workers, who were mainly Cocos Islanders, to take a limited number of turtles from the islands of Sipadan, Ligitan, Kapalan, Mabul, Danawan and Si Amil. This permit to allow the company workers to take turtles for consumption was the first of its kind. Previously permits had often been issued for the collection of turtle eggs, not for catching turtles. The local turtle egg collectors were unhappy with the issuing of this licence as they feared that their collection of turtle eggs would decline if more and more turtles were caught for consumption by the Cocos Islanders. Their concerted complaints finally led to the revocation of this licence by the same officer in September 1954.[10]

7.3.2 Establishment of a Bird Sanctuary on Sipadan Island
On 1 February 1933, the Government of North Borneo declared Pulau Sipadan a bird sanctuary. The declaration was published as a notification in the state's official paper, the *British North Borneo Official Gazette*.[11]

7.3.3 Construction and Maintenance of Lighthouses
Further evidence of Malaysia's *effectivités* on the two islands is shown by the decision of the Government of the Colony of North Borneo to construct

lighthouses in the area. In 1962 a 75 foot Light Tower was constructed at
Alice Channel on Sipadan Island. A notice concerning the presence of the
lighthouse was issued on 10 July 1963. On 17 July 1963, another notice
was issued concerning the operation of a lighthouse in the southern part
of Ligitan Reef. The coordinates given were those of Pulau Ligitan. There
was no reaction from Indonesia pertaining to both these public notices.
The lighthouses still exist today and have been regularly maintained and
administered by the Sabah Marine Department.[12]

7.4 NETHERLANDS AND INDONESIAN INACTIVITY IN RELATION TO SIPADAN AND LIGITAN

7.4.1 Introduction

The Malaysian Government contended that before 1969, neither the
Netherlands nor Indonesia ever laid claim to the two islands based on a
valid title. Malaysia further attested that in contrast to its own position,
both the Netherlands and Indonesia also did not have any administration or
control over the two islands. Malaysia then put forward various arguments
and evidence to support these two contentions.

7.4.2 Absence of Any Claim by the Netherlands to the Two Islands

One important evidence adduced by the Malaysian side to prove that the
Netherlands never made any claim to the two islands was the "Contract
of Vassalage" of 12 November 1850 between the Dutch East Indies
Government and the Sultan of Bulungan. Malaysia argued that in this
document, the territorial limits of the Kingdom of Bulungan were clearly
stated, but "none of the places identified in the Contract of 1850 were
anywhere near Ligitan or Sipadan".[13]

In this context, Malaysia also made reference to the following passage
in the Contract of Vassalage of 1850:[14]

> The following islands shall belong to Boeloengan, namely, Terakkan,
> Nenoekkan, and Sebittikh, together with the small islands belonging to
> them.

Malaysia was of the view that the "small islands" mentioned here referred
to such small features surrounding and lying between the three big islands
named in the passage and could not have at all alluded to the islands of
Sipadan and Ligitan which were situated some 40 to 50 nautical miles
away to the east of Sebatik and geographically closer to the Semporna

Peninsular in Sabah. When the ODA obtained the Sulu Grants of 22 July 1878, a boundary dispute soon developed between British Borneo and Dutch Borneo. As discussed in Chapter 3, the Sulu territorial concessions to the ODA extended on the east coast of Borneo to the Sibuku River, whereas the Dutch claimed jurisdiction farther north to Batu Tinagat and the Tawau River. Malaysia attested that though this was the case, the Dutch did not make any claim to territories to the east of Batu Tinagat. In fact, the Dutch considered Batu Tinagat as the "extreme easterly point" of its claim.[15] Malaysia summed up this heading by pointing out that in fact the boundary dispute was settled by the Boundary Convention of 1891 whereby the Dutch conceded Batu Tinagat and the northern half of Sebatik Island to Britain. In effect, this tantamounted to a "withdrawal of the Dutch claim to the north, not a further extension well to the north-east".[16]

7.4.3 Absence of Administration of the Islands by the Netherlands
In highlighting the issue of inactivity by the Netherlands and Indonesia pertaining to the two islands, Malaysia pointed out in its Memorial that the Netherlands never exercised any territorial administration over Sipadan and Ligitan.[17]

The Dutch navy, Malaysia conceded, did make occasional visits to the region, including to the islands of Sipadan and Ligitan, but these voyages were made either for purposes of conducting surveys, as was done by the *H.M.S. Macassar* in 1903; or for suppressing piracy, as was undertaken by the Dutch torpedo boat the *Lynx* in 1921. Malaysia stressed that the action of the *Lynx* did not involve activities pertaining to sovereignty or administration. It argued as follows:[18]

> There was no indication that the voyage of the *Lynx* involved the lodging of a territorial claim ... Nor was there any such follow-up activity (e.g. the publication of maps proclaiming sovereignty over the area or diplomatic correspondence) ...

7.4.4 Absence of Protest by the Netherlands
Malaysia contended that the Netherlands had not only failed to take any action to administer the islands in question, but it also did not protest at their administration by North Borneo. In this context, administrative activities relating to the two islands were undertaken by the North Borneo Government since the Sulu Grants of 1878 and included the issuing of turtle eggs collection licences since 1917 and the establishment of a bird sanctuary on Sipadan Island in 1933.[19]

7.4.5 Absence of Administration of the Islands by Indonesia after Independence

Malaysia then went on to point out that Indonesia did not include Sipadan and Ligitan within its jurisdiction when it proclaimed Act No. 4 of 18 February 1960 defining its territorial and archipelagic waters.[20]

7.4.6 Absence of Protest by Indonesia

Just like the Netherlands before it, Indonesia did not register any protest at acts of administration undertaken by the British Government and then Malaysia, pertaining to the two islands.

Malaysia concluded this section by reiterating that neither the Netherlands nor Indonesia ever exercised any administration over the two islands from the time of the Sulu Grants (1878) to 1969. There were also no protests against the BNBC, the British Government, and Malaysia concerning their continuous administration of the said islands and this tantamounted to their acquiesce of British and Malaysian jurisdiction over the islands.

During the Oral Pleadings on 5 June 2002, Counsel for Malaysia, Sir Elihu Lauterpacht strengthened Malaysia's arguments on this point by submitting that Malaysia's continuous presence and administration of the islands since before 1891 would prevail in international law over a title of acquisition of Sovereignty not followed by an actual display of state authority.

He argued further that there was no evidence of a single item of Dutch administration, legislation or assertion of title in respect of both islands. He emphasized as follows:[21]

> For 78 years [from 1891 to 1969] Indonesia remained totally silent and inactive regarding title to the islands, as well as in the ensuring 33 years [1969 to 2002].

On 7 June 2002, Sir Elihu again emphasized the strength of Malaysia's *effectivités*. With reference to the visit of the Dutch destroyer, the *Lynx* to Sipadan Island in 1921, he said although Indonesia had made a big deal of it, the Commander of the Dutch ship, however, was careful to keep in touch with Tawau as he knew he was in British waters. On the other hand, Malaysia (and its predecessors) had conducted "classic governmental activities" such as resolving disputes over the collection of turtle eggs on Sipadan, the issuing of licences, and the enactment of the Turtle Preservation Ordinance in 1917. He emphasized that the "enactment of legislation was one of the most obvious and accepted displays of sovereign authority". Going further, he made the following remark:[22]

> Surely, it [Malaysia's legislation] is every bit as cogent as, or indeed infinitely more than, the solitary voyage of the *Lynx*.

7.5 Lack of Support of the Boundary Convention of 1891 for Indonesia's Claims

Malaysia's contended that the linchpin of Indonesia's case, which was the Anglo-Dutch Boundary Convention of 1891 and the negotiations preceding it, did not support Indonesia's claim to the two islands.

7.5.1 Article IV of The Boundary Convention of 1891 did not Support Indonesia's Arguments

Malaysia argued that Article IV of the Boundary Convention of 1891 was crafted "solely to deal with Sebatik" island and was not intended to allocate islands far out in the sea to either power. Moreover, at the material time, "neither Britain nor the Netherlands claimed to exercise sovereignty beyond the three-mile belt of territorial waters". The plain and ordinary meaning of the words "the boundary line shall be continued .... across the island of Sebittik" Malaysia insisted, meant that the line cut Sebatik Island into two halves and went no further. The Indonesian interpretation of the word "across" which meant that the line "crossed" Sebatik to a distant point in the sea was therefore erroneous.[23] In his Oral Submissions on 5 June 2002, Counsel for Malaysia, Sir Elihu Lauterpacht argued that if the intention of Article IV of the Boundary Convention of 1891 had been to divide territories lying in the sea, it would have clearly spelt out, indicating which islands belonged to the Dutch and which to the British. He emphasized further as follows:[24]

> There is no word of reference, expressed or implied, to the extention of the boundary eastwards of Sebatik.

7.5.2 The Preparatory Work Leading to the Conclusion of the Anglo-Dutch Boundary Convention of 1891 Did Not Concern the Islands of Sipadan and Ligitan

Malaysia provided further evidence that the negotiations leading to the Boundary Convention of 1891 were not at all concerned with the allocation of offshore islands more than the three marine leagues limit of territorial waters. Malaysia pointed out that during the course of the negotiations between the Dutch and British Governments from 1889 to 1891, although the Dutch claimed territories as far north as Batu Tinagat, the representatives had agreed that regions to the eastward of the said point were under the Sulu rule. Moreover, Malaysia argued that it was clear from the correspondence between the two sides, that the issue at stake was the ownership of Sebatik Island which both sides wanted. The provision for the extension of the boundary line along the parallel of 4°10′ N, eastwards and westwards from Broershoek in Article IV was therefore made with the express purpose of accepting the compromise of dividing Sebatik Island equally between the two powers. The *travaux pre'paratoires* therefore, confirm that the question of the division of offshore islands more than the three marine league limit was not a point of discussion. Moreover, Britain had no jurisdiction at the time over islands beyond the three mile marine leagues limit and was therefore in no position to cede to the Netherlands islands (including Sipadan and Ligitan) falling in that zone.[25]

7.6 Malaysia's Sovereignty Confirmed by the Implementation of the Boundary Convention of 1891 and the Boundary Demarcation Agreement of 1915 (The Anglo-Dutch Boundary Treaty of 1915)

The issues Malaysia wished to consider under this heading were (i) the process of ratification of the Boundary Convention of 1891 by the Netherlands, and (ii) the process of demarcation of the boundary which ended in 1915 with the signing of the Boundary Demarcation Agreement of 28 September 1915.

7.6.1 The Process of Ratification by the Dutch, the Explanatory Memorandum Map and Subsequent Implementation Actions

(i) The Explanatory Memorandum Map of 1891
The first item that Malaysia reviewed under this heading was the Internal Dutch Map or the Explanatory Memorandum Map which was attached to the Explanatory Memorandum No. 3 dated 25 July 1891, presented to the Dutch Parliament for the purpose of ratification of the Boundary

Convention of 1891. Indonesia relied heavily on this map to support its case. This map showed a line in red colour which extended eastwards into the sea from the east coast of Sebatik Island along the parallel of 4°10′ N for a rough distance of 50 miles (see Figure 3.2). Indonesia contended that this was part of the boundary line as agreed in the Boundary Convention of 1891 and it was intended to allocate islands south of the line to the Dutch. Malaysia cited a number of reasons for rejecting Indonesia's claim. These may be tabulated as follows:[26]

(a) The Explanatory Memorandum Map was not part of the Boundary Convention of 1891. It was a unilateral map produced by the Dutch.
(b) The Boundary Convention of 1891 did not agree on any map, and no map was attached to the treaty to pinpoint the exact position of the boundary line which was to be determined later.
(c) The Explanatory Memorandum Map did not show the islands in dispute.

(ii) The Dutch Explanatory Memorandum, 1891
Malaysia also submitted that the Dutch Explanatory Memorandum presented to the Dutch Parliament for the purpose of ratification of the Boundary Convention of 1891 was silent on the question of an allocation line concerning offshore islands. The Memorandum was concerned only with the determination of a land boundary and the division of Sebatik Island into the Dutch and British halves.[27]

7.6.2 The Boundary Demarcation Process and the Boundary Demarcation Agreement of 1915 (The Anglo-Dutch Boundary Treaty of 1915)

Malaysia consolidated its case concerning the argument that the boundary line did not go beyond the east coast of Sebatik Island by presenting concrete evidence from the actual process of demarcation and the resulting Boundary Demarcation Agreement of 1915 between the Netherlands and Britain. As discussed in Chapter 3, the process of actual demarcation of the boundary on the spot began in 1912 and was undertaken by a joint Anglo-Dutch Commission consisting of two representatives from each side. After the job of surveying and marking the main boundary on Borneo Island was completed in January 1913, a separate exercise for surveying and marking the boundary line on Sebatik Island was undertaken by another joint team from 1913 to 1914.[28]

In relation to the actual process of demarcation of the boundary and the Boundary Demarcation Agreement of 1915, Malaysia cited the following evidence to support its contention that the boundary line did not go beyond the east coast of Sebatik Island into the sea:[29]

(i) The report of the Joint Commission on the boundary demarcated on Sebatik Island clearly stated that "the boundary [was] the straight line between the granite pillars on the East and West of Sebatik Island ...". No mention was ever made by Commissioners of both sides that the boundary line extended into the sea beyond the granite pillar on the east side of Sebatik.

(ii) The Commission Report was accompanied by a signed map which clearly showed that the boundary line stopped on the east coast of Sebatik and went no further.

(iii) Both the Commission Report and the signed map were endorsed and accepted by a formal Agreement signed on 28 September 1915 between the Netherlands and British Governments called the Boundary Demarcation Agreement of 1915. The map, therefore, is a treaty map. The Boundary Demarcation Agreement of 1915 and the map were subsequently published.

Malaysia concluded this section by emphasizing that the Boundary Demarcation Agreement of 1915 was indeed relevant for interpreting the text of the Boundary Convention of 1891. In this context, the Boundary Demarcation Agreement of 1915 confirmed that the Boundary Convention of 1891 did not provide for an allocation line in the seas to the east of Sebatik. The 1915 treaty was an agreed document, while the papers presented to the Dutch Parliament were internal documents and therefore did not have the same status.[30]

7.7 Map Evidence

In presenting relevant maps to prop up its case, Malaysia wished to emphasize two points:[31]

(a) that the boundary line did not extend into the sea east of Sebatik Island; and

(b) that both the islands of Sipadan and Ligitan were regarded as belonging to Britain or Malaysia.

To support these contentions, Malaysia tendered a number of maps as evidence. These included the important treaty-based map attached to the Boundary Demarcation Agreement of 1915. Other maps submitted to corroborate the two points mentioned above included British Admiralty charts Nos. 1681; 2576; and 2660B; BNBC's Map of North Borneo of 1906, and the 1935 Map of Semporna District issued by the Survey Department at Jesselton; the 1958 Map of Lahad Datu Police District; the 1979 Map of Malaysia; and a number of others maps.[32]

Malaysia concluded this section by submitting that map evidence did not support Indonesia's claim. On the other hand, the said map evidence overwhelmingly lent credence to Malaysia's claim of having obtained title to these islands through treaty transactions with other powers in the region and through long, uninterrupted administration of the said islands for more than a century.[33]

7.8 CONCLUSION

Malaysia therefore basically presented its case based on two elements. One was that it had obtained a title to the two islands through a chain of treaty transactions with other powers in the region, especially the United States. The second major basis for its claim was *effectivités* evidenced by a long, uninterrupted administration of the said islands since 1878. The rest of its case was primarily devoted to destroying the validity of Indonesia's arguments, principally relating to the interpretation of the Anglo-Dutch Boundary Convention of 1891 and the Dutch Explanatory Memorandum Map of 1891. Malaysia rounded up its case by using the Boundary Demarcation Agreement of 1915 (The Anglo-Dutch Boundary Treaty of 1915) as solid evidence to prove that the Boundary Convention of 1891 did not provide for an allocation line in the seas east of Sebatik Island. All in all, Malaysia presented quite a compelling case in support of its claim.

Notes

1. International Court of Justice (ICJ), *Case Concerning Sovereignty over Pulau Ligitan and Pulau Sipadan (Indonesia/Malaysia), Memorial of Malaysia*, vol. 1, 2 November 1999, para. 2.3, p. 3 (hereafter cited as *Memorial of Malaysia*, vol. 1).
2. Ibid., para. 2.9, p. 7.
3. Ibid., paras. 5.4–5.8, pp. 29–35.
4. Ibid., paras. 5.10–5.11, pp. 36–37.

5. Ibid., paras. 5.17–5.19, pp. 40–41.
6. Ibid., para. 5.20(b), p. 42.
7. Ibid., paras. 5.39–5.40, p. 55.
8. Ibid., paras. 5.43–5.44, pp. 56–58.
9. Ibid., para. 5.47, p. 59.
10. Ibid., pp. 63–69. For more details, see Chapter 2.
11. Notification No. 69, *British North Borneo Official Gazette*, 1 February 1933, p. 28, C.O. 855.
12. *Memorial of Malaysia*, vol. 1, pp. 69–70.
13. Ibid., paras. 7.2–7.3, pp. 72–73.
14. Ibid., para. 7.2, p. 73.
15. Ibid., para. 7.9, p. 78.
16. Ibid., para. 7.9, p. 78.
17. Ibid., para. 7.13, p. 7.
18. Ibid., para. 7.16, p. 82.
19. Ibid., paras. 7.17–7.18, pp. 83–84.
20. Ibid., paras. 7.19–7.20, pp. 84–85.
21. *The Star*, 8 June 2002. Based on Report of Oral Pleadings at The Hague by Tan Kah Peng.
22. *New Sunday Times*, 9 June 2002. Based on Report of Oral Pleadings at The Hague by Carolyn Hong.
23. *Memorial of Malaysia*, vol. 1, paras. 8.8–8.12, pp. 89–91.
24. *The Star*, 8 June 2002. Based on Report of Oral Pleadings at The Hague by Tan Kah Peng.
25. *Memorial of Malaysia*, vol. 1, pp. 91–95. For more details, see Chapter 3.
26. *Memorial of Malaysia*, vol. 1, paras. 9.2–9.9, pp. 96–99.
27. Ibid., paras. 9.10–9.15, pp. 99–102.
28. Ibid., para. 9.18, p. 103. For more details, see Chapter 3.
29. *Memorial of Malaysia*, vol. 1, para. 9.19 and 9.20, pp. 103–4.
30. Ibid., paras. 9.21–9.24, pp. 103–4.
31. Ibid., para. 10.4, p. 108.
32. Ibid., paras. 10.2–10.19, pp. 108–12.
33. Ibid., para. 10.20, p. 113.

8

The International Court of Justice (ICJ) Judgment

8.1 INTRODUCTION

As has been discussed in Chapter 1, both Indonesia and Malaysia agreed to refer the dispute concerning ownership of Pulau Sipadan and Pulau Ligitan to the International Court of Justice (ICJ) on 7 October 1996. Subsequently, on 31 May 1997, both countries signed a Special Agreement for this purpose and filed the said Agreement with the ICJ on 2 November 1998. In the Special Agreement, the two parties requested the ICJ to determine, on the basis of treaties, agreements, and other evidence to be furnished by them, whether sovereignty over the two islands belonged to the Republic of Indonesia or to Malaysia. Each of the Parties subsequently submitted a Memorial, a Counter-Memorial and a Reply as required by the Court. The Court delivered its verdict on 17 December 2002.

The Court comprised of seventeen judges. They included the President, Guilbert Guillaume, the Vice-President, Shi, and Judges Shigeru Oda, Ranjeva, Herczegh, Fleischhauer, Koroma, Vereshchetin, Higgins, Parra-Aranguren, Kooijmans, Rezek, Al-Khasawneh, Buergenthal and Elaraby; and Judges ad hoc Christopher Weeramantry and Thomas Franck. The Registrar was Philippe Couvreur. Since the Court did not include any judge of the nationality of either of the Parties, each Party proceeded to choose a judge ad hoc to sit on the case: Indonesia chose Mr Mohamed Shahabuddeen and Malaysia Mr Christopher Gregory Weeramantry of Sri Lanka. Mr Shahabuddeen later resigned, and Indonesia chose Mr Thomas Franck of the United States to replace him. Public hearings were held from

3 to 12 June 2002.[1] At the Oral Presentation held from 3 to 12 June 2002, the two sides advanced the following submissions to support their claims to the two islands.

On behalf of the Government of Indonesia:[2]

> On the basis of the facts and legal considerations presented in Indonesia's written pleadings and its oral presentation, the Government of the Republic of Indonesia respectfully requests the Court to adjudge and declare that:
> (i) Sovereignty over Pulau Ligitan belongs to the Republic of Indonesia; and
> (ii) Sovereignty over Pulau Sipadan belongs to the Republic of Indonesia

On behalf of the Government of Malaysia:[3]

> The Government of Malaysia respectfully requests the Court to adjudge, and declare that sovereignty over Pulau Ligitan and Pulau Sipadan belongs to Malaysia.

The verdict was delivered on 17 December 2002. In its Judgment, the Court found, by sixteen votes to one that "sovereignty over Pulau Ligitan and Pulau Sipadan belongs to Malaysia".

8.2 A Review of the Bases of the Parties' Claims

It may be useful to briefly review each country's standpoint before proceeding to a detailed analysis of the ICJ's verdict on the various arguments raised by both Indonesia and Malaysia in support of their respective claims over the two islands. The linchpin of Indonesia's case was that it held sovereignty over the two disputed islands on the basis of the Anglo-Dutch Boundary Convention of 1891 and the process of ratification of the said Convention; and some *effectivités*. Indonesia maintained that legal title was paramount and no amount of subsequent *effectivités* could displace such a title; they could only enhance it. Indonesia, therefore, rested its case almost entirely on the interpretation of the Boundary Convention of 1891 which was said to have given it a legal title. At the Oral Hearings, Indonesia further contended, by way of alternative argument, that if the Court were to reject its title based on the Boundary Convention of 1891, it could still claim sovereignty over the disputed islands as successor to the Sultan of Bulungan, who was the original owner of the islands.[4] On the other hand, Malaysia claimed that it had acquired sovereignty over the two islands by virtue of a series of treaties and engagements made since 1878 with states and parties with interests in the area. The title over the islands of Sipadan and Ligitan, originally held by the Sultan of Sulu, subsequently passed, in succession, to Spain, to the United States, to Great Britain, and finally to Malaysia itself. Malaysia's strong point was however *effectivités*. Malaysia contended that its title, based on international treaty transactions, was confirmed by a number of *effectivités* conducted by the British North Borneo Company (BNBC), the British Government, and itself over the two islands through a process of a long, uninterrupted possession and administration since 1878. Malaysia emphasized that Indonesia's predecessor in title did not contest these transactions which were open and made public at the material time. In fact, the Netherlands itself did not advance any claim to the two islands. The claim was advanced by Indonesia only in 1969.[5] Malaysia further argued that, if the Court were to conclude that the disputed islands had originally belonged to the Netherlands, its *effectivités* would, in any event, have displaced any such Netherlands title.[6] The order in which the contending parties presented their arguments was arranged according to their own priorities, but the ICJ rearranged the evidence firstly in support of a treaty-based title which it considered as paramount, and secondly in support of *effectivités*. The presentation here follows the ICJ structure.

8.3 THE COURT'S CONSIDERATION OF A TREATY-BASED TITLE

As mentioned, the Court gave priority consideration to a treaty-based title. In deciding on this issue, it first dealt with the arguments presented by Indonesia followed by Malaysia in support of their respective claims.

8.3.1 The Court's Views and Ruling on Indonesia's Claim to a Treaty-Based Title

The Court observed that Indonesia's claim to a treaty-based title was anchored on two major foundations: the Boundary Convention of 1891; and succession to the territories of the Sultan of Bulungan.

8.3.1.1 The Boundary Convention of 1891

The Court noted that Indonesia's main claim to sovereignty to the islands of Sipadan and Ligitan was based on the Boundary Convention of 1891.

In deciding whether the Boundary Convention of 1891 gave a legal title to Indonesia, the Court took into consideration a number of points. These included the interpretation of the text of the Boundary Convention of 1891; the legality of the Dutch Explanatory Memorandum Map of 1891; the object and purpose of the Boundary Convention of 1891; prior negotiations and the circumstances leading to the conclusion of the said Convention, and subsequent practice.

Concerning the text and interpretation of the provisions of the Boundary Convention of 1891, Indonesia claimed in its submissions that the said Convention gave it definitive title over the two islands. Indonesia emphatically argued that the 1891 Convention "defined" the boundaries between the colonial possessions of the British and the Dutch in northeastern Borneo and that the terms of the Convention and its "contemporaneous" interpretation by the two parties concerned, left no doubt as to the inclusion of both Sipadan and Ligitan "within the colonial domains of the Netherlands".[7]

In support of this contention, Indonesia argued as follows:[8]

> The Convention, by its terms, its context, and its object and purpose, established the 4°10′ N parallel of latitude as the dividing line between the Parties' respective possessions in the area now in question.

In this context, Indonesia maintained that the 4°10′ parallel was an allocation line and stated this position on follows:[9]

> The line must be considered an allocation line: land areas, including islands located to the north of 4°10′ N latitude were ... considered to be British, and those lying to the south were Dutch.

Indonesia depended heavily on the wording and interpretation of Article IV of the Boundary Convention of 1891 to support its case. The full text of this article reads as follows:

> From 4°10′ north latitude on the east coast the boundary-line shall be continued eastward along the parallel, across the Island of Sebatik; that portion of the island situated to the north of that parallel shall belong unreservedly to the British North Borneo Company, and the portion south of that parallel to the Netherlands.

Indonesia insisted that the words "shall be continued eastward" and "across the island of Sebatik" meant "through and beyond" the island of Sebatik "out to sea".[10]

Malaysia rejected Indonesia's interpretation of the Boundary Convention of 1891 on the grounds that the said Convention was a boundary treaty and not an allocation treaty; that Article IV was meant to divide the island of Sebatik into two equal halves; and that the plain and ordinary meaning of the words "across the island of Sebatik" was to describe, "in English and in Dutch, a line that crosses Sebatik from the west coast to the east coast and goes no further".[11] Malaysia also referred to Article V of the Boundary Convention of 1891 which was manifestly clear that the exact boundary line had not been settled in 1891, and that "the exact position of the boundary line, as described in the four preceding articles shall be determined hereafter by mutual agreement ..."[12]

In reviewing these submissions, the Court was of the view that the boundary line envisaged in the Boundary Convention of 1891 was not an allocation line; the said line was intended to be a land boundary only, and that Article IV did not support Indonesia's argument that the boundary line proceeded beyond Sebatik Island eastward out to sea so as to divide or allocate distant offshore islands.[13]

8.3.1.2 The Dutch Explanatory Memorandum Map of 1891

The next point of reference advanced by Indonesia was the argument that the Dutch Explanatory Memorandum Map of 1891 had a legal standing and was therefore binding since it was approved by the Dutch States-General.[14]

Indonesia also alleged that the British Government had acquired copies of the Explanatory Memorandum and the map, but there was no dissent.[15] This, according to Indonesia, implied Great Britain's concurrence in the content of the map which in turn amounted to the adoption of the map "as part of their treaty settlement" by both parties.[16] Malaysia described Indonesia's interpretation of the 1891 Dutch map as extravagant and rejected it on the following grounds:[17]

(a) That the Dutch Explanatory Memorandum Map of 1891 was not attached to the Boundary Convention of 1891 and was not referred to in the said treaty or in the negotiations leading to the Boundary Convention of 1891. It was entirely a unilateral document of the Netherlands Government, and

(b) That the said map was never formally delivered to the British negotiators. It did not exist at the conclusion of the Boundary Convention of 1891.

The Court's ruling on the importance of the Dutch Explanatory Memorandum Map of 1891 was that it could not accept Indonesia's argument regarding its "legal value" as the map was never transmitted by the Dutch Government to the British Government, though the latter was aware of it. The lack of reaction from the British Government could not, therefore, be deemed "to constitute acquiescence in this line". The Court concluded that under these circumstances, the map could not be considered both as "an agreement" relating to the treaty between the parties concerned, or as an "instrument" made by one party and accepted by the other within the context of the original treaty.[18] The Court also gave judgment concerning the Dutch Memorandum Map of 1891 under the category of subsequent practice of the parties to the Boundary Convention of 1891. On this point, the Court again rejected Indonesia's contention that the 1891 Dutch map could be considered as "a subsequent agreement or as a subsequent practice for the purposes of Article 31.2(a) and (b) of the Vienna Convention".[19]

8.3.1.3 The Object and Purpose of the Boundary Convention of 1891

The next item to come under the Court's consideration was the purpose and intention of the Boundary Convention of 1891. In this context, Indonesia had submitted that the purpose and intention of the Anglo-Dutch negotiations and the Boundary Convention of 1891 was to "settle definitely the whole problem of the limits of the British and Dutch possessions in the area" and as the Dutch also possessed the islands of Sipadan and Ligitan, the eastward boundary line was meant to extend out to the sea as far as these islands so as to complete the process of division.[20]

On this issue, the Court's judgment was similar to the point concerning the interpretation of the text of the said Convention as follows:[21]

> The Court accordingly concludes that the text or Article IV of the 1891 Convention, when read in context and in the light of the Convention's object and purpose, cannot be interpreted as establishing an allocation line determining sovereignty over the islands out to sea, to the east of the island of Sebatik.

8.3.1.4 Subsequent Practice

The Court next turned its attention to arguments pertaining to subsequent practice advanced by Indonesia. One such argument was Indonesia's claim that the 1893 amendment to the 1850 and 1878 Contracts of Vassalage with the Sultan of Bulungan gave the Dutch title over Sipadan and Ligitan. The 1893 amended text reads as follows:[22]

> the Islands of Tarakan and Nanoekan [Nanukan], and that portion of the Island of Sebatik situated to the south of the above boundary-line ..., belong to Boeloengan [Bulungan], as well as the small islands belonging to the above islands, so far as they are situated to the south of the boundary-line...

Indonesia claimed that both Sipadan and Ligitan were part of the "small islands" and they were under Dutch jurisdiction.[23] The Court ruled that Sipadan and Ligitan could not be part of these small group of islands as they were some 40 nautical miles away from the three bigger islands in question. The Court further stipulated that in any case Britain was not in a position to have apportioned them to the Dutch, as Britain had no sovereignty over the islands at the material time.[24]

In relation to subsequent practice, Indonesia also argued that the Demarcation Agreement of 1915 between Britain and the Netherlands supported its interpretation of the Boundary Convention of 1891 to the effect that the boundary line extended east of Sebatik Island into the sea. The Court rejected this view on the grounds that if the boundary was meant to continue in any way to the east of Sebatik, at the very least some mention of that could have been expected in the Agreement. The Court, in addition, considered that an examination of the map annexed to the Demarcation Agreement of 1915 reinforced its interpretation of the Agreement that the boundary line on Sebatik Island ended on the east coast of that island.[25]

With reference to the argument advanced by Indonesia concerning the practice of granting oil concessions whereby both parties had respected the 4°10′ north line, the Court ruled that it was unable to draw any conclusion for purposes of interpreting Article IV of the Boundary Convention of 1891 from these acts.[26]

The Court concluded the section on Indonesia's arguments pertaining to the subsequent practice of the parties to the Boundary Convention of 1891 by confirming the conclusion arrived by the Court earlier concerning the interpretation of the Article IV of that Convention. Basically, this conclusion was that the Boundary Convention of 1891 did not establish an allocation line determining sovereignty over the islands out to sea to the east of Sebatik Island.[27]

8.3.1.5 Map Evidence

The Court finally reviewed the effect of maps produced by both parties in respect of their respective interpretations of Article IV of the Boundary Convention of 1891. In this context, Indonesia referred to various maps which supported its contention that the islands of Sipadan and Ligitan lay on their side of the boundary line. Some of the maps submitted by Indonesia included the Dutch Explanatory Memorandum Map of 1891; the 1903 BNBC map entitled "Borneo" published by Stanford, the official cartographer for the BNBC; the "Colony of North Borneo" map of 1953; the 1964 and 1965 maps published by the Survey Department of the British Ministry of Defence; the 1964, 1967 and 1972 maps published by the Malaysian Directorate of National Mapping; and the 1968 map published by Malaysian's Ministry of Lands and Mines.[28] Malaysia also submitted a number of maps, but it relied particularly on the map annexed to the Boundary Demarcation Agreement of 1915 between Britain and the Netherlands. According to Malaysia, this was the only official map agreed upon by the parties concerning the delimitation of the boundary between the State of North Borneo and Dutch Borneo. In addition to the 1915 map, Malaysia also submitted a number of Dutch maps; maps of British origin; a Malaysian map of 1976; and finally an Indonesian map of 1960. Malaysia contended that all these maps showed that the boundary line between the Dutch and British possessions in the area did not extend into the sea east of Sebatik and that Sipadan and Ligitan were regarded as belonging to Malaysia or its predecessor in title.[29]

The Court's view concerning the map evidence produced by both parties was that with the exception of the map annexed to the Boundary Demarcation Agreement of 1915, the cartographic material submitted by both parties was "inconclusive in respect of the interpretation of Article IV of the Boundary Convention of 1891".[30]

The Court summed up its findings on Indonesia's claim to possession of title based on the Boundary Convention of 1891 as follows:[31]

> The Court ultimately comes to the conclusion that Article IV, interpreted in its context and in the light of the object and purpose of the Convention, determines the boundary between the two Parties up to the eastern extremity of Sebatik Island and does not establish any allocation line further eastwards. That conclusion is confirmed both by the *travaux préparatoires* and by the subsequent conduct of the parties to the 1891 Convention.

8.3.1.6 Title by Succession

Indonesia had also claimed that it possessed the title to the two islands of Sipadan and Ligitan by virtue of being the successor to the Netherlands, which in turn acquired its title through contracts with the Sultan of Bulungan, the original title holder.[32] In this respect, Indonesia had also claimed that the islands of Sipadan and Ligitan were part of the "islets" belonging to the bigger islands of Tarakan, Nanukan, and Sebatik owned by the Sultanate of Bulungan. The Court rejected this contention of Indonesia on similar grounds, as explained earlier, that the islands of Sipadan and Ligitan did not belong to the group of "small islands" belonging to the bigger islands of Tarakan, Nanukan, and Sebatik. In concluding this section, the Court ruled that it could not accept Indonesian's contention "that it inherited title to the disputed islands from the Netherlands through these contracts, which stated that the Sultanate of Bulungan as described in the contracts formed part of the Netherlands Indies".[33]

8.3.1.7 The Court's Verdict on Indonesia's Claim to a Treaty-Based Title

The Court's judgment pertaining to the issue of a treaty-based title by Indonesia was as follows:[34]

> The Court .... found that the 1891 Convention does not provide Indonesia with a treaty-based title and that title to the islands did not pass to Indonesia as successor to the Netherlands and the Sultanate of Bulungan.

8.3.1.8 The Court's Views on Malaysia's Claim to a Treaty-Based Title

Having disposed of Indonesia's claims to a treaty-based title, the Court then considered Malaysia's claim to such a title.

(i) Succession and Chain of Transfers of Title

Malaysia's claim was also based on succession and a series of transfers of title from the purported original title-holder, the Sultan of Sulu. In this "chain" of transfers, the original title for Sipadan and Ligitan allegedly passed from Sulu in turn to Spain, the United States, Great Britain and finally to Malaysia. Malaysia substantiated the authenticity of this "chain" of transfers by referring to the Sulu Grants of 1878; the 1885 Madrid Protocol between Spain, Germany and Great Britain; the 1898 Treaty of Paris; the 1900 Convention between Spain and the United States; the 1907 Exchange of Notes between Britain and the United States; and the

Boundary Convention of 1930 between the last two parties mentioned.[35] From the onset, the Court observed that the islands of Sipadan and Ligitan were not mentioned by name in any of the international legal agreements presented by Malaysia to prove its case concerning the "chain" of transfers. Concerning Sulu's ownership of the two islands, the Court ruled that there was no documentary evidence showing conclusively that Sipadan and Ligitan were part of domains of the Sultan of Sulu. There was no evidence that Spain ever laid claim to the two islands. In the case of the United States, the Court was of the opinion that the events of 1903 showed that the State Department had "no clear idea of the territorial and maritime extent of the Philippine Archipelago" and the 1907 Exchange of Notes was ambiguous on the question of sovereignty. Concerning the Boundary Convention of 1930, the Court noted that the document did not mention any island by name, apart from the Turtle and Mangsee Islands.[36] The Court then delivered its views on the Boundary Convention of 1930 as follows:[37]

> By concluding the 1930 Convention, the United States relinquished any claim it might have had to Ligitan and Sipadan and to the neighbouring islands. But the Court cannot conclude either from the 1907 Exchange of Notes or from the 1930 Convention or from any document emanating from the United States Administration in the intervening period that the United State did claim sovereignty over these islands. It can, therefore, not be said with any degree of certainty that by the 1930 Convention the United States transferred title to Ligitan and Sipadan to Great Britain, as Malaysia asserts.

And then the Court made a rather contradictory observation which reads as follows:[38]

> On the other hand, the Court cannot let go unnoticed that Great Britain was of the opinion that as a result of the 1930 Convention it acquired, on behalf of the BNBC, title to all the islands beyond the 3-marine-league zone which had been administered by the Company, with the exception of the Turtle and the Mangsee Islands. To none of the islands lying beyond the 3-marine-league zone had it ever before laid a formal claim. Whether such title in the case of Ligitan and Sipadan and the neighbouring islands was indeed acquired as a result of the 1930 Convention is less relevant than the fact that Great Britain's position on the effect of this Convention was not contested by any other State.

(ii) The Court's Verdict on Malaysia's Claim to a Treaty-Based Title

The ICJ also rejected Malaysia's claim to a treaty-based title. Its verdict reads as follows:[39]

> the Court concludes that it cannot accept Malaysia's contention that there is an uninterrupted series of transfers of title from the alleged original title-holder, the Sultan of Sulu, to Malaysia as the present one. It has not been established with certainty that Ligitan and Sipadan belonged to the possessions of the Sultan of Sulu nor that any of the alleged subsequent title-holders had a treaty-based title to these two islands. The Court can therefore not find that Malaysia has inherited a treaty-based title from its predecessor, the United Kingdom of Great Britain and Northern Ireland.

Both the contending parties therefore failed to prove that they possessed a treaty-based title to the two disputed islands.

8.4 THE COURT'S CONSIDERATION OF *EFFECTIVITÉS*

Having dismissed the claims of both parties to a treaty-based title, the Court was therefore obliged to consider whether *effectivités* could provide the basis for a decision as to who had sovereignty over Sipadan and Ligitan. The Court observed that both parties had presented their submissions on *effectivités* merely as confirming a treaty-based title. The Court, however, decided to treat *effectivités* as an independent and separate issue altogether in the light of its findings that neither party had a treaty-based title to the two islands.[40]

Both Indonesia and Malaysia relied on *effectivités* to support each other's claims. Indonesia's case based on *effectivités*, however, was rather weak, as it and its predecessors in title, had not been in occupation of the two islands of Sipadan and Ligitan. On the other hand, *effectivités* was the linchpin of Malaysia's case as it argued convincingly that it, and its predecessors in title, the BNBC, and Britain had continuous and uninterrupted control and administration of the two islands since 1878.

8.4.1 Indonesia's *Effectivités*

Indonesia tried to salvage the situation by capitalizing on rather isolated acts of state activity pertaining to the two islands. One such highlighted incident was the visit of the Dutch destroyer, the *Lynx* to the two islands in November and December 1921. The naval expedition, Indonesia claimed,

"Constituted acts par excellence of the exercise of governmental authority with respect to the islands", thus confirming Dutch sovereignty over the islands. Indonesia further stated that between 1965 and 1969 its naval units made a number of visits to the islands. Moreover, Indonesian fisherman had traditionally conducted fishing activities on and around the two islands and sometimes stayed overnight on Sipadan Island.[41]

8.4.1.1 *The Court's Verdict on Indonesia's Effectivités*

Turning to *effectivités* relied upon by Indonesia, the Court observed from the onset that none of them were of a "legislative or regulatory nature." Referring to the cruise of the *Lynx* and other Dutch or Indonesian naval surveillance and patrol activities, the Court was of the view that it was unable to deduce whether the naval authorities concerned considered Ligitan and Sipadan to be under Dutch or Indonesian sovereignty. Concerning the traditional activities of Indonesian fishermen on the two islands, the Court ruled that these were activities by private persons and therefore could not be construed as constituting *effectivités* "if they do not take place on the basis of official regulations or under governmental authority."[42] The final verdict of the Court on Indonesian *effectivités* was as follows:[43]

> The Court concludes that the activities relied upon by Indonesia do not constitute acts *à titre de souverain* reflecting the intention and will to act in that capacity.

8.4.2 Malaysia's *Effectivités*

Malaysia, on the other hand, was able to present an impressive record of *effectivités* to support its claim of long and undisputed occupation and administration of the two islands since 1878. One of the *effectivités* cited by Malaysia was the control and regulation of the collection of turtle eggs on the two islands. From 1913 onwards, Company officials began issuing *surat kuasa* (licences) to well-known native residents of Semporna and Danawan Island for the collection of turtle eggs on Sipadan Island. In 1917, the Government of North Borneo passed the Turtle Preservation Ordinance. This ordinance was applied to Sipadan in 1919 when that island was declared a native reserve. From 1919 onwards, there was continuous enforcement of the Turtle Preservation Ordinance of 1917 on Sipadan Island.

Another example of state *effectivités* on the islands was the establishment of a bird sanctuary on Sipadan Island on 1 February 1933.

Further evidence of Malaysia's *effectivités* on the two islands was the construction of lighthouses by the Government of North Borneo on Sipadan and Ligitan in 1962 and 1963 respectively. These lighthouses still exist today and have been regularly maintained and administered by the Sabah Marine Department.[44]

8.4.2.1 *The Court's Verdict on Malaysia's Effectivités*

In the case of Malaysia, the Court accepted the measures to regulate and control the collection of turtle eggs and the establishment of a bird reserve "as regulatory and administrative assertions of authority" over the two islands. The maintenance of lighthouses by Malaysia and its predecessor, the Colony of North Borneo since 1962 and 1963 on the two islands was also accepted as a manifestation of state authority.

The Court further observed that the activities relied upon by Malaysia were modest in number, but they were "diverse in character" and included "legitimate, administrative and quasi-judicial acts". They were also spread over a considerable period of time and showed an intention to exercise state authority. The Court further observed that neither Indonesia nor the Netherlands ever protested against these activities till the dispute surfaced in 1969.[45] The verdict of the Court concerning Malaysia's *effectivités* was as follows:[46]

> Given the circumstances of the case, and in particular in view of the evidence furnished by the Parties, the Court concludes that Malaysia has title to Ligitan and Sipadan on the basis of the *effectivités* referred to above.

8.5 THE COURT'S FINAL VERDICT ON THE CASE

In its final judgment, the Court ruled, by sixteen votes to one, that sovereignty over the two islands of Sipadan and Ligitan belonged to Malaysia. The full text of the operative paragraph of the Judgment reads as follows:[47]

> For these reasons,
>
> THE COURT,
>
> By sixteen votes to one,
>
> Finds that sovereignty over Pulau Ligitan and Pulau Sipadan belongs to Malaysia.

IN FAVOUR: President Guillaume; Vice-President Shi; Judges Oda, Ranjeva, Herczegh, Fleischhauer, Koroma, Vereshchetin, Higgins, Parra-Aranguren, Kooijmans, Rezek, Al-Khasawneh, Buergenthal, Elaraby; Judge ad hoc Weeramantry:

AGAINST: Judge ad hoc Franck.

Notes

1. International Court of Justice (ICJ), *Judgment, Case Concerning Sovereignty Over Pulau Ligitan and Pulau Sipadan (Indonesia/Malaysia)*, The Hague, Netherlands, 17 December 2002, paras. 1–11, pp. 1–12 (hereafter cited as *ICJ Judgment, Case Concerning Ligitan and Sipadan*).
2. Ibid., para. 13, p. 12.
3. Ibid., para. 13, p. 12.
4. Ibid., para. 32, p. 21.
5. ICJ, *Case Concerning Sovereignty Over Pulau Ligitan and Pulau Sipadan (Indonesia/Malaysia), Memorial of Malaysia*, vol. 1, 1999, para. 2–3, p. 3 (hereafter cited as *Memorial of Malaysia*, vol. 1).
6. *ICJ Judgment, Case Concerning Ligitan and Sipadan*, para. 33, p. 21.
7. ICJ, *Case Concerning Sovereignty over Pulau Ligitan and Pulau Sipadan (Indonesia/Malaysia), Memorial Submitted by the Government of the Republic of Indonesia*, vol. 1, 2 November 1999, para. 5.1, p. 61 (hereafter cited as the *Memorial of Indonesia*, vol. 1).
8. *ICJ Judgment, Case Concerning Ligitan and Sipadan*, para. 34, p. 21.
9. Ibid., para. 34, p. 22.
10. *Memorial of Indonesia*, vol. 1, para. 5.43, pp. 83–86.
11. *ICJ Judgment, Case Concerning Ligitan and Sipadan*, para. 40, p. 24.
12. *Memorial of Malaysia*, vol. 1, para. 8.1–8.12, pp. 87–91.
13. *ICJ Judgment, Case Concerning Ligitan and Sipadan*, paras. 41, 42 and 43, pp. 25–26.
14. *Memorial of Indonesia*, vol. 1, paras. 5.50 and 5.51, p. 88; and ICJ, *Verbatim Record in the Case Concerning Sovereignty over Pulau Ligitan and Pulau Sipadan (Indonesia/Malaysia)*, 3 June 2002, 3.00 p.m., para. 60, p. 22 (hereafter cited as *Verbatim Record*).
15. *Memorial of Indonesia*, vol. 1, para. 5.63, pp. 95–96.
16. *Verbatim Record*, 3 June 2002, para. 66, p. 23.
17. *Memorial of Malaysia*, vol. 1, paras. 9.4–9.5, p. 97.
18. *ICJ Judgment, Case Concerning Ligitan and Sipadan*, paras. 47 and 48, pp. 27 and 28.
19. Ibid., paras. 59–61, pp. 32–33.
20. *Memorial of Indonesia*, vol. 1, para. 5.43(c) and (d), p. 84; and *Verbatim Record*, 3 June 2002, 10.00 a.m., p. 22.

21. *ICJ Judgment, Case Concerning Ligitan and Sipadan*, para. 52, p. 30.
22. Ibid., para. 62, p. 33.
23. *Memorial of Indonesia*, vol. 1, paras. 4.66–4.71, pp. 58–60; and *Verbatim Record*, 3 June 2002, 10.00 a.m., p. 21.
24. *ICJ Judgment, Case Concerning Ligitan and Sipadan*, para. 64, pp. 33–34.
25. Ibid., para. 71–72, pp. 36–38.
26. Ibid., para. 79, p. 40. For more details of Indonesia's submissions see *Memorial of Indonesia*, vol. 1, pp. 104–9.
27. *ICJ Judgment, Case Concerning Ligitan and Sipadan*, para. 80, p. 40. See para. 52, p. 30 for the Court's earlier judgment on the interpretation of the Boundary Convention of 1891.
28. See *Memorial of Indonesia*, vol. 1, pp. 113–27.
29. For more details, see *Memorial of Malaysia*, vol. 1, pp. 107–13.
30. *ICJ Judgment, Case Concerning Ligitan and Sipadan*, para. 91, p. 44.
31. Ibid., para. 92, p. 44.
32. For more details, see *Memorial of Indonesia*, vol. 1, pp. 55–60. Also see *Verbatim Record*, 3 June 2002, 10.00 a.m., pp. 21–37.
33. *ICJ Judgment, Case Concerning Ligitan and Sipadan*, para. 96, pp. 44–45.
34. Ibid., para. 125, p. 52.
35. Ibid., para. 97, p. 45. Also see *Memorial of Malaysia*, vol. 1, pp. 29–59.
36. *ICJ Judgment, Case Concerning Ligitan and Sipadan*, paras. 117–19, pp. 51–52.
37. Ibid., para. 120, p. 52.
38. Ibid., para. 121, p. 52.
39. Ibid., para. 124, p. 52.
40. Ibid., para. 127, p. 53.
41. For more details, see *Memorial of Indonesia*, vol. 1, pp. 101–4.
42. *ICJ Judgment, Case Concerning Ligitan and Sipadan*, paras. 137–40, p. 57.
43. Ibid., para. 141, p. 57.
44. *Memorial of Malaysia*, vol. 1, pp. 60–71.
45. *ICJ Judgment, Case Concerning Ligitan and Sipadan*, paras. 145–48, pp. 58 and 59.
46. Ibid., para. 149, p. 59.
47. Ibid., para. 150, p. 60.

9

Conclusion

9.1 INTRODUCTION

Malaysia has had the experience of submitting two cases to the International Court of Justice (ICJ) for resolution. One involved the Sipadan and Ligitan case between Malaysia and Indonesia. This dispute between Malaysia and Indonesia over the ownership of these two islands developed in 1969, which is called the "critical date". The case was filed with the ICJ for arbitration on 2 November 1998. The ICJ delivered its verdict on 17 December 2002 awarding Malaysia sovereignty over the two disputed islands.[1]

The second case involved the question of disputed sovereignty between Malaysia and Singapore over three maritime features, that is, Pulau Batu Puteh (Pedra Branca), Middle Rocks and South Ledge. In this case, the dispute emerged on 14 February 1980 when Singapore protested against the 1979 Malaysian map which showed Pulau Batu Puteh lying within Malaysian territorial waters. The issue of sovereignty over Middle Rocks and South Ledge emerged much later on 6 February 1993 when Singapore first brought it up in conjunction with the Pulau Batu Puteh claim. The dispute over these three marine features was filed with the Registry of the ICJ on 24 July 2003. Judgment day was 23 May 2008, but because of the nature of the case, and due to differing circumstances, three separate judgments were delivered. The court ruled, by a vote of 12-4, that sovereignty over Pulau Batu Puteh belonged to Singapore. Sovereignty over Middle Rocks was awarded to Malaysia with fifteen judges ruling in favour of Malaysia and one judge, dissenting. In the case of South Ledge, the court concluded, 15-1, that sovereignty over this feature belonged to the state in the territorial waters of which it is located.[2]

9.2 CARDINAL PRINCIPLES OF INTERNATIONAL LAW

A number of important prerequisites and cardinal principles may be noted concerning the operation of International Law and the preferences of the ICJ pertaining to cases involving territorial disputes by using these two cases as a referral point. These are presented below.

9.2.1 Prerequisites for Proving Ownership

A country has to fulfil the following requirements in order to show that it has ownership or sovereignty over a piece of disputed territory:

(a) It must possess an original legal title to the said territory.
(b) It has had long control of the territory concerned and has conducted substantial and continuous *effectivités*.
(c) It acquired the said territory (islands and maritime features) through the operation of the United Nations Law of the Sea (UNCLOS).

9.2.2 Possession of an Original Legal Title is Paramount

A country may use the following bases to prove possession of a legal title which is considered paramount by the ICJ:

(a) Historical ownership
(b) A treaty or treaties
(c) Succession
(d) Or any combination of the above three sources.

To prove the possession of a valid title, a contestant must advance convincing arguments and evidence concerning the following items to support its case:

i. Solid and unassailable evidence regarding historical ownership.
ii. Detailed contextual interpretation of the terms of a relevant treaty or treaties.
iii. The purpose and intent of a treaty or treaties.
iv. The initial discussions and agreements prior to the conclusion of a treaty or treaties.
v. Subsequent agreements.
vi. Subsequent practice.
vii. Succession.

Maps attached to and forming part of the relevant treaty or treaties should also be tendered as evidence as they are considered vital for a more accurate interpretation and validation of the text and contents of treaties used.

9.2.3 A Country May Lose an Original Title
A country may have an original title to a territory, but may eventually lose it due to the following circumstances:

(a) An absence of a proper agreement, as was the case with Malaysia's title over Pulau Batu Puteh.
(b) Through transfer by a treaty.
(c) Through lack of exercise of *effectivités* (Malaysia's lack of *effectivités* over Pulau Batu Puteh after 1844; Sulu's and Philippine's lack of *effectivités* over Sabah since 1878).
(d) Or any combination of the above.
(e) Through silence or acquiesce. According to the ICJ, the law on silence is as follows:[3]

> Under certain circumstances, sovereignty over territory might pass as a result of the failure of the State which has sovereignty to respond to conduct *á titre de souverain* of the other State or, as Judge Huber put it in *Island of Palmas* case, to concrete manifestations of the display of territorial sovereignty by the other State (*Island of Palmas Case (Netherlands/United States of America)*, Award of 4 April 1928, *RIAA*, vol. II, p. 839). Such manifestations of the display of sovereignty may call for a response if they are not to be opposable to the State in question. The absence of reaction may well amount to acquiescence. The concept of acquiescence "is equivalent to tacit recognition manifested by unilateral conduct which the other party may interpret as consent…" *(Delimitation of the Maritime Boundary in the Gulf Maine Area (Canada/United States of America), Judgment, I.C.J. Report 1984, p. 305, para. 130)*. That is to say, silence may also speak, but only if the conduct of the State calls for a response.

9.2.4 The Importance of *Effectivités* or Conduct of the Parties
This principle gains prominence when both the parties are unable to prove possession of a title. (A good example is the Sipadan and Ligitan case.)

9.2.5 The "Critical Date"
In cases involving disputes concerning sovereignty over contested territories, the ICJ gives particular importance to the date on which a dispute

crystallized. This date is called the "Critical Date". The Critical Date is important because in awarding sovereignty, the ICJ takes into consideration only those acts performed by the contestants before that date and not after. With regards to the Sipadan and Ligitan case, the ICJ fixed 1969 as the Critical Date and observed as follows:[4]

> The Court further observes that it cannot take into consideration acts having taken place after the date on which the dispute between the Parties crystallized unless such acts are a normal continuation of prior acts and are not undertaken for the purpose of improving the legal position of the Party which relies on them (see the Arbitral Award in the *Palena* case, 38 International Law reports *(ILR)*, pp. 79–80). The Court will, therefore, primarily, analyse the *effectivités* which date from the period before 1969, the year in which the Parties asserted conflicting claims to Ligitan and Sipadan.

In the case involving sovereignty over Pulau Batu Puteh, Middle Rocks, and South Ledge, the ICJ decided that the Critical Date for Pulau Batu Puteh was 14 February 1980, while for Middle Rocks and South Ledge, it was 6 February 1993.[5] Rival claimants, therefore, must take particular cognizance of this rule as activity undertaken after the Critical Date will not strengthen their claims.

9.2.6 Provision for a Revision of an ICJ Judgment
Under Article 61 of the Statute of the ICJ, a party to a dispute is allowed to make an application for revision of an ICJ judgment if it fulfills the following conditions:[6]

(a) a new fact of a decisive nature is discovered by the party seeking revision; that this new fact was unknown to the Court and the party claiming revision at the time the Judgment was given; and that such ignorance was not due to negligence (Article 61/1)
(b) the request for revision must be made within six months of the discovery of the new fact (Article 61/4)
(c) an application for revision must be made within ten years of the ICJ Judgment (Article 61/5)

The Court will then decide whether an application for revision has fulfilled the conditions laid down and is therefore admissible for revision. Once it decides that the application is admissible, then only will proceedings for revision be opened by the court (Article 61/2).

9.2.7 Congruence of *Effectivités* and Principle of Self-Determination

Effectivités may justifiably be used to award sovereignty over unoccupied islands and other maritime features. What about large territories with substantial populations such as Sabah and Indian Kashmir? Here the principle of self-determination may also be taken into consideration in addition to *effectivités*. In the case of Sabah, there is a happy congruence of *effectivités* (long rule by the BNBC and the British Government) and self-determination.

9.3 A Review of the Application of These Principles with Reference to the Two Cases under Consideration

9.3.1 The Paramountcy of a Valid Title Based on Historical Ownership, a Treaty or Treaties, or Succession

It is manifestly clear from an analysis of the two cases mentioned above that the ICJ gives priority preference to possession of a valid title. The two contestants in the first case, that is, Indonesia and Malaysia knew fully well of the importance of holding and proving a valid title.

In this context it must be noted, as discussed in Chapter 6, that Indonesia believed that legal title was paramount and no amount of subsequent *effectivités* could displace such a title, they could only enhance it. As such the linchpin of its submissions was that it held legal title over these two islands as a result of succession; the Anglo-Dutch Boundary Convention of 1891; and the process of ratification of the said Convention which involved proceedings in the Dutch Parliament especially those pertaining to the Explanatory Memorandum Map of 1891. It also submitted a number of maps. Its pretensions to such a title, however, were weak; its interpretation of the Boundary Convention of 1891 was punctuated with loopholes; the Dutch Explanatory Memorandum Map of 1891 was an internal map, not a treaty map; and the historical basis for the ownership of the two islands as a result of succession to the territorial possessions of the Sultan of Bulungan, was rather dubious. In these circumstances, the ICJ rejected Indonesia's claims of possessing a valid title.

Malaysia, too, presented a strong case pertaining to the issue of holding a valid title. Malaysia's case was based on a long "chain" of transfers and eventual succession. Malaysia attempted to prove that it was the Sulu Sultanate which was the original owner of the two islands. This ownership changed hands from the Sulu Sultanate to Spain, from Spain to the United States and eventually to the British (the Boundary Convention of 1930). As discussed in Chapter 8, the ICJ rejected the authenticity of the chain of transfers. The end result was that the ICJ rejected both Indonesia's and Malaysia's claims to possession of a valid title to the two islands.

My own view is that the ICJ's judgment pertaining to Malaysia's claim of possessing a legal title was unfortunate as the claim was based on solid documentary evidence since at least 1903. In that year, the United States proclaimed sovereignty over the islands of Sipadan and Ligitan by name. This event, together with the 1907 Exchange of Notes and the "Durand" Map attached to them, clearly showed that the United States exercised sovereignty over these islands. By the Boundary Convention of 1930, the United States in effect transferred its sovereignty over the two islands to Britain, although the two islands were not mentioned by name. The title held by the United States and its transfer to Britain was grounded on strong documentary evidence. The rejection of this well-documented and valid title by the ICJ is even more confounding when the Court itself viewed that it could not totally neglect Great Britain's claims. The Court had this to say on the matter:[7]

> On the other hand, the Court cannot let go unnoticed that Great Britain was of the opinion that as a result of the 1930 Convention it acquired, on behalf of the BNBC, title to all islands beyond the 3-marine-league zone which had been administered by the Company ... Whether such title in the case of Ligitan and Sipadan and the neighbouring islands was indeed acquired as a result of the 1930 Convention is less relevant than the fact that Great Britain's position on the effect of this Convention was not contested by any other State.

So, if the Court could not disregard Britain's "opinion" pertaining to its acquisition of title over all the islands beyond the three marine leagues zone which had been administered by the BNBC [and these definitely included the islands of Sipadan and Ligitan], then the Court's verdict on this matter stood in stark contradiction to its own views.

A good example of the paramountcy of a legal title for awarding of sovereignty is the case of Middle Rocks. In this case, Malaysia proved that it had the original title to Middle Rocks through historical circumstances and never lost it. On the strength of continued possession of this original title, the ICJ awarded sovereignty over the disputed feature of Middle Rocks to Malaysia. The Court's view on the matter was as follows:[8]

> Since Middle Rocks should be understood to have had the same legal status as Pedra Branca/Pulau Batu Puteh as far as the ancient original title held by the Sultan of Johor was concerned, and since the particular circumstances which have come to effect the passing of title to Pedra Branca/Pulau Batu Puteh to Singapore do not apply to this maritime feature, original title to Middle Rocks should remain with Malaysia as the successor to the Sultan of Johor, unless proven otherwise, which the Court finds Singapore has not done.

A country may obtain a valid title to a piece of territory through the instrument of an International Treaty. Good examples of such instances include the acquisition of sovereignty by the United States over the Philippines from Spain through the Treaty of Paris of 1898 and the Convention of 1900. Another case that has been causing strained relations between Malaysia and the Philippines is the ongoing Sabah claim by the latter. The Philippine claim to Sabah is basically rooted in the 1878 Grants by the Sultan of Sulu to the Overbeck-Dent Association (ODA). In the same year, six months later, Sulu capitulated to Spain which therefore acquired sovereign powers over the former possessions of the Sulu Sultanate. Whatever the controversy over the interpretation of the terms of the 1878 Sulu Grants to the ODA, it is eminently clear that Spain surrendered her sovereignty over all the former possessions of the Sultan of Sulu in Borneo to Britain by the Madrid Protocol of 7 March 1885. It is valid to conclude that Britain acquired a legal title over the former territorial possessions of the Sulu Sultanate in Borneo, that is, Sabah, through the Protocol of 1885 which was a recognized International Treaty between Britain, Spain, and Germany. Another example that may be useful to examine is the case of the Senkaku/Diaoyu Islands which are presently controlled by Japan, but China is staking a claim to them. In this case, it may be said that these islands originally belonged to China on historical grounds. However, as a result of the Sino-Japanese War of 1894–95, China lost the war and was forced to sign the Treaty of Shimonoseki. Although the Diaoyu Islands were not part of the treaty concessions, Japan annexed these islands as war booty. Conflicting claims by these two powers over these islands have heightened security concerns in the region.[9]

9.3.2 Losing a Valid Original Title

Another principle to bear in mind is that a country may have a valid original title to a territory but may lose it due to failure in entering into a binding agreement with a tenant or failure to produce such an agreement. A good example is the case of Pulau Batu Puteh. In this case, the ICJ accepted Malaysia's contention that it had indeed possessed the original title to the island, but only till 1844. In this context, the Court held the following view:[10]

> In the light of the forgoing, the Court concludes that Malaysia has established to the satisfaction of the Court that as of the time when the British started their preparations for the construction of the lighthouse on Pedra Branca/Pulau Batu Puteh in 1844, this island was under the sovereignty of the Sultan of Johor.

The situation after 1844 became different. In 1844, the British, who were then ruling Singapore, obtained permission from the Government of Johor (Malaysia) to build and operate a lighthouse on Pulau Batu Puteh. Documentary evidence, however, was unable to furnish the exact terms of the permission given by the Johor Government for the construction of the lighthouse on Pulau Batu Puteh. In these circumstances, the Court was of the view that the 1844 correspondence was extremely vague and inconclusive as to whether Pulau Batu Puteh was ceded to the British as claimed by Singapore, or whether it was only leased as claimed by Malaysia. In the absence of such evidence, the Court could not accept Malaysia's contention that Singapore was only given the rights of a lighthouse operator. The Court's views on the matter were as follows:[11]

> Against the background of extensive legal regulation in agreements between the sovereign of the territory where the lighthouse was to operate and European States, the Court observes the lack, in the case of Pedra Branca/Pulau Batu Puteh, of any written agreement between the Johor and the British authorities regulating in some detail the relationship between them and their related rights and obligations. The Johor authorities did not provide for instance for the maintenance of their sovereignty and their rights to repossess the land in the event that conditions relating to the operation of the lighthouse were not satisfied. Further, while at the hearing before the Court the Agent of Malaysia stated that "Malaysia has always respected the position of Singapore as operator of Horsburgh lighthouse and I would like to place formally on

record that Malaysia will continue to do so," Malaysia has at no time attempted to spell out in any detail at all the rights and obligations of "Singapore as operator".

Since the question of title could now no longer be determined definitely and was considered an unsafe ground to rely upon, the Court decided to judge the case based on the conduct of the Parties after 1844. It may be concluded that the failure of the Johor Government to either conclude or produce (if it indeed had such an agreement) a legal written agreement with Singapore, clearly spelling out that Pulau Batu Puteh was leased and not ceded, cost Malaysia its title.[12]

9.3.3 *Effectivités* and *À titre de Souverain* Gain Prominence

Next in importance to a valid title is the principle of *effectivités* and *à titre de souverain*. The first pertains to the acts of a state in instituting or exercising legal and administrative authority over a disputed territory. *À titre de Souverain* refers to the intention, the will and the capacity to act as a sovereign and the actual exercise of authority as a sovereign over a piece of territory. In considering *effectivités* and *à titre de souverain*, the ICJ first determines whether a party to a conflict had the legal status to act as a Sovereign over the disputed territory. In the Sipadan and Ligitan case, the Court decided that Britain did not have that capacity over the two islands before the Boundary Convention of 1930, as it was the United States which had sovereignty over these two islands till then. Despite holding this view, the Court was, however, unwilling to ignore the administrative activities undertaken by the BNBC pertaining to the two islands since at least 1907. The Court's position on this issue was as follows:[13]

> With regard to the *effectivités* relied upon by Malaysia, the Court first observes that pursuant to the 1930 Convention, the United States relinquished any claim it might have had to Ligitan and Sipadan and that no other State asserted its sovereignty over those islands at that time or objected to their continued administration by the State of North Borneo. The Court further observes that those activities which took place before the conclusion of that Convention cannot be seen as acts "*à titre de souverain*", as Great Britain did not at that time claim sovereignty on behalf of the State of North Borneo over the islands beyond the 3-marine-league limit. Since it, however, took the position that the BNBC was entitled to administer the islands, a position which after 1907 was formally recognized by the United States, these administrative activities cannot be ignored either.

In the Sipadan and Ligitan case, both Indonesia and Malaysia used *effectivités* to support their respective claims. Indonesia, however, gave greater emphasis to a title and had very little to offer in terms of administrative or legal activities over the two islands. This was mainly due to the fact that Indonesia and its predecessors in title were not in actual control of the two islands. Malaysia, on the other hand, gave greater prominence to *effectivités*, although it also presented a strong case pertaining to the possession of a title. Malaysia's *effectivités* were strong because the BNBC began to administer these two islands and another twenty or so from its inception in 1882 under the mistaken notion that they were part of the territorial concessions granted to the ODA in 1878 by the Sultan of Sulu, although they were beyond the three marine leagues limit. Even when this mistake was discovered by the US authorities in the Philippines in 1903, the BNBC was allowed to continue administering these islands by the United States which however reserved sovereignty for itself. In the circumstances, the BNBC, and then the Colonial Government and even Malaysia conducted various legal and administrative activities in a continuous fashion on the two islands from 1882 to 1969. Malaysia's *effectivités* were therefore substantial and continuous compared to Indonesia's which were weak and almost lacking. The fact is Malaysia's predecessors in title exercised jurisdiction over the two islands in a persistent, active, and conscious manner, while Indonesia's *effectivités*, if there were any, were incidental. This is an important cue for keeping control over a piece of territory.

This very same principle operated in the Pulau Batu Puteh case. Malaysia did not show any strong inclination, interest, will or capacity to take control of jurisdiction over Pulau Batu Puteh after 1844. As had been discussed earlier in this chapter, the ICJ decided to judge the case based on the conduct of the Parties after 1844. In considering Malaysia's *effectivités* after this date, the Court first paid attention to the period from 1844 to 1953. On an overall basis, the Court did not find much to support Malaysia's *effectivités*, not even the presence of any Johor dignitary or representative at the stone laying ceremony of the Horsburgh lighthouse on 15 October 1851. The Court was also of the opinion that correspondence, legislation, and historical developments from 1844 to 1952 were inconclusive to prove either Malaysia's or Singapore's sovereignty over Pulau Batu Puteh.[14]

The Court then turned its attention to the 1953 correspondence which was given a great deal of prominence by both parties. On 12 June 1953, the Colonial Secretary of Singapore wrote the following letter addressed to the British Adviser to the Government of Johor:[15]

I am directed to ask for information about the rock some 40 miles from Singapore known as Pedra Branca on which the Horsburgh Lighthouse stands. The matter is relevant to the determination of the boundaries of the Colony's territorial waters. It appears this rock is outside the limits ceded by Sultan Hussain and the Dato Tumunggong to the East India Company with the island of Singapore in the Treaty of 1824 (extract at "A"). It was however mentioned in a despatch from the Governor of Singapore on 28th November 1844 (extract at "B"). The Lighthouse was built in 1850 by the Colony Government who have maintained it ever since. This by international usage no doubt confers some rights and obligations on the Colony.

2. In the case of Pulau Pisang which is also outside the Treaty limits of the colony it has been possible to trace an indenture in the Johore Registry of Deeds dated 6th October, 1900. This shows that a part of Pulau Pisang was granted to the Crown for the purposes of building a lighthouse. Certain conditions were attached and it is clear that there was no abrogation of the sovereignty of Johore. The status of Pisang is quite clear.

3. In is how [now] desired to clarify the status of Pedra Branca. I would therefore be most grateful to know whether there is any document showing a lease or grant of the rock or whether it has been ceded by the Government of the State of Johore or in any other way disposed of.

4. A copy of this letter is being sent to the Chief Secretary, Kuala Lumpur.

Three months later, the Acting State Secretary of Johor replied as follows:[16]

I have the honour to refer to your letter...dated 12th June 1953, addressed to the British Adviser, Johore, on the question of the status of Pedra Branca Rock some 40 miles from Singapore and to inform you that the Johore Government does not claim ownership of Pedra Branca.

This reply from the Acting State Secretary of Johor was detrimental to Malaysia's case. Although the Court ruled that the denial by Johor "cannot be interpreted as a binding undertaking," it was of the opinion that the statement "has major significance".[17] What is more disturbing, however, is the inaction of the Chief Secretary of the Federation of Malaya who was sent a copy of the Colonial Secretary of Singapore's letter of 12 June 1953. A reply from him was of paramount importance to Malaysia's case as the jurisdiction over territorial sovereignty now rested with the Federal Government and not the State of Johor (Malaya had become a Federation in

1948 and Johor was part of the new federation). Silence can be detrimental. Or was there a reply from the Chief Secretary of the Federation and the research team failed to locate it?

Another point to note is that Malaysian officials or citizens wishing to undertake visits to Pulau Batu Puteh were required to obtain permission from the Singapore authorities. Singapore contended that it exercised exclusive control on visits to the island, whether undertaken by Singapore or Malaysian officials, citizens, and institutions. At no time, Singapore argued, did Malaysia protest against Singapore's regulations requiring those officials to obtain permits from it. In fact, in 1978, Malaysian officials from the Survey Department were told to leave the island as they had not obtained proper permits from the relevant Singapore authorities. The Court accordingly ruled that Singapore's conduct in this matter tantamounted to acts *à titre de souverain*.

In evaluating the Conduct of the Parties from 1953 to 1980 it may be noted that Singapore's activities during the later phase were numerous, and many had the character of acts *à titre de souverain*, which is, not just related to the operation and maintenance of the lighthouse. On the other hand, Malaysia had few such activities, and in many cases, such as the Acting State Secretary of Johor's letter of 1953, and the maps of 1962–75, they were detrimental to Malaysia's interest.[18] In the final analysis, Malaysia lost its case over Pulau Batu Puteh firstly because it lost its historical title due to the absence of a proper agreement of lease and secondly due to lack of activities tantamounting to acts *à titre de souverain*.

9.3.4 Activating the Process for Revision of Judgment

On 2 February 2017, Malaysia filed an application for revision of the judgment delivered by the ICJ on 23 May 2008 in which the said Court found, *inter alia*, that sovereignty over the island of Pedra Branca/Pulau Batu Puteh belonged to Singapore.[19] In its application, Malaysia contended that "there exists a new fact of such a nature as to be a decisive factor within the meaning of Article 61". In this context, Malaysia referred to the discovery of three important documents which were not at all known to its team at the time of the 2008 judgment as they were only released to the public by the National Archives of the United Kingdom after the said judgment was made. As such, it contended that its ignorance of the new fact was not due to negligence and so its application also fulfilled this particular requirement of Article 61 of the Statute. Malaysia further submitted that its application for revision complied with the Court's provision concerning the timing of the application, that is, it was submitted within six months of the discovery of the new fact (4 August 2016) and within ten years of the judgment being made (2008). In conclusion, Malaysia requested the Court to adjudge and declare that its application for revision of the 2008 judgment was admissible and to fix the schedule to proceed with consideration of the merits of the application. On 24 May 2017, Singapore filed its rebuttal contending that the documents relied upon by Malaysia did not satisfy the criteria under which it applied for revision of the judgment.

On 30 June 2017, Malaysia filed a second application for revision of the 2008 judgment. In its second application, Malaysia asked the ICJ to declare the waters around Pedra Branca to be Malaysian waters, and by extension that South Ledge belonged to Malaysia. On 30 October 2017, Singapore filed its rebuttal to Malaysia's second application. The ICJ fixed public hearings from 11 to 13 and 18 June 2018 for the first case and 18 to 19 and 21 to 22 June 2018 for the second case. However, in an interesting twist to the whole episode, the Malaysian Government for reasons as yet unknown, suddenly informed the ICJ on 28 May 2018 that it was withdrawing its application for revision of the 2008 judgment. On 29 May 2018, the ICJ informed both Singapore and Malaysia that it had placed on record the discontinuance of the case. Malaysia's withdrawal means that it can no longer challenge Singapore's sovereignty over Pedra Branca as the ten-year window for revision lapsed on 23 May 2018.[20]

9.3.5 Mandating the ICJ to Delimit National Maritime Zones

Another lesson we can learn from the two cases discussed above is that it is not sufficient to request the ICJ to rule on the sovereignty issue alone, without also mandating it to resolve the problem of overlapping maritime zones between the contending parties. This is because even after the sovereignty issue has been settled, the problem of unresolved maritime boundaries continue to cause intense friction and tension between the parties concerned. In fact, in the Pulau Batu Puteh, Middle Rocks and South Ledge case, the Court implied that the absence of such a mandate led it to deliver a rather inconclusive judgment on South Ledge. The Court recorded its views on this matter as follows:[21]

> The Court recalls that in the Special Agreement and in the final submissions it has been specifically asked to decide the matter of sovereignty separately for each of the three maritime features. At the same time the Court has not been mandated by the Parties to draw the line of delimitation with

respect to the territorial waters of Malaysia and Singapore in the area in question.

In these circumstances, the Court concludes that for the reasons explained above sovereignty over South Ledge, as a low-tide elevation, belongs to the State in the territorial waters of which it is located.

To sum up, we may say that in cases involving territorial disputes, a contestant's position becomes immediately stronger if it possesses a valid title based on historical grounds, a valid treaty or succession. However, such a title can be lost if a lease is made without a proper comprehensive agreement. A lease agreement should also spell out clearly the retention of sovereignty, a definite time span of the lease (unlike the Sulu Grants of 1878), and the payment of a rental. In the eventuality that both parties are unable to prove possession of a valid title, then strong *effectivités*, and the operation of the Law of the Sea become powerful bases for winning sovereignty. The principle of self-determination can become an additional factor in territories which have a substantial population.

Notes

1. For a general review of the Sipadan and Ligitan Case, see D.S. Ranjit Singh, "Boundary Delineation in the Sabah-Indonesia-Philippine Region: The Sipadan and Ligitan Case at the ICJ", *AdRem, Journal of the Selangor Bar* 1 (2006): 31–41.
2. See International Court of Justice (ICJ), *Judgment, Sovereignty over Pedra Branca/ Pulau Batu Puteh, Middle Rocks and South Ledge (Malaysia/Singapore)*, The Hague, Netherlands, 23 May 2008, pp. 80–81 (hereafter cited as *ICJ Judgment, Sovereignty over Pedra Branca*).
3. Ibid., para. 121, p. 37.
4. ICJ, *Judgment, Case Concerning Sovereignty over Pulau Ligitan and Pulau Sipadan (Indonesia/Malaysia)*, The Hague, Netherlands, 17 December 2002, para. 135, p. 56 (hereafter cited as *ICJ Judgment, Case Concerning Ligitan and Sipadan*).
5. ICJ, *Judgment, Sovereignty over Pedra Branca*, para. 34, p. 17.
6. For more details, see *ICJ Press Release*, 3 February 2017, No. 2017/6, The Hague, Netherlands (www.icj-cij.org). Also see Article 61 of the Statute of the ICJ, ibid.
7. ICJ, *Judgment, Case Concerning Ligitan and Sipadan*, para. 121, p. 52.
8. ICJ, *Judgment, Sovereignty over Pedra Branca*, para. 290, p. 78.
9. For details of the Sino-Japanese War of 1894–95 and the Treaty of Shimonoseki, 1895, see Warren I. Cohen, *East Asia At the Center* (New York: Colombia University Press, 2000), pp. 285–91.
10. ICJ, *Judgment, Sovereignty over Pedra Branca*, para. 117, p. 36.

11. Ibid., para. 144, p. 44.
12. See D.S. Ranjit Singh, "The Pedra Branca/Pulau Batu Puteh Case at the International Court of Justice (ICJ): Some Observations", in *The Seas Divide: Geopolitics and Maritime Issues in Southeast Asia*, edited by Jatswan S. Sidhu and K.S. Balakrishnan (Kuala Lumpur: Institute of Ocean and Earth Sciences, University of Malaya, 2008), pp. 83–96.
13. ICJ, *Judgment, Case Concerning Ligitan and Sipadan*, para. 142, p. 58.
14. Ranjit Singh, "The Pedra Branca/Pulau Batu Puteh Case at the ICJ", p. 86.
15. ICJ, *Judgment, Sovereignty over Pedra Branca*, para. 192, pp. 55–56.
16. Ibid., para. 196, p. 56.
17. Ibid., paras. 227 and 275, pp. 53 and 75.
18. Ibid., paras. 238 and 239, pp. 65 and 66.
19. For details, see *ICJ Press Release*, 3 February 2017, No. 2017/6, The Hague, Netherlands.
20. *Straits Times*, 30 May 2018.
21. ICJ, *Judgment, Sovereignty over Pedra Branca*, paras. 298 and 299, p. 80.

APPENDIXES

APPENDIX A

The Madrid Protocol, 1885

PROTOCOL BETWEEN GREAT BRITAIN, GERMANY AND SPAIN, SIGNED AT MADRID, 7 MARCH 1885

The undersigned, Sir Robert B.D. Morier, Envoy Extra-ordinary and Minister Plenipotentiary of Her Britannic Majesty, his Excellency Don Jose Elduayen, Marquis del Pazo de la Merced, Minister of State of his Majesty the King of Spain, and Count Soloms Sonnenwale, Envoy Extraordinary and Minister Plenipotentairy of His Majesty the German Emperor, duly authorized to bring to a close the negotiations conducted in London and at Berlin during the years 1881–82 by the Representatives of His Majesty the King of Spain at the Courts of Great Britain and Germany, for the purpose of obtaining from these two Powers the formal recognition of the sovereignty of Spain over the Archipelago of Sulu (Jolo), have agreed upon the following Articles:-

ARTICLE I

The Government of Great Britain and of Germany recognize the sovereignty of Spain over the places effectively occupied, as well as over those places not yet occupied, of the Archipelago of Sulu (Jolo), of which the limits are laid down in Article II.

Source: J. de V. Allen, A.J. Stockwell and L.R. Wright, eds., *A Collection of Treaties and Other Documents Affecting the States of Malaysia, 1791–1963*, vol. 2 (London: Oceana Publications, 1981), pp. 465–68.

ARTICLE II

The Archipelago of Sulu (Jolo), conformably to the definition contained in Article I of the treaty signed September 23rd, 1836, between the Spanish Government and the Sultan of Sulu (Jolo), comprises all the islands which are found between the western extremity of the island of Mindanao on the one side, and the continent of Borneo and the Island of Paragua on the other side, with the exception of those which are indicated in Article III.

It is understood that the Islands of Balabac and of Cagayan-Jolo from part of the archipelago.

ARTICLE III

The Spanish Government renounces, as far as regards the British Government, all claims of sovereignty over the territories of the Continent of Borneo, which belong, or which have belonged in the past to the Sultan of Sulu (Jolo), and which comprise the neighbouring islands of Balambangan, Banguey, and Malawali, as well as all those comprised within a zone of three maritime leagues from the coast, and which form part of the territories administered by the company styled the "British North Borneo Company".

ARTICLE IV

The Spanish Government engages to carry out, in the Archipelago of Sulu (Jolo), the stipulations contained in Articles I, II, and III of the Protocol signed at Madrid, March 11th, 1877, that is to say:- "(1) The commerce and the direct traffic of vessels and subjects of Great Britain, Germany, and the other powers, with the Archipelago of Sulu (Jolo), and in all parts thereof, are declared to be, and shall be, absolutely free; as well as the right of fishing without prejudice to the rights of Spain recognised by the present Protocol, conformably to the following declarations. (2) The Spanish authorities shall not be able to require in future that vessels and subjects of Great Britain, Germany, and the other Powers, freely repairing to the Archipelago of Sulu, or from one point of it to another indiscriminately, or thence to any other part of the world, shall be under the necessity of touching, before or after, at a point indicated in the archipelago or elsewhere; or of paying any dues whatsoever; or of procuring permission from the said authorities; who, on their side, shall abstain from all obstruction and all intervention in the above-named traffic. It is well understood that the Spanish authorities shall not hinder in any manner, or under any pretext, the free importation and exportation of all kinds of merchandise without exception, save at such places as are occupied, and conformably to Declaration III; and that in all the places not effectively occupied by Spain, neither the vessels, nor the subjects above-mentioned, nor their merchandise, shall be submitted to any tax or duty or payment whatever, nor to any regulation, sanitary or otherwise. (3) In those places in the Archipelago of Sulu, which are occupied by Spain, the Spanish Government shall be able to establish taxes and regulations, sanitary or otherwise, during the effective occupation of the places indicated. But Spain, on its side, engages to maintain in those places the establishment and employees necessary for the needs of commerce, and for the application of the said regulations.

"It is, nevertheless, expressly understood, and the Spanish Government being resolved on its side not to apply restrictive regulations to the places occupied, undertakes the engagement willingly, that it shall not introduce in the said places any taxes or duties greater than those fixed by Spain tariffs, or by the Treaties or Conventions between Spain and any other Power. It shall not, moreover, put into force exceptional regulations applicable to the commerce or to the subjects of Great Britain, Germany, or the other Powers.

"In case Spain shall effectively occupy other places in the Archipelago of Sulu, maintaining there the establishments and employees necessary for the needs of commerce, the Government of Great Britain and of Germany shall make no objection to the application of the same rules agreed upon for the places already occupied. But in order to prevent new cases of claims which might arise from the uncertainty as to trade with places which are occupied, and which are subject to regulations and tariffs, the Spanish Government shall communicate in each case the effective occupation of a place in the Archipelago of Sulu to the Government of Great Britain and of Germany, and shall, at the same time, inform the trading interest concerned by a suitable notification published in the official journals of Madrid and Manila. As regards the tariffs and regulations for commerce agreed upon for the places actually occupied, they shall not be applicable to the places subsequently occupied by Spain until after a period of six months, dating from the said publication in the official journal of Madrid. It is agreed, however, that no vessel or subject of Great Britain, of Germany, or of other Powers shall be obliged to touch at one of the places occupied, either in going or returning from a place not occupied by Spain, and that no prejudice will be caused to them on this account, nor in respect of any kind of merchandise destined for a place in the archipelago which is not occupied".

ARTICLE V

The Government of Her Britannic Majesty engages to see that there is entire freedom of commerce and navigation, without distinction of flag, in the territory of North Borneo administered by the company styled "British North Borneo Company".

ARTICLE VI

If the Government of Great Britain and of Germany have not refused their adhesion to the present Protocol within a period of fifteen days from this date or if they notify their adhesion before the expiration of this period through their undersigned representatives, the present declarations shall immediately come into force.

Done at Madrid, March 7th, 1885.

Seals of

R.B.D. MORIER
J. ELDUAYEN
P.C. SOLMS

APPENDIX B

Convention between Great Britain and the Netherlands Defining Boundaries in Borneo

Signed at London, 20 June 1891

[Ratifications exchanged at London, 11 May 1892]

HER Majesty the Queen of the United Kingdom of Great Britain and Ireland, Empress of India, and Her Majesty the Queen-Dowager, Regent of the Netherlands, in the name of Her Majesty Wilhelmina, Queen of the Netherlands, being desirous of defining the boundaries between the Netherland possessions in the Island of Borneo and the States in that island which are under British protection, have resolved to conclude a Convention to that effect, and have appointed as their Plenipotentiaries for that purpose, that it to say:

Her Majesty the Queen of the United Kingdom of Great Britain and Ireland, Empress of India, the Right Honourable Robert Arthur Talbot Gascoyne Cecil, Marquis of Salisbury, Earl of Salisbury, Viscount Cranborne, Baron Cecil, Peer of the United Kingdom, Knight of the Most Noble Order of the Garter, Member of Her Majesty's Most Honourable Privy Council, Her Majesty's Principal Secretary of State for Foreign Affairs, & c.; and Her Majesty the Queen Dowager Regent of the Netherlands, Count Charles

---

Source: C.O. 874/503, ff. 232–34; and F.O. 12/98, ff. 286–88.

Malcolm Ernest Georges de Bylandt, Knight Grand Cross of the Order of the Netherland Lion, Her Majesty's Envoy Extraordinary and Minister Plenipotentiary at the Court of St. James': who, having produced their Full Powers, found in good and due form, have agreed upon the following Articles:-

ARTICLE I

The boundary between the Netherland possessions in Borneo and those of the British protected States in the same island shall start from 4°10′ north latitude on the east coast of Borneo.

ARTICLE II

The boundary-line shall be continued westward from 4°10′ north latitude, and follow in a west-north-west direction, between the Rivers Simengaris and Soedang, up to the point where the meridian 117° east longitude crosses the parallel 4°20′ north latitude, with the view of including the Simengaris River within Dutch territory. The boundary-line shall then follow westward the parallel 4°20′ north latitude until it reaches the summit of the range of mountains which forms on that parallel the watershed between the rivers running to the North-West coast and those running to the east coast of Borneo, it being understood that, in the event of the Simengaris River or any other river flowing into the sea below 4°10′, being found on survey to cross the proposed boundary-line within a radius of 5 geographical miles, the line shall be diverted so as to include such small portions or bends of rivers within Dutch territory; a similar concession being made by the Netherland Government with regard to any river debouching above 4°10′ on the territory of the British North Borneo Company, but turning southwards.

ARTICLE III

From the summit of the range of mountains mentioned in Article II, to Tandjong-Datoe on the west coast of Borneo, the boundary-line shall follow the watershed of the rivers running to the north-west and west coasts, north of Tandjong-Datoe, and of those running to the west coast south of Tandjong-Datoe, the south coast, and the east coast south of 4°10′ north latitude.

ARTICLE IV

From 4°10′ north latitude on the east coast the boundary-line shall be continued eastward along that parallel, across the Island of Sebittik; that portion of the island situated to the north of that parallel shall belong unreservedly to the British North Borneo Company, and the portion south of that parallel to the Netherlands.

ARTICLE V

The exact positions of the boundary-line, as described in the four preceding Articles, shall be determined hereafter by mutual agreement, at such times as the Netherland and the British Governments may think fit.

ARTICLE VI

The navigation of all rivers flowing into the sea between Batoe-Tinagat and the River Siboekoe shall be free, expect for the transport of war material; and no transport duties shall be levied on other goods passing up those rivers.

ARTICLE VII

The population of Boelongan shall be allowed to collect jungle produce in the territory between the Simengaris and the Tawao Rivers for fifteen years from the date of the signature of the present Convention, free from any tax or duty.

ARTICLE VIII

The present Convention shall be ratified, and it shall come into force three months after the exchange of the ratifications, which shall take place at London one month, or sooner if possible, after the said Convention shall have received the approval of the Netherland States-General.

In witness whereof the Undersigned have signed the sent Convention, and have affixed thereto their seals.

Done at London, in duplicate, this 20th day of June, 1891.

(L.S.)	(Signed)	SALISBURY
(L.S.)	(Signed)	C. De BYLANDT

APPENDIX C

Agreement between the United Kingdom and the Netherlands Relating to the Boundary between the State of North Borneo and the Netherland Possessions in Borneo

Signed at London, 28 September 1915

His Britannic Majesty's Government and the Government of Her Majesty the Queen of the Netherlands having agreed in a spirit of mutual goodwill to confirm the joint Report with the accompanying map prepared by their respective Commissioners in accordance with Article 5 of the Convention signed at London on the 20th June, 1891, for the delimitation of the boundary line between the States in the Island of Borneo which are under British protection and the Netherland possessions in that island, and relating to the boundary between the State of North Borneo and the Netherland possessions in the island; the undersigned duly authorized to that effect, hereby confirm the aforesaid joint Report and map, as signed by their Commissioners at Tawao on the 17th February, 1913.

The text of this joint Report, signed in English only, is as follows:-

We, the undersigned: J.H.G. Schepers, engineer of the Triangulation Brigade, Netherland India, E.A. Vreede, 2nd Lieutenant of the Netherland Royal Navy, appointed by Netherland India Government Resolution No. 1 of the 9th April 1912, and No. 38 of the 30th October 1912, respectively,

---

Source: C.O. 874/503, ff. 251–53.

as leader and Joint Commissioner of the Netherland Commission to delimitate on the spot the frontier between Netherland territory and the State of British North Borneo; H.W.L. Bunbury, officer of the First Class, British North Borneo Civil Service, G. St. V. Keddell, surveyor, appointed by commission from his Excellency the Governor of British North Borneo, dated the 30th May 1912, respectively, as Civil Commissioner and Surveyor representing the Government of British North Borneo; have the honour to report as follows:-

1. We have travelled in the neighborhood of the frontier from the 8th June 1912, to the 30th January 1913, during which period the Netherland Commission has made the necessary astronomical observations and topographical surveys, the results of which we declare to be correct and sufficient for the determination of the boundary.

2. Where physical features did not present natural boundaries conformable with the provisions of the Boundary Treaty of the 20th June 1891, we have erected the following pillars:-

    (a) Two pillars on the opposite banks of the Pentjiangan River, both marked "G.P.1."

    (b) One pillar on the right bank of the Agisan River, marked "G.P. 3."

    (c) One pillar on the left bank of the Seboeda River, marked "G.P. 2."

    All being on the parallel 4°20′ north latitude.

3. We have determined the boundary between the Netherland territory and the State of British North Borneo, as described in the Boundary Treaty supplemented by the interpretation of Article 2 of the Treaty mutually accepted by the Netherlands and British Government in 1905 as taking the following course:-

    (1.) Traversing the island of Sibetik, the frontier line follows the parallel of 4°10′ north latitude, as already fixed by Article 4 of the Boundary Treaty and marked on the east and west coasts by boundary pillars.

    (2.) Starting from the boundary pillar on the west coast of the island of Sibetik, the boundary follows the parallel of 4°10′ north latitude westward until it reaches the middle of the channel, thence keeping a mid-channel course until it reaches the middle of the mouth of Troesan Tamboe.

(3.)   From the mouth of Troesan Tamboe the boundary line is continued up the middle of this Troesan until it is intersected by a similar line running through Troesan Sikapal; it then follows this line through Troesan Sikapal as far as the point where the latter meets the watershed between the Simengaris and Seroedong Rivers (Sikapal hill), and is connected finally with this watershed by a line taken perpendicular to the center line of Troesan Sikapal.

(4.)   From the point where this watershed (Sikapal hill) meets Troesan Sikapal the boundary line follows the watershed until the latter joins Mount Bemboeding.
[*Note.* – There is thus included in the Netherland territory all the country that is drained by the Simengaris River and its tributaries, while all the country that is drained by the Seroedong River and its tributaries is included in the territory of British North Borneo].

(5.)   Leaving the junction point of the Simengaris- Seroedong watershed with Mount Bemboeding, the boundary line follow successively—
(a.)   Mount Bemboeding in a northerly direction.
(b.)   Mount Pemantoengan Bagas and Mount Meliat in a westerly direction.
(c.)   Mount Keblajoeng in a south-easterly direction.
(d.)   The watershed between the Karawangan and Apat Rivers in a south-westerly direction.
(e.)   The Inoeloeh Ketek hill in a northerly direction.
(f.)   The watershed between the Loeloewejen and Siangan streams in a western direction.
(g.)   The most western spur of this watershed, intersected by a straight line running due east from boundary pillar "G.P.2."
(h.)   Along this straight line as far as pillar "G.P.2."
[*Note.*—There is thus included in the Netherland territory all the country that is drained by any of the following rivers and their tributaries: Soboeloeh, Mesaloei, Tempilan, Apat, and Toelit, together with the Seboeda south of 4°20′ north latitude and its eastern tributaries debouching south of that parallel; and in the territory of British North Borneo all the country drained by the Seroedong and its tributaries,

and by the Seboeda north of 4°20′ north latitude, and by the tributaries of the Seboeda debouching above that parallel.]

(6.)   From the pillar "G.P.2." the boundary line follows successively —

(a.)   A straight line running due west as far as the most eastern spur of the watershed between the Linemoejoe and Labau streams, intersected by this straight line.

(b.)   The above-mentioned spur.

(c.)   The watershed between the Linemoejoe and Labau streams.

(d.)   The watershed between the Labau and Balang streams.

(e.)   The watershed (the Sinogo ridge) between the Agisan and Seboeda Rivers.

(f.)   The watershed between the Lakoetan and Makalap streams.

(g.)   The most western spur of the latter watershed, intersected by a straight line running due east from boundary pillar "G.P.3."

(h.)   This straight line itself as far as pillar "G.P.3."

[Note.—There is thus included in the Netherland territory all the country drained by the western tributaries of the Seboeda and the eastern tributaries of the Agisan debouching below 4°20′ north latitude, and in the territory of British North Borneo the country drained by the corresponding tributaries debouching above that parallel.]

(7.)   From the pillar "G.P.3." the boundary line follows successively—

(a.)   A straight line running due west as far as the most eastern spur of the watershed between the Klawasan and Mesaloei streams intersected by this line.

(b.)   The above – mentioned spur.

(c.)   The watershed between the Klawasan and Mesoloei streams.

(d.)   The watershed (Peloetan ridge) between the Sesoegon and Agisan streams.

(e.)   The main watershed between the Sembakoeng and Seboekoe Rivers in a south-westerly direction.

(f.)   The watershed (Mount Boedjoek Bah) between the

Sementebel, with its tributaries, and the Semantaloen, with their tributaries.

(g.) The watershed (Mount Boedjoek Bah) between the Sementebel, with its tributaries, and the Seliman and Semanganwat, with their tributaries.

(h.) The watershed (Poegisiai hill) between the Semandapi, with its tributaries, and the Sementebel, with their tributaries, as far as the Toenangan hill.

(i.) The watershed between the Semandapi, with its tributaries, and the eastern tributaries of the Pentjiangan River debouching below 4°20′ north latitude, as far as the intersection of this watershed with a straight line running due east from the pillar "G.P.1" on the left bank of the Pentjiangan.

(j.) This straight line itself.

[Note.—There is thus included in the Netherland territory all the country drained by the Agisan River south of 4°20′ north latitude, and by the western tributaries of the Agisan debouching below that parallel, and by the eastern tributaries of the Pentjiangan debouching below the same parallel; and in the territory of British North Borneo all the country drained by the Agisan River north of 4°20′ north latitude, and by the western tributaries of the Agisan and eastern tributaries of the Pentjiangan River debouching above 4°20′ north latitude.]

(8.) From the pillar "G.P.1" on the left bank of the Pentjiangan River the boundary line follows successively-

(a.) A line running due west to the pillar "G.P.1" on the right bank.

(b.) The first hill-spur south of the Lombai stream as far as its junction with the main watershed between the tributaries of the Pentjiangan debouching above 4°20′ north latitude and the tributaries that debouch south of that latitude.

(c.) The last-named watershed as far as the Seselatan hill.

(d.) The watershed, or series of watershed, dividing the northern tributaries of the Sedalir that debouch above 4°20′ north latitude from those that debouch below that parallel.

(e.) The most western spur of this watershed, or series of the watershed, intersected by parallel 4°20′ north latitude.

(f.) The parallel 4°20′ north latitude, crossing the Sedalir River until it meets the most eastern spur of the watershed, or series of watersheds, between the southern tributaries of the Sedalir that debouch above 4°20′ north latitude from those that debouch below that parallel, in conformity with Article 2 of the Treaty.

(g.) The last-named watershed, or series of watersheds (and, if necessary, the watershed between the Sedalir and the Sesajap Rivers), until they meet the main watershed described in Article 3 of the Treaty.

[Note.- There is thus included in the Netherland territory all the country drained by the Pentjiangan below 4°20′ north latitude, by the Sedalir below that parallel, by the tributaries of both of these rivers debouching below 4°20′ north latitude, and by the Sesajap River; and in the territory of British North Borneo any country that is drained by the Pentjiangan north of 4°20′ north latitude, by the Sedalir north of that parallel, and by the tributaries of both of these rivers debouching north of 4°20′ north latitude.]

To the above we have all agreed and appended our signatures at Tawao, British North Borneo, this 17th day of February, 1913.

J.H.G.SCHEPERS
E.A. VREEDE.
H.W.L.BUNBURY.
G.ST.V.KEDDELL.

In witness whereof the undersigned have signed the present Agreement and have affixed thereto their seals.

Done at London, the 28th day of September, 1915.

(L.S.)   E. GREY.
(L.S.)   R. DE MAREES VAN SWINDEREN.

APPENDIX D

H.M. Durand's Memorandum 1906

MEMORANDUM, H.M. DURAND, BRITISH AMBASSADOR TO THE UNITED STATES, TO THE SECRETARY OF STATE, U.S.A.

BRITISH EMBASSY,
Washington, 23 June 1906

The Secretary of State's semiofficial note of January 12 in regard to the control of certain islands in North Borneo was duly forwarded by His Majesty's embassy to Sir Edward Grey, who has now replied, giving the views of the British North Borneo Company on the four points raised in that note.

In regard to the first point, the company deprecate having to submit a chart showing the line dividing North Borneo from American territory. They point out that to prepare such a chart would necessitate the dispatch of a joint delimitation commission, which would involve considerable expense. His Majesty's embassy is, however, authorized to communicate to the State Department the inclosed map as showing the limits within which the company desire to carry on the administration.

2. The company would like to be left undisturbed in the administration of the islands without any detailed agreement, the United States Government simply waiving in favour of the company their right to administer, which it is believed they have no special desire to exercise; but if this is not

---

Source: C.O. 874/1002.

possible the company would prefer to continue the administration on leases renewable say every twenty-five years, paying the annual rent of $150 as suggested before.

3. The company suggest that in case of denunciation the United States Government should agree to recognize titles and concessions granted in the islands by the company and should pay the company for improvements.

4. In the event of the United States Government agreeing to refrain from administering the islands, the company will, as a matter of course, agree to the exemption of the United States Government from any claim or allegation of responsibility arising out of acts done in or from any islands within the proposed line of demarcation.

They do not suppose that it was the intention of the Department of State to disclaim responsibility for the consequences of acts done in or from American islands under the direct control of the United States administration.

APPENDIX E

The Secretary of State (U.S.A.) to the British Ambassador

DEPARTMENT OF STATE,
Washington, 19 December 1906

DEAR MR. AMBASSADOR: Your note of November 6 reminded me that a respond has not yet been forthcoming to the memorandum which you left with me on the 23rd June last in relation to the administration or leasing of certain small islands on the North Bornean coast by the British North Borneo Company.

The matter has required much consideration and involved delay which I regret, and even at this late day I am not at all clear as to the most practical way to give effect to the desire of your Government by a formal agreement.

I apprehend that the difficulty in the way of a conventional delimitation of the boundary between the former possessions of Spain in the Sulu Archipelago, now belonging to the United States, and the North Bornean territories on or adjacent to the mainland of Borneo, may lie in the circumstance that the North Bornean domain is not an imperial possession of Great Britain, but is held by a British Chartered Company under grant of the native Sultans and under the protection of the Crown in virtue of such grant. If this be so, I can discern impediments to an international convention between our two countries for establishing a boundary line between their respective sovereignties—and I can equally

---

Source: C.O. 874/1002.

see that objections might be raised to undertaking to fix that boundary by agreement between this Government and a chartered corporation having per se no national status.

Something of the same difficulty might arise in the case of the United States undertaking to lease the islands to a chartered company not having the standing of a government. The third condition of your memorandum illustrates this point, suggesting, as it does in effect, that such a lease should carry with it power to the company to grant titles and concessions binding upon the United States and to make valuable improvements, which would be an eventual charge upon this Government should the United States terminate the lease and reenter upon the property.

The second proposition of the company seems, on the whole, to be preferable and safer, namely, that the company be left undisturbed in the administration of the islands, without any detailed agreement, the United States Government simply waiving in favour of the company their right to such administration in the meantime—in other words, that the existing status be continued indefinitely at the pleasure of the parties. It might be agreed that such an understanding shall be with the British Government, acting on behalf of the interests of British subjects; that it shall not carry with it territorial rights (such as those of grants and concessions), that the waiver shall cover the islands to the westward and southwestward of the line traced on the map which accompanied your memorandum of June 23; that the company (through the British Government) shall agree to the exemption of the United States from any claim or allegation of responsibility arising out of acts done in or from any islands within the said line, and that the understanding shall continue until the two Governments may by treaty delimit the boundary between their respective domains in that quarter, or until one year's notice of termination, to be given by either to the other.

I should be glad to have the views of your Government on these suggestions.

I am, my dear Sir Mortimer,
      Very faithfully yours,

                                        ELIHU ROOT

APPENDIX F

Exchange of Note of 3 July 1907 between Britain and the United States

The British Ambassador to the Secretary of State.

BRITISH EMBASSY,
Intervale, N. H.,
3 July 1907

SIR, I have the honor to inform you that His Majesty's Government, acting at the request and on behalf of the British North Borneo Company, are prepared to acquiesce in the last proposal stated in your letter to Sir H.M. Durand of the 19th of December last, respecting the administration of certain islands on the east coast of Borneo. I am therefore instructed by His Majesty's principal secretary of state for foreign affairs to place the proposed arrangement formally on record without further delay.

His Majesty's Government understands the terms of the arrangement to be as follows:

Firstly. That the said company be left undisturbed in the administration of the islands in question without any agreement specifying details, the United States Government simply waiving in favour of the said company the right to such administration in the meantime; in other words, that the existing status be continued indefinitely at the pleasure of the two Governments concerned.

Secondly. That such privilege of administration shall not carry with it in question to extend beyond the temporary occupation of the company;

Source: C.O. 874/1002. See also *Papers Relating to the Foreign Relations of the United States For 1907*, vol. 1, pp. 542–49.

and any grant, concession, or license made by the company shall cease upon the termination of the company's occupation.

Thirdly. That the temporary waiver of the right of administration on the part of the United States Government shall cover all the islands to the westward and southwestward of the line traced on the map which accompanied Sir H.M. Durand's memorandum of the 23rd of June, 1906, and which is annexed to and to be deemed part of this note.

Fourthly. That the British North Borneo Company, through His Majesty's Government, shall agree to the exemption of the United States Government from any claim or allegation that the latter Government has incurred any responsibility in respect of acts done in or from any island within the said line.

Fifthly. That the understanding shall continue until the said two Governments may by treaty delimit the boundary between their respective domains in that quarter or until the expiry of one year from the date when notice of termination be given by either to the other.

Sixthly. That in case of denunciation, the United States Government shall not be responsible for the value of any buildings or other permanent improvements which may have been erected or made by the company upon the islands, but permission is hereby given to the company to remove, at its own expense, any buildings or improvements erected by it, provided the interests of the United States be not injured thereby.

I have therefore the honor to request you to be so good as to inform me whether the United States adhere to the terms of the arrangement above described, and I shall be glad to receive an assurance from you at the same time that this note will be considered by the United States Government as sufficient ratification of the above arrangement on the part of His Majesty's Government.

I have the honor, etc ...,

JAMES BRYCE

APPENDIX G

Exchange of Note of 10 July 1907 between Britain and the United States

The Acting Secretary of State to the British Ambassador

DEPARTMENT OF STATE,
Washington, 10 July 1907

EXCELLENCY: I have the honor to acknowledge the receipt of your note No. 151 of the 3d instant, by which you inform me that His Majesty's Government, acting at the request and on behalf of the British North Borneo Company, are prepared to acquiesce in the last proposal stated in the letter of December 19, 1906, from the Secretary of State to Sir H.M. Durand, respecting the administration of certain islands on the east coast of Borneo and that you are therefore instructed by His Majesty's principal secretary of state for foreign affairs to place the proposed arrangement formally on record without further delay.

The understanding of His Majesty's Government of the terms of the arrangement is stated by you to be as follows:

Firstly. That the said company be left undisturbed in the administration of the islands in question without any agreement specifying details, the United States Government simply waiving in favour of the said company the right to such administration in the meantime; in other words, that the existing status be continued indefinitely at the pleasure of the two Governments concerned.

Source: C.O. 874/1002. See also *Papers Relating to the Foreign Relations of the United States For 1907*, vol. 1, pp. 542–49.

Secondly. That such privilege of administration shall not carry with it territorial rights, such as those of making grants or concessions in the islands in question to extend beyond the temporary occupation of the company; and any grant, concession, or license made by the company shall cease upon the termination of the company's occupation.

Thirdly. That the temporary waiver of the right of administration on the part of the United States Government shall cover all the islands to the westward and southwestward of the line traced on the map which accompanied Sir H.M. Durand's memorandum of the 23rd of June, 1906, and which is annexed to and to be deemed part of this note.

Fourthly. That the British North Borneo Company, through His Majesty's Government, shall agree to the exemption of the United States Government from any claim or allegation that the latter Government has incurred any responsibility in respect of acts done in or from any island within the said line.

Fifthly. That the understanding shall continue until the said two Governments may by treaty delimit the boundary between their respective domains in that quarter or until the expiry of one year from the date when notice of termination be given by either to the other.

Sixthly. That in case of denunciation, the United States Government shall not be responsible for the value of any buildings or other permanent improvements which may have been erected or made by the company upon the islands; but permission is hereby given to the company to remove, at its own expense, any buildings or improvements erected by it, provided the interests of the United States be not injured thereby.

The understanding of His Majesty's Government as above recited agreeing with that of the United States, I have the honor formally to announce the adherence of the United States to the arrangement and the acceptance of your note as sufficient ratification of the arrangement on the part of His Majesty's Government.

I have, etc … ,

ROBERT BACON

APPENDIX H

Boundary Convention between Great Britain and the United States, 2 January 1930, and Exchange of Notes, 2 January 1930 and 6 July 1932

BOUNDARIES: PHILIPPINES AND NORTH BORNEO

Convention signed at Washington January 2, 1930: exchanges of notes at Washington January 2, 1930 and July 6, 1932
Senate advice and consent to ratification February 11, 1930
Ratified by the President of the United States February 21, 1930
Ratified by the United Kingdom November 2, 1932
Ratifications exchanged at Washington December 13, 1932
Entered into force December 13, 1932
Proclaimed by the President of the United States December 15, 1932

47 Stat.2198; Treaty Series 856

CONVENTION

The President of the United States of America and His Majesty the King of Great Britain, Ireland, and the British Dominions beyond the Seas, Emperor of India,

---

Source: Charles Bevans, *Treaties and other International Agreements of the United States, (1776–1949)*, vol. 2, pp. 473–81. See also *Papers Relating to the Foreign Relations of the United States, 1930*, vol. 3, pp. 147–55. Also in C.O. 531/22, ff. 22–28.

Being desirous of delimiting definitely the boundary between the Philippine Archipelago (the territory acquired by the United States of America by virtue of the Treaties of December 10, 1898, and November 7,1900, with Her Majesty the Queen Regent of Spain) and the State of North Borneo which is under British protection,

Have resolved to conclude a Convention for that purpose and have appointed as their plenipotentiaries:

The President of the United States of America,

Henry L. Stimson, Secretary of State of the United States of America; and

His Majesty the King of Great Britain, Ireland and the British Dominions beyond the Seas, Emperor of India,

For Great Britain and Northern Ireland:

The Right Honorable Sir Esme Howard, G.C.B., G.C.M.G., C.V.O., His Majesty's Ambassador Extraordinary and Plenipotentiary at Washington;

Who, having communicated to each other their respective full powers found in good and due form have agreed upon and concluded the following Articles:

ARTICLE I

It is hereby agreed and declared that the line separating the islands belonging to the Philippine Archipelago on the one hand and the islands belonging to the State of North Borneo which is under British protection on the other hand shall be and is hereby established as follows:

From the point of intersection of the parallel of four degrees forty-five minutes (4°45′) north latitude and the meridian of longitude one hundred twenty degrees (120°0′) east of Greenwich, (being a point on the boundary defined by the Treaty between the United States of America and Spain signed at Paris, December 10, 1898), a line due south along the meridian of longitude one hundred twenty degrees (120°0′) east of Greenwich to its points of intersection with the parallel of four degrees twenty-three minutes (4°43′) north latitude;

thence due west along the parallel of four degrees twenty-three minutes (4°43′) north latitude to its intersection with the meridian of longitude one hundred nineteen degrees (119°0′) east of Greenwich;

thence due north along the meridian of longitude one hundred nineteen degrees (119°0′) east of Greenwich to its intersection with the parallel of four forty-two minutes (4°42′) north latitude;

thence in a straight line approximately 45°54′ true (N45°54′E) to the intersection with the parallel of five degrees sixteen minutes (5°16′) north latitude and the meridian of longitude one hundred nineteen degrees thirty-five minutes (119°35′) east of Greenwich;

thence in a straight line approximately 314°19′ true (N45°41′W) to the intersection with the parallel of six degrees (6°0′) north latitude and the meridian of longitude one hundred eighteen degrees fifty minutes (118°50′) east of Greenwich;

thence due west along the parallel of six degrees (6°0′) north latitude to the intersection with the meridian of longitude one hundred eighteen degrees twenty minutes (118°20′) east of Greenwich;

thence in a straight line approximately 307°40′ true (N52°20′W) passing between Little Bakkungaan Island and Great Bakkungaan Island to the intersection of the parallel of six degrees seventeen minutes (6°17′) north latitude and the meridian of longitude one hundred seventeen degrees fifty-eight minutes (117°58′) east of Greenwich;

thence due north along the meridian of longitude one hundred seventeen degrees fifty- eight minutes (117°58′) east of Greenwich to the intersection of the parallel of six degrees fifty-two minutes (6°52′) north latitude;

thence in a straight line approximately 315°16′ true (N44°44′W) to the intersection with the parallel of seven degrees twenty-four minutes forty-five seconds (7°24′45″ north latitude and the meridian of longitude one hundred seventeen degrees twenty minutes thirty seconds (117°25′30″) east of Greenwich;

thence in a straight line approximately 300°56′ true (N59°4′W) through the Mangsee Channel between Mangsee Great Reef and Mangsee Islands to the intersection with the parallel of seven degrees forty minutes (7°40′) north latitude and the meridian of longitude one hundred seventeen degrees (117°0′) east of Greenwich; the latter point being on the boundary defined by the Treaty between the United States of America and Spain signed at Paris, December 10, 1898.

ARTICLE II

The line described above has been indicated on Charts Nos. 4707 and 4720, published by the United States Coast and Geodetic Survey, corrected to July 24, 1929, portions of both charts so marked being attached to this treaty and made a part thereof. It is agreed that if more accurate surveying and mapping of North Borneo, the Philippine Islands, and intervening islands shall in the future show that the line described above does not pass between Little Bakkungaan and Great Bakkungaan islands, substantially as indicated on Charts No. 4720, the boundary line shall be understood to be defined in that area as a line passing between Little Bakkungaan and Great Bakkungaan Islands as indicated on the chart, said portion of the line being a straight line approximately 370°40′ true drawn from a point on the parallel of six degrees 6°0′ north latitude to a point on the meridian of longitude of 117°58′ east of Greenwich.

It is likewise agreed that if more accurate surveying and mapping shall show that the line describe above does not pass between the Mangsee Islands and Mangsee Great Reef as indicated on Charts No. 4720, the boundary line shall be understood to be defined in that area as a straight line drawn from the intersection of the parallel of 7°24′45″ north latitude and the meridian of longitude 117°25′30″ east of Greenwich, passing through Mangsee Channel as indicated on attached Chart No. 4720 to a point on the parallel of 7°40′ north latitude.

ARTICLE III

All islands to the north and east of the said line and all islands and rocks traversed by the said line, should there be any such, shall belong to the Philippine Archipelago and all islands to the south and west of the said line shall belong to the State of North Borneo.

ARTICLE IV

The provisions of Article 19 of the Treaty between the United States of America, the British Empire, France, Italy and Japan limiting naval armament, signed at Washington on February 6, 1922, shall, so long as that Treaty remains in force, apply in respect of all islands in the Turtle and Mangsee Groups which are or may be deemed to be comprised within the territories of the Philippine Archipelago on the one hand and of the State of North Borneo on the other hand in consequence of the establishment of the line fixed by the preceding articles of the present Convention. In the event of either High Contracting Party ceding, selling; leasing or transferring any of the islands in question to a third party provision shall be made for the continued application to such island of the aforementioned Article-19 of the Treaty between the United States of America, the British Empire, France, Italy and Japan limiting naval armament, signed at Washington on

February 6, 1922, provided that Treaty is still in force at the time of such cession, sale, lease or transfer.

ARTICLE V

The present Convention shall be ratified by the President of The Unites States of America, by and with the advice and consent of the Senate thereof, and by His Britannic Majesty, and shall come into force on the exchange of the acts of ratification which shall take place at Washington as soon as possible.

In witness whereof the respective Plenipotentiaries have signed the same and have affixed thereof their respective seals.

Done in duplicate at Washington the second day of January in the year of our Lord one thousand nine hundred and thirty.

HENRY L. STIMSON   [SEAL]

ESME HOWARD   [SEAL]

EXCHANGES OF NOTES

The British Ambassador to the Secretary of State

BRITISH EMBASSY,
Washington, D.C., 2nd January, 1930

No. 679

SIR,

By the convention concluded between the President of the United States of America and His Britannic Majesty for the purpose of delimiting the boundary between the Philippines archipelago on the one hand and the State of North Borneo which is under British protection on the other hand, the sovereignty over certain islands which have for many years past been administered by the British North Borneo Company has been definitely recognized as pertaining to the United States of America. These islands which formed the subject of the arrangement effected by an exchange of notes between His Majesty's Government and the United States Government of July 3rd and July 10th, 1907, are:

1. Sibuang, Boaan, Lihiman, Langaan, Great Bakkungaan, Taganak and Baguan in the group of islands known as the Turtle Islands.
2. The Mangsee Islands.

His Majesty's Government in the United Kingdom understand that the Government of the Unites States of America are prepared to conclude an arrangement in regard to these islands, supplementary to the above-mentioned convention, in the following terms:

FIRSTLY. That the said company be left undisturbed in the administration of the islands in questions unless or until the United States Government give notice to His Majesty's Government of their desire that the administration of the islands should be transferred to them. The transfer of administration shall be effected within one year after such notice is given on a day and in a manner to be mutually arranged.

SECONDLY. That when the administration of any island is transferred in accordance with the foregoing the said Company will deliver to the United States Government all records relating to administration prior to the date of transfer.

THIRDLY. The United States of America shall not be responsible for the value of any buildings which have been or may be erected or other permanent improvements which have been or may be made in any island the administration of which is subject to transfer but any buildings or improvements erected or made by the administrative authorities prior to the transfer of administration may be removed provided the interests of the United States of America are not thereby injured. In the event, however, of the Island of Taganak being so transferred, the United States Government will give favourable consideration to the question of the compensation to be paid to the said company in respect of the capital expenditure incurred by the company in connection with the lighthouse situated on the island, and the United States Government will provide for the future maintenance of the lighthouse.

FOURTHLY. That such privilege of administration shall not carry with it territorial rights, such as those of making grants or concessions in the islands in question to extend beyond the temporary occupation of the company; and any grant, concession, or license made by the company shall cease upon the termination of the company's occupation.

The United States Government, however, take note of the desire of His Majesty's Government that the following titles to land in certain of the islands which were in good faith granted by the Government of North Borneo prior to the arrangement of 1907, be allowed to stand on the terms on which they were issued by that Government.

PARTICULARS

Titles	Date of Alienation	Period	Approximate Total Acreage
Boaan Island 26 Native Titles	1.6.1907	In perpetuity	146 acres
Lihiman Island 7 Native Titles	1.6.1907	" "	37 "
1 Provisional Lease 2416	1.6.1907	999 years	13 "
		Total	50 "
Longaan Island 4 Native Titles	1.6.1907	In perpetuity	
Great Bakkungaan 3 Provisional Leases	26.9.1903	999 years	118 "

FIFTHLY. It is agreed that the United States Government shall be exempt from responsibility in respect of acts done in or from any of the islands in question the administration of which has not been transferred to the United States.

SIXTHLY. The stipulation of the extradition treaties between the United States Government and His Majesty's Government shall be applicable within the limits provided for in the exchange of notes which took place in Washington on September 1st/23rd, 1913, to the islands in question and the Unites States Government takes note of the importance which, in view of the proximity of the islands to North Borneo, the said company attaches to the establishment and maintenance of an adequate police post thereon, in the event of the administration being transferred to the United States Government.

SEVENTHLY. In the event of the cession, sale, lease or transfer of the islands in question to any third party, the United States Government undertake to use their good offices in commending to the favourable consideration of such third party the desires expressed by His Majesty's Government in the United Kingdom and the British North Borneo Company, as set out in the preceding articles of the present arrangement.

I have the honour under instructions from His Majesty's Principal Secretary of State for Foreign Affairs to request you to be so good as to inform me whether the United States adhere to the terms of the arrangement above described and I shall be glad to receive an assurance from you at the time that this note will be considered by the United States Government as sufficient acceptance of the above arrangement on the part of His Majesty's Government in the United Kingdom.

I have the honour to be, with the highest consideration, Sir. Your most obedient, humble servant,

ESME HOWARD

The Honourable
HENRY L. STIMSON
Secretary of State of the Unites States,
Washington, D.C.

Mr. Stimson to Sir Esme Howard.
Department of State,
Washington, January 2, 1930.

Excellency,

In your Excellency's note of to-day's date you stated that His Majesty's Government in the United Kingdom understands that the Government of the United States of America is prepared to conclude an arrangement in the following terms regarding certain islands off the coast of Borneo which have been administered by the British North Borneo Company in accordance with the arrangement effected by an exchange of notes between His Majesty's Government and the Government of the Unites States of America on the 3rd and 10th July, 1907:-

Firstly.- That the said company be left undisturbed in the administration of the islands in question unless or until the United States Government give notice to His Majesty's Government of its desire that the administration of the islands should be transferred to it. The transfer of administration shall be effected within one year after such notice is given on a day and in a manner to be mutually arranged.

Secondly.- That when the administration of any island is transferred in accordance with the foregoing the said Company will deliver to the United States Government all records relating to administration prior to the date of transfer.

Thirdly.- The United States of America shall not be responsible for the value of any buildings which have been or may be erected or other permanent improvements which have been or may be made in any island the administration of which is subject to transfer but any buildings or improvements erected or made by the administrative authorities prior to the transfer of administration may be removed provided the interests of the United States of America are not thereby injured. In the event, however, of the Island of Taganak being so transferred, the United States Government will give favourable consideration to the question of the compensation to be paid to the said company in respect of the capital expenditure incurred by the company in connection with the lighthouse situated on the island, and the United States Government will provide for the future maintenance of the lighthouse.

Fourthly.- That such privilege of administration shall not carry with it territorial rights, such as those of making grants or concessions in the islands in question to extend beyond the temporary occupation of the company; and any grant, concession, or licence made by the company shall cease upon the termination of the company's occupation.

The United States Government however, takes note of the desire of His Majesty's Government that the following titles to land in certain of the islands which were in good faith granted by the Government of North Borneo prior to the arrangement of 1907, be allowed to stand on the terms on which they were issued by that Government:-

PARTICULARS

Titles	Date of Alienation	Period	Approximate Total Acreage
Boaan Island- 26 native titles	June 1, 1907	In perpetuity	Acres 146
Lihiman Island- 7 native titles	June 1, 1907	" "	37
1 provisional lease 2416	June 1, 1907	999 years	13
			Total 50

Longaan Island- 4 native titles	June 1, 1907	In perpetuity	12
Great Bakkungaan- 3 provisional leases	September 26, 1903	999 years	118

Fifthly.- It is agreed that the United States Government shall be exempt from responsibility is respect of acts done in or from any of the islands in question the administration of which has not been transferred to the United States of America.

Sixthly.- The stipulations of the extradition treaties between the United States Government and His Majesty's Government shall be applicable within the limits provided for in the exchange of notes which took place in Washington on the 1st to 23rd September, 1913, to the islands in question and the United States Government takes note of the importance which, in view of the proximity of the islands to North Borneo, the said company attached to the establishment and maintenance of an adequate police post thereon, in the event of the administration being transferred to the United States Government.

Seventhly.- In the event of the cession, sale, lease or transfer of the islands in question to any third party, the United States Government undertakes to use its good offices in commending to the favourable consideration of such third party to desires expressed by His Majesty's Government in the United Kingdom and the British North Borneo Company, as set out in the preceding articles of the present arrangement.

In reply to the enquiry made on behalf of your Excellency's Government in the last paragraph of your note of to-day's date, I take pleasure in informing you that the Government of the United States of America adheres to the terms of the arrangement above described, and in assuring you that your note under acknowledgment in considered by the Government of the United States of America as sufficient acceptance of the arrangement on the part of His Majesty's Government in the United Kingdom.

Accept, &c.

HENRY L. STIMSON.
The Secretary of State to the British Ambassador

DEPARTMENT OF STATE,
Washington, July 6, 1932

EXCELLENCY:

I have the honor to acknowledge the receipt of Your Excellency's note of this day's date in which Your Excellency refers to the fact that in the notes exchanged between the Government of the United States of America and His Majesty's Government in the United Kingdom on January 2nd, 1930, constituting an arrangement regarding certain islands off the coast of Borneo which have been administered by the British North Borneo Company in accordance with the arrangement effected by an exchange of notes between His Majesty's Government and the Government of the United States on July 3 and July 10, 1907, the Government of the United States took note of the desire of His Majesty's Government that certain titles to land in certain of the islands which were in good faith granted by the Government. In relation to this matter Your Excellency states that His Majesty's Government regrets that the following title was inadvertently omitted from the list of land titles included in the above arrangement:

Lihiman Island	Date of Alienation	Period	Area
Provisional Lease No. 2417	1.6.1907	999 years	13 acres 0 roods 24 perches

Under instructions from His Majesty's Principal Secretary of State for Foreign Affairs Your Excellency requests that I be so good as to inform you whether the Government of the United States will agree to regard this title as included in those mentioned in the arrangement concluded on January 2, 1930.

In reply I am pleased to inform Your Excellency that the Government of the United States agrees to the extension of the arrangement of January 2, 1930, to include the above-mentioned title, and I take pleasure also in assuring Your Excellency that your note under acknowledgement is considered by the Government of the United States as a sufficient confirmation on the part of His Majesty's Government in the United Kingdom of the aforesaid extension.

Accept, Excellency, the renewed assurances of my highest consideration.

For the Secretary of State:
W.R. CASTLE, Jr.
His Excellency
    The Honorable Sir RONALD LINDSAY,
        P.C., G.C.M.G., K.C.B., C.V. O.,
            British Ambassador.

Bibliography

PRIMARY SOURCES

1. **Unpublished Primary Sources**
   A. *United Kingdom*
   (a) National Archives, London
       (i) Colonial Office Records

C.O. 531	Original Correspondence, North Borneo.
20	Files for 1926, 1927.
21	Files for 1928, 1929.
22	Files for 1930.
33	Files for 1947–49.
C.O. 648	Administration Reports, North Borneo.
(a)	Administration Reports, North Borneo, 1–22, 1908–1940.
(b)	Administration and Annual Reports, North Borneo, 1909.
C.O. 855	British North Borneo Herald and Official Gazette, Nos. 1–54, 1883–1955.
C.O. 874	British North Borneo Company Papers.
1.	11 August 1865. Lease of Northern Borneo from Abdul Mumin (Sultan of Brunei) to C. Lee Moses.
2.	11 August 1865. Lease of various territories and islands from Pangeran Temengong (of Brunei) to C. Lee Moses.
3.	9 September 1865. Memorandun of agreement between C. Lee Moses, J.W. Torrey and others of the American Trading Company of Borneo.
12.	19 January 1875. Agreement of sale by J.W. Torrey of the American Trading Company to Baron de Overbeck.
16.	27 March 1877. Articles of agreement between Alfred Dent and Baron Von Overbeck.
31.	4 April 1881. Agreement for Sale by A. Dent to the British North Borneo Provisional Association.
33.	Deed of Settlement (of the British North Borneo Company).
53.	22 April 1903. Confirmation by the Sultan of Sulu of cession of certain islands.
54.	1877–1903. Cession Deeds.

72.   2 May–5 February 1878. Diary of W. Pretyman, Resident of Tempassuk.
117.   31 May 1881. Out-letters. British North Borneo Provisional Association to Governor.
170.   1881. Copy of agreement for sale between A. Dent and the British North Borneo Provisional Association.
191.   1846–1889. Correspondence regarding the Dutch boundary.
228.   1 August, 1881–31 December 1881. Inward despatches from the Company's Governor.
292.   13 May 1882–13 April 1883. Outward despatches to the Company's Governor.
499.   1891–1912. Demarcation of the Anglo-Dutch Boundary.
500.   1913–1914. Demarcation of the Anglo-Dutch Boundary.
503.   1915: Anglo-Dutch Boundary Agreement.
1001. 1900–1903. Sovereignty over certain islands.
1002. 1906–1923. Sovereignty over certain islands.
1003. 1922–1927. Sovereignty over certain islands.
1004. 1927–1929. Sovereignty over certain islands.
1005. 1925–1931. Sovereignty over certain islands.
1006. 1932–1947. Sovereignty over certain islands.

(ii)   Foreign Office Records
F.O. 12.   Foreign Office Borneo Correspondence.
86.   Papers Relating to the Affairs of Sulu and Borneo Part I (Spain No. 1, 1882): Borneo and Sulu.
       Papers Relating to the Affairs of Sulu and Borneo Part II (Netherlands No. 1, 1882): Borneo and Sulu.

B.   *Netherlands*
   (a)   Algemeen Rijksarchief
   (i)   Dutch Document Box A 60, File 791: Proceedings of the Joint Commission appointed by the British and Netherland Governments for considering the question of the Boundary between the Netherland Indian Possessions on the Island of Borneo and the Territory belonging to the British North Borneo Company, First, Second and Third Meetings held at the Foreign Office, London, 1889.
   (ii) Official Parliamentary Reports, The Netherlands, Session 1890–1891: 187:
         "Explanatory Memorandum No. 3, Ratification of the Agreement made in London between the Netherlands and Great Britain and Ireland for the Fixing of the Boundaries between the Possessions of the Netherlands

on the Island of Borneo and the States on that Island which are under British Protectorate."

(b) International Court of Justice, The Hague.
(i) International Court of Justice,
Case Concerning Sovereignty over Pulau Ligitan and Pulau Sipadan (Indonesia/Malaysia), Memorial of Malaysia, volumes 1 and 2, 2 November 1999.
(ii) *Case Concerning Sovereignty over Pulau Ligitan and Pulau Sipadan (Indonesia/Malaysia), Memorial Submitted By the Government of the Republic of Indonesia*, volume I, 2 November 1999.
(iii) *Verbatim Record in the Case Concerning Sovereignty over Pulau Ligitan and Pulau Sipadan (Indonesia/Malaysia)*, 3 June 2002.
(iv) *Judgment, Case Concerning Sovereignty over Pulau Ligitan and Pulau Sipadan (Indonesia/Malaysia)*, 17 December 2002.
(v) *Judgment, Sovereignty over Pedra Branca/Pulau Batu Puteh, Middle Rocks and South Ledge (Indonesia/Singapore)*, 23 May 2008.

C. *United States*
(a) National Archives of the United States, Washington D.C.
(i) Hydrographic Office Survey Correspondence (U.S.A), 1854–1907, R.G. 37, File 161.34, Box 9.
Ibid., File 563.49, Box 66.
(ii) U.S Department of State Series, entitled *Limits In The Sea*, No. 1.
(iii) General Correspondence of the Office of the Secretary of the Navy, 1891–1926, R.G. 80, File 15826/7 Box 642.
(iv) General Records of the Department of the Navy (U.S.A), 1900–1947, R.G. 80, File G.B. 424, 1900–1907, Box 122.
(v) Records of the Department of State, U.S.A, 1910–1929, R.G. 29, Micro 581, Roll 5; R.G. 59, Micro 581.
(vi) Records of the Bureau of Insular Affairs Relating to the Philippine Islands, 1898–1935, R.G. 350, File 907/10, Box 130–131.
Ibid., 1893–1935, R.G. 350, File 907/17, Box 130–131.
(vii) Papers Relating to the Foreign Relations of the United States for 1900, vol. I.
Ibid., 1907, vol. I, pp. 542–49.
Ibid., 1927 and 1928, vol. II, pp. 724–986.

D. *Malaysia*
(a) Sabah State Archives (SSA) Files
(i) Resident of The East Coast Files (R.O.E.C) 324/10; 39/16.

E. *ASEAN Secretarial Files and Documents, Jakarta, 2003*

2. **Unpublished Theses, Dissertations and Research Reports**

Ranjit Singh, D.S., et al. "Kajian Sejarah Labuan, 1800–1984". Unit Perundingan Universiti Malaya, Kuala Lumpur, 2006.

Reynolds, J.K. "Towards an Account of Sulu and its Borneo Dependencies, 1700–1878", Thesis submitted as partial fulfilment of M.A., University of Wisconsin, 1970.

Report of the Committee of Investigation, (State of Sabah), Re: Sipadan and Ligitan, Kota Kinabalu, 1975, vol. 2.

Sanib Said. "Anti-Cession Movement, 1946 to 1951: The Birth of Nationalism in Sarawak". Graduation Exercise, Department of History, University of Malaya, Kuala Lumpur, 1976.

3. **Newspapers**

Asia Week, 23 July 1982.

International Herald Tribune, 20 August 2012.

New Straits Times, 12 October 1991; 18 October 1991; 15 September 2012; 25 September 2012; 11 May 2015; 4 June 2015; 2 December 2015; 3 December 2015; 23 June 2016; 13 July 2016.

New *Sunday Times*, 2 June 2002; 9 June 2002; 3 April 2016.

Straits Times, 7 July 1982.

Sunday Star, 3 February 2013; 1 November 2015.

The Star, 7 June 1991; 11 October 1991; 8 June 2002; 26 September 2012; 6 February 2013; 22 January 2015; 29 May 2015; 7 August 2015; 5 April 2016.

The Wall Street Journal, 20 August 2012.

SECONDARY SOURCES

Books, Journals, Articles and Conference Papers

Abdul Rahman, T.P. *Looking Back: Monday Musings and Memories*. Kuala Lumpur: Pustaka Press, 1977.

Allen, J. de V. *The Malayan Union*. New Haven: Yale University, Southeast Asia Studies, 1967.

Allen, J. de V., A.J. Stockwell and L.R. Wright. *A Collection of Treaties and Other Documents Affecting the States of Malaysia, 1761–1963*, vol. 2, London: Oceana Publications, 1961.

Andaya, Barbara Watson, and Leonard Y. Andaya. *A History of Malaysia*. Basingstoke: Macmillan, 1982.

Ariff, M.O. *The Philippines Claim to Sabah: Its Historical, Legal and Political Implications*, Singapore: Oxford University Press, 1970.

Bevans, Charles I. *Treaties and Other International Agreements of the United States, 1776–1949*, vol. 2. Washington, D.C.: Department of State Publication, 1968.

Blair, E.H., and J.A. Robertson, eds. *The Philippine Islands*, vol. 4. Cleveland, 1903–9.

Bonney, R. *Kedah 1771–1821: The Search for Security and Independence*. Kuala Lumpur: Oxford University Press, 1974.

Brown, D.E. *Brunei: The Structure and History of a Bornean Malay Sultanate*. Monograph of the Brunei Museum Journal, vol. 2, no. 2, 1970.

Burrough, Josephine Boenisch. "Ference Xavier Witti: Two Narratives by G.C. Woolley and Owen Rutter". *Sabah Society Journal* V, no. 3 (December 1971).

Cady, John F. *Southeast Asia: Its Historical Development*. New York: McGraw-Hill Inc. 1964.

Cheah Boon Kheng. *Red Star over Malaya: Resistance and Social Conflict During and After the Japanese Occupation of Malaya, 1941–1946*. Singapore: Singapore University Press, 1983.

Cohen, Warren I. *East Asia at the Center*. New York: Colombia University Press, 2000.

Cowan, C.D. *Nineteenth Century Malaya: The Origins of British Political Control*. London: Oxford University Press, 1961.

Dalrymple, Alexander. "Essay Towards an Account of Sooloo". In *Journal of the Indian Archipelago and Eastern Asia*, edited by J.R. Logan. Singapore, 1849.

Fernando, Joseph M., *The Making of the Malayan Constitution*. JMBRAS Monograph No. 31. Kuala Lumpur: JMBRAS, 2002.

Funston, John, ed. *Government and Politics in Southeast Asia*. Singapore: Institute of Southeast Asian, Studies, 2001.

Hall, D.G.E. *A History of South-East Asia*. London: Macmillan, 1981.

Haller-Trost, R. *The Territorial Dispute between Indonesia and Malaysia over Pulau Sipadan and Ligitan in the Celebes Sea: A Study in International Law*. Durham: International Boundaries Research Unit, University of Durham, 1995.

———. *The Contested Maritime and Territorial Boundaries of Malaysia: An International Law Perspective*. London: Kluwer Law International, 1998.

Harrison, Tom, ed. "The Diary of Mr. W. Pretyman, First Resident of Tempasuk, North Borneo (1878–1880)". *Sarawak Museum Journal* VII (1956).

Hashim Abdul Wahab. *Adventure Journeys in Sabah*. Kuala Lumpur: Alafhakam Sdn Bhd, 2001.

Holsti, K.J. *International Politics: A Framework for Analysis*, 7th ed. Englewood Cliff, New Jersey: Prentice-Hall, 1995.

Irwin, Graham. *Nineteenth-Century Borneo: A Study in Diplomatic Rivalry*. Singapore: Donald Moore Books, 1965.

Kahin, G.M., ed. *Governments and Politics of Southeast Asia*. New York: Cornell University Press, 1967.

Komer, R.W. *The Malayan Emergency in Retrospect: Organization of a Successful Counterinsurgency Effort*. Santa Monica: The Rand Corporation, 1972.

Kriangsak Kittichaisaree. *The Law of the Sea and Maritime Boundary Delimitation in South-East Asia*. Singapore: Oxford University Press, 1987.

Lau, Albert. *The Malayan Union Controversy, 1942-1948*. Singapore: Oxford University Press, 1991.

Low, H. "Selesilah (Book of Descent) of the Rajas of Bruni". *Journal of the Straits Branch, Royal Asiatic Society (JSBRAS)*, no. 5 (June 1880).

Luping, Herman J. *Sabah's Dilemma: The Political History of Sabah (1960-1994)*. Kuala Lumpur: Magnus Books, 1994.

Mackie, J.A.C. *Konfrantasi: The Indonesia-Malaysia Dispute 1963-1966*. Kuala Lumpur: Oxford University Press, 1974.

Maier, Pauline, et al. *Inventing America: A History of the United States*. New York: W.W. Norton and Co., 2003.

Maxwell, W.G., and W.S. Gibson. *Treaties and Engagements Affecting the Malay States and Borneo*. London: Jes. Truscott, 1924.

Mills, L.A. *British Malaya 1824-67*. Kuala Lumpur: Malaysian Branch of the Royal Asiatic Society, 2003.

Mohamed Noordin Sopiee. *From Malayan Union to Singapore Separation: Political Unification in the Malaysian Region, 1945-1965*. Kuala Lumpur: Penerbit Universiti Malaya, 1976.

Navaratnam, A. *The Spear and the Kerambit: The Exploits of VAT 69, Malaysia's Elite Fighting Force 1968-1989*. Kuala Lumpur: Utusan Publications and Distributors, 2001.

O'balance, Edgar. *Malaya: The Communist Insurgent War, 1948-60*. London: Faber and Faber 1966.

Ongkili, J.P. *The Borneo Response to Malaysia, 1961-1963*. Singapore: Donald Moore Press, 1967.

Palmer, R.R., and Joel Colton. *A History of the Modern World*. New York: Alfred A. Knopf, 1978.

Parkinson, C.N. *British Intervention in Malaya, 1867-77*. Singapore: University of Malaya Press, 1959.

Poulgrain, Greg. *The Genesis of Konfrantasi: Malaysia, Brunei and Indonesia, 1945-1965*. Bathurst, N.S.W: Crawford House Publishing, 1998.

Ranjit Singh, D.S. *Brunei 1839-1983: The Problems of Political Survival*. Singapore: Oxford University Press, 1984, reprinted, 1991.

———. "A Dominion of Southeast Asia". *JMBRAS* LXXI, pt. 1 (1998).

———. *The Making of Sabah, 1865-1941: The Dynamics of Indigenous Society*, 3rd ed. Kota Kinabalu: Sabah State Government, 2011.

———. "Boundary Delineation in the Sabah-Indonesia-Philippine Region: The Sipadan and Ligitan Case at the ICJ". *AdRem, Journal of the Selangor Bar* 1 (2006).

———. "The Pedra Branca/Pulau Batu Puteh Case at the International Court of Justice (ICJ): Some Observations". In *The Seas Divide: Geopolitics and Maritime Issues in Southeast Asia*, edited by Jatswan S. Sidhu and K.S. Balakrishnan. Kuala Lumpur: Institute of Ocean and Earth Sciences (IOES), University of Malaya, 2008.

Reece, R.H.W. *The Name of Brooke: End of White Rajah Rule in Sarawak.* Kuala Lumpur: Oxford University Press, 1982.

Runciman, Steven. *The White Rajahs: A History of Sarawak from 1841 to 1946.* Cambridge: Cambridge University Press, 1960.

Sarawak Museum Journal VII, 1956.

SarDesai, D.R. *Southeast Asia, Past and Present.* Basingstoke: Macmillan, 1989.

Short, Anthony. *The Communist Insurrection in Malaya, 1948–1960.* London: Frederick Muller, 1975.

Spear, Percival. *A History of India,* vol. 2. Harmondsworth: Penguin Books, 1975.

Stockwell, A.J. *British Policy and Malay Politics During the Malayan Union Experiment 1942–1948.* JMBRAS Monograph No. 8. Kuala Lumpur: JMBRAS, 1979.

Stubbs, Richard. *Hearts and Minds in Guerrilla Warfare: The Malayan Emergency 1948–1960.* Singapore: Eastern Universities Press, 2004.

Tarling, Nicholas. *Britain, the Brookes and Brunei.* Kuala Lumpur: Oxford University Press, 1971.

———. "Borneo and British Intervention in Malaya". *Journal of Southeast Asian Studies* V, no. 2 (September 1974).

———, ed. *The Cambridge History of Southeast Asia, vol. 2. The Nineteenth and Twentieth Centuries.* Cambridge: Cambridge University Press, 1992.

———. *Southeast Asia: A Modern History.* South Melbourne: Oxford University Press, Australia, 2001.

Teixeira, Manual. "Early Portuguese and Spanish Contacts with Borneo". *Da Sociedade De Geografia De Lisboa* (July–December, 1964).

Tregonning, K.G. *A History of Modern Malaya.* London: Eastern Universities Press, 1964.

———. "American Activity in North Borneo, 1865–1881". *Pacific Historical Review* XXIII (November 1954).

———. *Under Chartered Company Rule (North Borneo 1881–1946).* Singapore: University of Malaya Press, 1959.

United Nations. *The Law of the Sea.* New York, 1983.

Valencia, Mark J. *Malaysia and the Law of the Sea: The Foreign Policy Issues, the Options and Their Implications.* Kuala Lumpur: Institute of Strategic and International Studies (ISIS), Malaysia, 1991.

Vlekke, Bernard, H.M. *Nusantara: A History of the East India Archipelago.* Cambridge, Mass.: Harvard University Press, 1943.

Warren, J.F. *The Sulu Zone, 1768–1898: The Dynamics of External Trade, Slavery and Ethnicity in the Transformation of a Southeast Asian Maritime State.* Singapore: Singapore University Press, 1981.

Willi of Gais, Johannes. *The Early Relations of England with Borneo to 1805.* Langensaiza: Druk von Herman Rayer & Sohne, 1992.

Wong Kim Min, James. *The Birth of Malaysia.* Kuching: 1995.

Wright, L.R. *The Origins of British Borneo.* Hong Kong: Hong Kong University Press, 1970.

Index

Note: Page numbers followed by "n" refer to endnotes.

Turtle Preservation Ordinance, 1917,
41, 150, 153–54
Tydings-McDuffie Act, 1934, 89, 108

U
Unfederated Malay States, 114
United Malays National Organization
(UMNO), 115
United Nations (UN), 10
United Nations Conference on the Law
of Sea (UNCLOS), 6, 9, 10, 123,
176
United Nations Continental Shelf
Convention, 1958, 9, 123
United States, 8, 10, 13, 32
cession of the Philippines from
Spain, 49, 107
sovereignty over North Bornean
islands, 80–81
takeover of the Philippines, 71,
74–79

Treaty of Paris, 1898, 49, 76, 107,
137, 147
Turtle Islands takeover, 88, 90, 96,
108
war with Spain, 106

V
Vienna Convention, 165
Villiers, F.H., 82, 84
Vreede, E.A., 62

W
Washington Naval Treaty, 90
Watts, Sir Arthur, 128–133
Weedon, W.C. Moores, 63
Weeramantry, Christopher Gregory, 160
West Coast Residency, 35, 39
"White Rajahs", 112, 113, 124n26
Witti, Ference Xavier, 51–52, 68n17
Wong Kim Min, James, 122, 126n57
Wood, Leonard, 108

About the Author

Emeritus Professor Dr D.S. Ranjit Singh is currently affiliated to the College of Law, Government and International Studies, Universiti Utara Malaysia, Sintok, Kedah. From 1973 to 2004, Ranjit served with the Department of History, Faculty of Arts and Social Science, University of Malaya in various positions, including as Tutor (1973–79), Lecturer (1979–90), Associate Professor (1991–97) and Professor (1998–2004). Since 2006, Ranjit has been attached to the School of International Studies (SoIS), Universiti Utara Malaysia. His areas of specialization include Malaysian History (Sabah and Sarawak); Political History of Southeast Asia, especially Brunei; International Relations; and Strategic Studies. Among his major publications are: *Brunei 1838–1983: The Problems of Political Survival* (Singapore: Oxford University Press, 1984; reprinted, 1991) and *The Making of Sabah 1865–1941: The Dynamics of Indigenous Society* (Kuala Lumpur: University of Malaya Press, 2000, 3rd ed., 2011, Government of Sabah).

Ranjit was Visiting Scholar/Visiting Professor at the following institutions: School of Oriental and African Studies, University of London (1984, 1991); University of Hiroshima (1996); University of Indiana and University of Utah (1997); and National University of La Plata, Argentina (2000). He was consultant to the Ministry of Foreign Affairs and was the leader of the team which prepared the historical evidence for Malaysia's case at the ICJ pertaining to the country's sovereignty over Pulau Sipadan and Pulau Ligitan. In 2002, Malaysia won the case when the ICJ, in a historic judgment, awarded sovereignty over the two islands to Malaysia. From 2011 to 2012, he served as a member of the Social Committee to study the history curriculum and textbooks for secondary schools. The report of the committee was submitted to the Ministry of Education on 15 May 2012. In October 2012, Universiti Utara Malaysia conferred upon him the prestigious title of Emeritus Professor.

www.ingramcontent.com/pod-product-compliance
Lightning Source LLC
Chambersburg PA
CBHW060354220326
41598CB00023B/2913